The Essential Jesus

The Man, His Message, His Mission

Edited by Bryan W. Ball and William G. Johnsson

Pacific Press Publishing Association
Boise, Idaho

Edited by Bryan W. Ball and William G. Johnsson

Designed by Dennis Ferree

Published jointly by:

Pacific Press Publishing Association
Nampa, Idaho
USA

Signs Publishing Company
Warburton, Victoria
Australia

Printed in Australia

ISBN: 0-8163-1929-4

02 03 04 05 06 • 5 4 3 2 1

Contents

For
those who believe,
those who would like to believe, and
those who used to believe and still waver between belief and
unbelief.

"I am more convinced than I am in my own existence that the view of life Christ came into the world to preach, and died to sanctify, remains as true and valid as ever, and that all who care to, young and old, healthy and infirm, wise and foolish . . . may live thereby, finding in our troubled, confused world, as in all circumstances and at all other times, an enlightenment and a serenity not otherwise attainable." (Malcolm Muggeridge, *Jesus Rediscovered, 1979*, p. 97).

Preface

I am convinced the time is right for this book.

There is a sense in which a careful, thorough book about Jesus of Nazareth is always welcome. Beyond question, Jesus is the most significant individual in the history of the world. His influence today continues to be profound. So great, widespread, and lasting has been the impact of this Man that everyone who thinks must make the effort to try to figure out who He was, what He thought about Himself, and what He hoped to accomplish. Not to face Jesus is to dodge the call of history and the challenge of rational thought.

But the times into which we suddenly have been plunged make this book all the more welcome. We are hardly into the new millennium, and we find ourselves facing terrible uncertainty, apprehension, and even fear. Does the essential Jesus have a word for these times? This book argues that He does, and that we do well to heed it.

There is yet another factor: Jesus is under attack as perhaps never before in the 2,000 or so years since He lived. A rather small group of biblical scholars have seized the opportunities afforded by the modern media to propagate a view of Jesus starkly at odds with that presented in the four Gospels and Christian history. It is time to set the record straight over against the press reports and books coming from these self-appointed reconstructionists.

Let me add a note about the writers of this volume. All are scholars with earned doctoral degrees, most have spent years teaching in disciplines related to the Bible and theology, and most are previously published authors. All take the Bible seriously, and they represent hundreds, perhaps thousands, of scholars the world over with similar considered views. A final word about the writers: all believe in Jesus Christ. While they reason carefully in view of the biblical evidence, they do not come to the text as skeptics or doubters. They have thought through for themselves the critical questions about Jesus of Nazareth.

I hope this work will encourage you to do likewise. This remarkable Person deserves it, and so do you.

Jan Paulsen, President
General Conference of Seventh-day Adventists
Silver Spring, Maryland, USA
January 30, 2002

Contributors

Roy Adams, M.Div., Ph.D. (Andrews University); Associate editor, *Adventist Review*; formerly Associate Professor of Systematic Theology, Adventist Institute of Advanced Studies, Philippines; Associate Secretary, Seventh-day Adventist Church in Canada.

Bryan W. Ball, M.A., Religion (Andrews University), Ph.D.(University of London); Honorary Research Fellow, Avondale College; formerly Head, Religion Dept., Newbold College; Principal, Avondale College; President, South Pacific Division, Seventh-day Adventist Church.

Ivan T. Blazen, M.A., M.Div. (Andrews University), Ph.D.(Princeton Theological Seminary); Professor of Biblical Interpretation and Theology, Loma Linda University; formerly Professor of New Testament and Theology, Seventh-day Adventist Theological Seminary, Andrews University; Professor of Religion, Pacific Union College.

Raoul F. Dederen, M.A.,(University of Geneva), Dr. ès. Sc. Morales (Ph.D., University of Geneva); Emeritus Professor of Theology, Seventh-day Adventist Theological Seminary, Andrews University; formerly Chair, Theology Dept., and Dean, Seventh-day Adventist Theological Seminary.

William G. Johnsson, M.A.(Andrews University), B.D.(University of London), M.A., Ph.D. (Vanderbilt University); Editor, *Adventist Review*; formerly Professor of New Testament and Associate Dean, Seventh-day Adventist Theological Seminary, Andrews University; Dean, School of Theology, Spicer Memorial College.

Andrea T. Luxton, M.A.(Andrews University), Ph.D.(Catholic University of America); Vice-President for Academic Administration, Canadian University College; formerly Head, English Dept. and Principal, Newbold College.

David N. Marshall, M.A.(University of Hull), Ph.D.(University of Hull); Editor, Stanborough Press, England and Editor of Autumn House Publications; formerly Senior Lecturer in History, Stanborough School.

Jan Paulsen, M.A., B.D.(Andrews University), D.Th.(Tubingen); President, General Conference, Seventh-day Adventist Church; formerly President, Trans-European Division; Head, Religion Dept., and Principal, Newbold College; Head, Religion Dept., and Principal, Adventist Seminary of West Africa.

Steven W. Thompson, M.Div.(Andrews University), Ph.D.(University of St. Andrews); Dean, Faculty of Theology, Avondale College; formerly Senior Lecturer, Religion Dept. and Principal, Newbold College.

Laurence A. Turner, M.Div.(Andrews University), Th.M.(Princeton Theological Seminary), Ph.D.(University of Sheffield); Senior Lecturer and Head, Dept. of Theological Studies, Newbold College; formerly Senior Lecturer, Theology Dept., Avondale College.

Nancy J. Vyhmeister, M.A., Religion(Andrews University), Ed.D.(Andrews University); Professor Emerita, Seventh-day Adventist Theological Seminary, Andrews University; formerly editor, *Andrews University Seminary Studies*.

Norman H. Young, M.Litt.(University of New England), Ph.D.(University of Manchester); Senior Lecturer, New Testament Studies, Avondale College; visiting lecturer, Andrews University.

Acknowledgments

No book, certainly not one such as this, can reach publication without the interest and help of a great many people.

Although the contributors have been mentioned elsewhere, thanks are due to them again, not only for providing readable, high quality material from a wide range of biblical, theological, and related disciplines, but also for their enthusiasm for the project from the beginning and for their willing cooperation throughout the writing and editorial process.

Muriel Rudge and Chitra Barnabas have provided invaluable assistance with keyboard, copy editing and proofreading skills, and have collectively been responsible for the bulk of the technical work in getting the manuscript ready for publication.

Special thanks are due to various people in the Avondale Information Technology Department, notably Peter King, Phil Page, and Graham Lloyd, for coming to the rescue on numerous occasions when the Australian-based coeditor's computer refused to take orders or otherwise misbehaved.

This book could not have come to reality without the support of the South Pacific Division of the Seventh-day Adventist Church which provided the initial funding to get the project off the ground. Alex Currie and Ray Coombe, successive Administrative Assistants to the Division President, deserve special mention for their liaison role and unfailing support throughout.

The staff at Pacific Press Publishing Association also merit thanks, particularly Russell Holt, Vice-President for Product Development, and his colleagues, for showing an early and sustained interest in a book entitled *The Essential Jesus*. In those early days all they had to go on was the word of two very convinced coeditors.

Credit is also due to the production team at The Signs Publishing Company in Warburton, Australia. They were latecomers to this project but rose to the occasion with enthusiasm and expertise. Dale Williams, Alan Holman, Michael Heath and Murray Howse deserve special mention for their committment to seeing the project come to fruition.

Finally, there have been a sequence of occurrences, of greater or lesser significance, from the very outset of this project, which can best be described as evidence of a providential interest in the finished product. As biblical scholars from earlier generations might have said in response to such indications, *Sola Gloria Dei*! That, indeed, has been the ultimate objective of this book, as it was for the Jesus whom it proposes as still being essential for men, women, and children everywhere.

Introduction

Jesus is under attack. This sobering fact has profound and far-reaching implications for both believers and unbelievers. It is one of the major reasons for the existence of this book.

Jesus has always been under attack, of course. From the day Herod the Great of Judea sought to destroy the infant Christ to the day of His judicial murder at the hands of the Roman Pontius Pilate, and on numerous occasions in between when the ruling Jewish authorities or the synagogue worshipers in His home town of Nazareth sought to kill Him, He was under attack. Even before that, if our traditional understanding is correct, before the foundations of the earth were laid in eons past He had been the object of Satanic jealousy and malice.

In more recent times, notably since the so-called Enlightenment of the late seventeenth and early eighteenth centuries, the attack on Jesus has been more ideologically oriented. Particularly since the mid-nineteenth century, when historical-critical scholarship began to be applied to the life and work of Jesus, the attack has been focused on the nature and reliability of the biblical record. If we could take only one example of post-Enlightenment theology to illustrate the point it would be that of Rudolph Bultmann, perhaps the most influential theologian of the twentieth century. Bultmann's radical thinking dispensed with much of the New Testament and called for the historical understanding of Jesus to be "demythologized," leaving a Christ barely recognizable from the Jesus of preceding centuries, to say nothing of the Jesus revealed in the Bible. Bultmann's legacy is almost incalculable. His followers and fellow-travelers are today numerous, widespread, educated, vocal, and influential.

"So," we might ask, "What's new? Why the fuss?" Jesus has always had His enemies. There have always been those who have attempted to explain Him away, undermine His credentials, weaken His influence, counter His teachings, dispense with His redemptive significance, in fact, to destroy Him.

The answer to this question, and the motivation for this sequence of essays, is that today Jesus is the object of a renewed offensive, more radical and intense and in some respects different from the attacks of previous generations. People are now talking openly for the first time, at least in the modern era, of the possibility that the Christian faith might be on its way out. A distinguished scholar expressed the conviction in a recent television documentary that Christianity would be finished by the first quarter of the twenty-first century. That could happen if the attack on Jesus were to prove successful.

The current offensive against Jesus began in earnest, or at least came into the open, in 1977 with the publication of the now well-known collection of essays, *The Myth of God Incarnate*. The Bultmannian overtones of this title clearly indicate the intention of the editor, John Hick, and his fellow liberal theologians—the complete dismantling of the historical, biblical doctrine of the incarnation and the debunking of the biblical Christ. The ripples from this bold assault on the very foundations of the faith are still being felt around the world. The ensuing attack on Jesus continued apace during the last two decades of the twentieth century and as yet shows no sign of abating. Dr. Paul Barnett, one of the most able contemporary defenders of the historical Jesus, warns "Christianity is currently facing one of its most profound challenges."[1]

Speaking of the current interest in the person of Christ, Barnett states that the redefinition of Jesus in the final quarter of the twentieth century was based on the "presumption that he cannot have been a supernatural figure," and that "he must be capable of other explanations." Barnett notes that in the 1980s and early 1990s no fewer than 260 books and articles were published relating to the life and teachings of Jesus, the greater part of which presented "a Jesus who is unrecognizable to the Christian faith as expressed in the historic creeds and confessions of the church."[2] That number now would almost certainly be well in excess of 300, most with the same intention of "redefining" the historical Jesus.

In another defense of the biblical Christ, *Jesus Under Fire*, the authors, Dr. Michael J. Wilkins and Dr. J. P. Moreland, point out that to many people of our time "the Jesus of Nazareth we find in the pages of the Bible is a fictitious creation of the early church" and not the real Jesus at all. The message today is that intelligent people must not "simplistically accept" the biblical record of Jesus at face value. According to the reinventors, "Jesus must be stripped of ancient myths that surrounded him . . . so that the modern person can hear his true message." He "must be brought down to earth . . . so that we can understand who he was as he walked under Palestinian skies and comprehend what, if any, religious relevance he has for us today."[3] The clear implication is that the biblical Jesus has little, if any, relevance for our contemporary world.

One outcome of this quite remarkable new interest in Jesus is a particular cause for concern. As Barnett puts it, there are today "as many Jesuses as there are people who write about him."[4] Having felt free to jettison the Christ of Scripture, those who seek to reinvent Him must at least be credited with imagination. He is variously portrayed as a Jewish sage, a religious genius, a misguided visionary, a social revolutionary, an itinerant philosopher, a Mediterranean peasant, a spiritual charismatic, an eschatological enthusiast, a healer, an exorcist, a magician, a story-teller, a rabbi, to mention only some. But not the traditional Son of God, the divine-human Saviour of sinful humanity. Anything but that.

Two of the most prominent contemporary assailants of the biblical Jesus are the Australian Dr. Barbara Thiering and the American Bishop John Spong. Thiering, whose work has been described by one eminent Jewish scholar as "fiction" and "sand-castles,"[5] proposes that Jesus was drugged at the time of His crucifixion (which took place by the Dead Sea and not at Jerusalem), and that He did not actually die on the cross but subsequently revived. He later married Mary Magdalene, fathered three children, then divorced Mary in favour of another woman, and eventually died in old age.[6] Barnett observes that Thiering has "done nothing more than create a historical fantasy" which appeals to many people "just because it is so fantastic."[7] The Oxford New Testament scholar, N. T. Wright, says that Thiering's book, *Jesus the Man*, is one of "the strangest" he has ever read and that the only scholar who takes Thiering seriously is Thiering herself.[8]

Bishop Spong wants to free Christians from "2000 years of misunderstanding." Believing that the Gospels and the Pauline writings should not be taken literally, Spong denies the virgin birth of

Christ, His miracles, and the recorded details of the crucifixion and the resurrection. In another flight into fancy Spong says that the marriage at Cana in Galilee was actually the marriage of Jesus and Mary Magdalene. Dismissing orthodox Christians and scholars who believe in the affirmations of Scripture and the definitions of the historic creeds as "uninformed, unquestioning and ignorant," Spong declares that the biblical teachings of human sin and divine redemption through Christ are "no longer believable."[9]

Probably the most influential group of contemporary theologians to attempt a massive shift away from traditional belief in Jesus is the so-called Jesus Seminar founded in 1985. While the views of the Jesus Seminar are examined more fully in chapter 2 of this book, it will be instructive to note here its main objective. The cofounders of the Seminar, Dr. Robert Funk and Dr. John Crossan, want "to liberate Jesus," that is to free the "mythic" Jesus from the traditional biblical stories that have "entrapped" Him. They maintain that the biblical records of Jesus' death, burial, and resurrection were the "wishful thinking of the early church."[10] As one critic rightly notes, "If the view of the Jesus Seminar is correct—that almost nothing definite can be known about the life of Jesus of Nazareth—the basis for all Christian belief is destroyed."[11] Barnett agrees. "To disprove these facts" (concerning the historical Jesus), he says, "would be to destroy the essential character of Christianity."[12]

Another disturbing feature of the renewed assault on Jesus is its entry into the public domain. A wide cross section of the general public now thinks that traditional beliefs about Jesus have been exposed as untrue. This is largely due to media attention frequently focused on the current radical views about Jesus. Whereas previously the Jesus debate has been largely confined to scholarly circles, attracting little public attention, the issues have now been turned into national, even international, headlines in newspapers, magazines, and on TV. It is undeniable, certainly in the Western world, that a greater proportion of the population today doubts the biblical record and the historic understanding of Jesus than at any previous time in history.

The exposure given in *Time* magazine is one example of this process. In April, 1994 and again in April, 1996 *Time* reported the findings of the Jesus Seminar, and in December, 1999 the *Time* lead article featured a controversial rewrite of parts of the Gospel entitled "Jesus of Nazareth: Then and Now." The April 8, 1996 issue reported that most of the Seminar group concurred that "not much of the New Testament can be trusted" and that "most Christians' picture of Jesus was radically misguided." Thus any statements reputed to have been made by Jesus on the cross, the description of His trial, the resurrection, and "any claim by Jesus to be the Messiah or the Son of God" are "inauthentic."[13]

Enough has been said to demonstrate the nature and the extent of the current attack on Jesus. However, it is also important to understand the underlying convictions that are driving the reinterpretation of history's most respected and revered figure. The presuppositions that lead to the radical conclusions proposed today are as significant as the conclusions themselves. There are at least four such guiding principles, most of them deriving from what N.T. Wright calls "the cultural imperialism of the Enlightenment."[14] They are:

    Rejection of the supernatural, including miracles.

    Rejection of the historicity and authority of the Bible, particularly the Gospels.

    A belief that it is impossible to know what Jesus said or did, or even who He was.

    A conviction that the Jesus of faith is not necessarily based on the Jesus of history.

It goes without saying that there can be no Christian faith in the traditional sense if presuppositions such as these drive the search for the "real Jesus." Fortunately, a number of credible dissenting voices has already been raised in defense of the biblical Christ, voices willing and able to point out the flaws and assumptions of the contemporary new gospelers.

In an essay entitled "Who is Jesus?" in *Jesus Under Fire,* Dr. Scot McNight underlines the fundamental importance of these matters. The Jesus question, now firmly in the spotlight and before the eyes of the reading public "could be the most critical issue of our day," he says.[15] McNight goes on to point out the real significance of these issues for Christianity and for the world at large. If the revised views of Jesus are correct, he says, "millions of Christians have been deluded into thinking that Jesus was and is their Saviour. They have bought into a myth that has no more roots in reality than the Wizard of Oz. They have trusted in a Christ who is not there and assumed a faith that is an illusion. Millions of Christians, throughout the world and throughout the history of the church, have begun their day, sustained their work, and laid their heads down at night in constant prayer to Jesus, the Lord; if that Jesus did not exist then their faith is a psychological trick and their prayers are no more than fanciful coping mechanisms."[16] McNight concludes, and we concur, that if we are going to be honest about Jesus "we have to choose a Jesus who satisfies all the evidence" and who will also explain why it is that so many people still worship Him.[17]

One further factor should perhaps be recognized. The attack on Jesus comes not only from without but also, and with equal cause for concern, from within. The Jesus of our own imagination frequently rises to replace the Jesus of the Bible. How easy it is to create a Jesus to our liking! A Jesus who corresponds to our own presuppositions, fears, prejudices, aversions, wants, likes and dislikes, expectations and priorities, a comfortable Jesus who never challenges us or disturbs us or seeks to change us, a pick-and-mix Jesus with whom we can leave out the things we don't like and try to convince ourselves they don't even exist. This Jesus, too, is a product of our times. He is the Jesus for a materialistic, narcissistic age, a Jesus who is sufficient to sustain our respectability, who just satisfies any qualms of conscience we may have about not going the extra mile or binding up the wounds of the nearest stricken Samaritan. The real Jesus wants us to be honest with ourselves as well as with the evidence. And that is not always as easy as it may sound.

Here, then, is the background and the reason for this book. It proposes that Jesus, the traditional, biblical Jesus, the complete biblical Jesus, is still essential to give meaning to human existence and richness to human experience. It argues in substance that this Jesus is at the same time the historical Jesus and the Jesus of faith. It aims to demonstrate the trustworthiness of the more traditional answers to fundamental questions about Jesus still being asked by millions around the world. Who was He? Are the Gospel accounts of His birth, life, death, and teachings reliable? Why did He die? Did He really rise from the dead? What does discipleship mean? Does Jesus have a future? Will He come again? Does He still call men, women, and young people to discipleship and, if so, what does He expect of those who respond?

The various chapters that follow address these and related issues, showing that there are still persuasive arguments to believe as Christians have always believed, even though the media prefer to parade the radical and the sensational as if equally arguable and intellectually respectable alternatives no longer exist. *The Essential Jesus* is for those who do not want to have the foundations washed completely away and who would prefer to believe, as millions through the centuries have believed, that the biblical Jesus is also the only real object of true faith. It is for those who are persuaded, or who are open to be persuaded, that this Jesus brings relevance, meaning, and purpose to life and a reasonably based hope of life to come.

While *The Essential Jesus* has been written by trained scholars it is not principally for academics. It is for people in all walks of life and in all cultures who think about life and death, faith and the future, and about this unique person, Jesus of Nazareth, who has so dramatically changed the course of history. And it is for those who, perhaps wistfully and tentatively, still look to Him and wonder if He is, indeed, the answer to the human predicament.

The various chapters in this volume each deal with an aspect of the person or work of Jesus that could itself easily take up a whole book. Indeed, most already have, as the "Further Reading" recommendations at the end of each chapter demonstrate. The contributors have each sought to present their topics with as much evidence and explanation as the limitations of space allowed, recognizing that much material had to be omitted but in the firm conviction that they had presented enough to dispel doubt and provide a basis for reasonable and satisfying belief. We believe they have succeeded. No additional evidence or argument would persuade the mind that chooses not to be convinced.

And finally, a word about timing. This book was still being written on September 11, 2001. The calculated and monstrous events of that horrific day have darkened the horizon forever. We have stood together on the rim of the crater and seen with our own eyes the abysmal depths of evil. We have witnessed the terrifying human propensity for aberration and willful annihilation and have heard the threats of worse to come. We have been compelled to contemplate the future—if any—and what meaning the past and present may have. Against this dark and foreboding background we, with millions of others, remain convinced that Jesus is still the Light of the world, the Way, the Truth, and the Life. We send out this volume in the hope that it will cause the Light to shine more brightly and the Way to be seen more clearly.

Bryan W. Ball and William G. Johnsson

Note: The *New International Version* of the Bible is the one used most frequently throughout. Where other versions have been used they are so indicated in the references: NEB, *New English Bible*; NKJV, *New King James Version* (or *Revised Authorised Version*); KJV, *King James Version* (or *Authorised Version*); REV, *Revised English Version*; RSV, *Revised Standard Version*.

Notes

1. Paul W. Barnett, *Jesus and the Logic of History* (London: Apollos, 1997), p. 15.
2. *Ibid.*, pp. 11, 15.
3. Michael J. Wilkins and J. P. Moreland, *Jesus Under Fire: Modern Scholarship Reinvents the Historical Jesus* (Grand Rapids: Zondervan, 1995), p. 1.
4. Barnett, p. 11.
5. A. D. Crown, *Annals,* 1992, pp. 14, 15, cited in Paul Barnett, *The Truth About Jesus* (Sydney: Aquila, 1994), p. 3; Barbara Thiering, *Jesus the Man: A New Interpretation from the Dead Sea Scrolls* (New York: Doubleday, 1992).
6. N. T. Wright, *Who Was Jesus?* (London: SPCK, 1992), p. 19.
7. Barnett, *The Truth About Jesus*, p. 3.
8. Wright, pp. 19, 23.
9. Grant R. Jeffrey, *Jesus: The Great Debate* (Toronto: Frontier, 1999), p. 23.

See also Wright, pp. 65 ff.

10. Wilkins and Moreland, p. 2.
11. Jeffrey, p. 21.
12. Barnett, *The Truth About Jesus,* p. 7.
13. *Time* Magazine, April 8,1996; Dec. 6, 1999.
14. N. T. Wright, *The New Testament and the People of God* (Minneapolis, MI: Fortress, 1992), p. 84.
15. Scot McNight, "Who Is Jesus? An Introduction to Jesus Studies," in Wilkins and Moreland, *Jesus Under Fire,* p. 52.
16. *Ibid.*
17. *Ibid.,* p. 68.

The Influence of Jesus
William G. Johnsson

Of all the names given children since the dawn of time, one stands alone, solitary, immovable. Although many men and women now take that name in oath or jest, one day every knee in heaven and earth will bow before Him who bears it and declare that He is King of kings and Lord of lords. That name is the sweetest sound to come from infant lips; it sustains us through life; and it will be our security when we embark on our final journey.

Jesus.

All our hopes—for this world and the next—center in Him. Our best joys, our highest aspirations, our cleanest motivations, spring from Him. Every other name will pass away; His, never.

In a recent book Lee Strobel describes a revealing moment during a conversation with a renowned atheist. Strobel, a trial lawyer and journalist, arranged to interview Charles Templeton in preparing the manuscript for what became *The Case for Faith*.[1] Templeton was once a Christian minister and a close friend and associate of Billy Graham. But he began to doubt the reliability of the Bible and shared his arguments with the young Graham. Graham wrestled with the concerns raised by his friend, decided that the Bible was trustworthy, and went into the Los Angeles evangelistic campaign that catapulted him on a long and remarkable career as the preacher who would speak to more people worldwide than any person in the history of Christianity. Templeton, however, chose the opposite course; he resigned from the ministry and devoted his life to attacking belief in God.

As Strobel probed the critical points in Templeton's journey, Templeton revealed that a picture of a starving child in drought-stricken Africa first led him to doubt the existence of God. If there were a God, all He had to do was send rain, but no rain came. So, Templeton concluded, God didn't exist, or if He did exist, He was either powerless to help or a monster. It would be the first of a plethora of arguments Templeton, now in his eighties, would marshal during the course of a long life.

It was late in the interview, and Templeton had laid out a compelling case for his rejection of faith. Then Strobel put a question that abruptly changed the tenor of the conversation: "And so how do you assess this Jesus?" The change in the avowed atheist was dramatic.

"Templeton's body language softened. It was as if he suddenly felt relaxed and comfortable in talking about an old and dear friend. His voice, which at times had displayed such a sharp and insistent edge, now took on a melancholy and reflective tone. His guard seemingly down, he spoke in an unhurried pace, almost nostalgically, carefully choosing his words as he talked about Jesus.

" 'He was,' Templeton began, 'the greatest human being who has ever lived. He was a moral genius. His ethical sense was unique. He was the intrinsically wisest person that I've ever encountered in my life or in my readings. His commitment was total and led to his own death, much to the detriment of the world. What could one say about him except that this was a form of greatness?'

"I was taken aback. 'You sound like you really care about him,' I said.

" 'Well, yes, he's the most important thing in my life,' came his reply. 'I . . . I . . . I,' he stuttered, searching for the right word, 'I know it may sound strange, but I have to say . . . I *adore* him!'

"I wasn't sure how to respond. 'You say that with some emotion,' I said.

" 'Well, yes. Everything good I know, everything decent I know, everything pure I know, I learned from Jesus. Yes . . . yes. And tough! Just look at Jesus. He castigated people. He was angry. People don't think of him that way, but they don't read the Bible. He had a righteous anger. He cared for the oppressed and exploited.

There's no question that he had the highest moral standard, the least duplicity, the greatest compassion, of any human being in history. There have been many other wonderful people, but Jesus is Jesus.'

" 'And so the world would do well to emulate him?'

" 'Oh, my goodness, yes! I have tried—and try is as far as I can go—to act as I have believed he would act. That doesn't mean I could read his mind, because one of the most fascinating things about him was that he often did the opposite thing you'd expect—'

"Abruptly, Templeton cut short his thoughts. There was a brief pause, almost as if he was uncertain whether he should continue.

" 'Uh . . . but . . . no,' he said slowly, 'he's the most . . .' He stopped, then started again. 'In my view,' he declared, 'he is the most important human being who has ever existed.'

"That's when Templeton uttered the words I never expected to hear from him. 'And if I may put it this way,' he said as his voice began to crack, '*I . . . miss . . . him!*'

"With that, tears flooded his eyes. He turned his head and looked downward, raising his left hand to shield his face from me. His shoulders bobbed as he wept."[2]

After more than half a century of convincing himself and trying to convince others that the Christian faith was nonsense, Templeton had not escaped the influence of Jesus Christ. The mention of Jesus' name brought back associations of a friendship once treasured but long severed and still longed for.

I agree with Templeton's assessment and would modify it only to assert that Jesus was not only the most important person who ever lived, but by far the most important.

A remarkable thing about this Man is that the centuries as they pass do not lessen His influence. He is the Man who will not go away. He still makes the cover of the world's leading news magazines. Thus, in a *Time* cover story titled "Jesus of Nazareth: Then and Now," biblical scholar Reynolds Price asserts:

"The memory of any stretch of years eventually resolves to a list of names, and one of the useful ways of recalling the past two millenniums is by listing the people who acquired great power. Muhammad, Catherine the Great, Marx, Gandhi, Hitler, Roosevelt,

Stalin and Mao come quickly to mind. There's no question that each of those figures changed the lives of millions and evoked responses from worship through hatred.

"It would require much exotic calculation, however, to deny that the single most powerful figure—not merely in these two millenniums but in all human history—has been Jesus of Nazareth. Not only is the prevalent system of denoting the years based on an erroneous sixth-century calculation of the date of his birth, but a serious argument can be made that no one else's life has proved remotely as powerful and enduring as that of Jesus."[3]

To attempt to chronicle the influence of this Man stretches the limits of the intellect and bursts the confines of a single chapter in this book. At best I can present slices of history, vignettes, episodes. The whole story is as marvelous and as far flung as the myriads of men and women, and boys and girls for whom Jesus of Nazareth has been, and is, Saviour and Lord. Of course, there are some negative voices also to be heard; and although I write as a confirmed believer in Jesus, I shall try to be fair to them.

In this brief overview of Jesus' influence, we shall focus on three periods: Jesus' influence during His lifetime, His influence after His death, and His influence in our times.

Jesus in His Own Times

Although occasionally during the course of history voices have been raised calling into question whether Jesus actually existed, these have never been taken seriously. Even by the most vehement critics of Christianity, the fact of Jesus is a given. The issues debated over the centuries have not been whether there was such a man but rather who He thought He was and who He really was.

The One whom subsequent generations would acclaim as the most important person of all time made only a minor impact on the world of His day—here is the supreme irony. The nature of His personality, the values for which He stood, and the purpose of His living and dying were alien to the Caesars and the empire they ruled. By far the greatest amount of material about Him was left, not by historians and poets, but by people whose lives were profoundly influenced by Him and for whom Jesus became the object of faith.

Nevertheless, Jesus left a trail in His own times outside the writings of the Bible. The Jewish historian Josephus, born A.D. 37, makes two references to Jesus in *The Antiquities*.[4] One of these, the *Testimonium Flavianum*, has been disputed over the years because of the explicitness of the material; today it is considered authentic overall, but with some doctoring by Christian copyists.

The Roman historian Tacitus likewise corroborated the death of "Christus" by crucifixion during the governorship of Pontius Pilate.[5] Other Jewish and Roman writings supply additional supporting references.[6]

The stark fact that emerges from these extra-biblical sources is: Jesus died on a Roman cross. *He was executed!* This was no ordinary Jew; in some way and at some level Jesus was considered a threat by the ruling authorities. Crucifixion was Rome's supreme deterrent for troublemakers: its painfully slow death was deliberately put on public display so that anyone who might harbor thoughts of rebellion or lawbreaking would get the message.

The barest factual minimum, then—that the Jew Jesus was crucified by the Romans—introduces us inexorably to a life that influenced those in its own day.

As we still seek to understand Jesus in His own time from outside the circle of faith, we are confronted with another historical datum—the Gospels. This Man spawned not one attempt to record His life and death and who He was, but four accounts. In fact, beyond the writings we know as Matthew, Mark, Luke and John, "many" efforts were made in the first century that centered in Him (see Luke 1:1-4). The Gospel enterprise continued into the second century and included increasingly legendary and fantastic material. The four Gospels of the New Testament with which we are familiar are the survivors of a sifting and winnowing process among the early Christians.

There is another historical fact in connection with these Gospels: the pagans attempted to produce their own counterpart, one based on an alleged miracle worker, Appolonius of Tyana. Although Appolonius lived in the first century, his biographer, Philostratus, only wrote a century and a half later when the Gospels had circulated widely.

What sort of life attracts a biographer? One that has influence.

What sort of life attracts not one biographer but many? One that influenced many other lives.

What sort of biography stirs the elements of the established religious order to countermand it by imitation? One that threatens the survival of the old order.

I have referred to "biographers" above, but the four Gospels of the New Testament are not biographies as we understand the term. They are selective, omitting large periods of Jesus' life; they concentrate on the brief period of His public ministry, but even here they do not attempt to follow strict order or to cover its various phases proportionately; they devote inordinate attention to the final week of His life and His death, and they proceed from a stance of faith in Jesus and invite the reader also to believe—they are faith histories.[7]

These four accounts overlap, repeat materials, disagree in some details but agree in major points. The overall outline of Jesus' life and death, and the impact of His person is the same for each: Jesus dominates every account.

Why four Gospels—why not only one? Each is different but complements the others. Each is powerful, but the combined effect is massive in the composite portrait of Jesus that emerges. It is as though this Man is too big to be comprehended in any one telling.

"There is variety in a tree; there are scarcely two leaves just alike. Yet this variety adds to the perfection of the tree as a whole.

"In our Bible, we might ask, Why need Matthew, Mark, Luke, and John in the Gospels, why need the Acts of the Apostles, and the variety of writers in the Epistles, go over the same thing?

"The Lord gave His word in just the way He wanted it to come. He gave it through different writers, each having his own individuality, though going over the same history. Their testimonies are brought together in one Book, and are like the testimonies in a social meeting. They do not represent things in just the same style. Each has an experience of his own, and this diversity broadens and deepens the knowledge that is brought out to meet the necessities of varied minds. The thoughts expressed have not a set uniformity, as if cast in an iron mold, making the very hearing monotonous. In such uniformity there would be a loss of grace and distinctive beauty."[8]

To these four accounts we now turn to gain a more accurate reading of Jesus' influence in His own day. Under the impact of rationalistic investigation generated by the Enlightenment, the Gospels have been intensely scrutinized for more than two hundred years. Some of the keenest intellects attempted to apply the "scientific method" to the Gospels with the supreme goal of unlocking the historical Jesus, an endeavor brilliantly described and critiqued by Dr. Albert Schweitzer in his *The Quest of the Historical Jesus*[9] in the early twentieth century. After Schweitzer, Bultmann reigned as king with a radical pessimism that relegated the New Testament accounts to myths generated by the early church, leaving Jesus essentially as an "X" who died on a Roman cross. But the disciples of Bultmann, notably Ernst Käsemann, turned away from their professor in a new quest of the historical Jesus that attempted to separate myth from history in the Gospel accounts; and the endeavor has recently taken on a new life in the work of the Jesus Seminar.

Despite all the effort expended, this two-centuries-long quest to recover the historical Jesus from the Gospels must be deemed to be flawed. The application of a detached, "scientific method" to these documents misses the most basic feature of the Gospels—that they proceed from a stance of faith and are written to awaken faith. Lacking this key ingredient the investigation employs a flawed methodology, incongruent with the subject matter. The absurd lengths to which its proponents are prepared to go has come to full flower in the work of the Jesus Seminar, where a group of self-selected scholars determine what is authentic in the Gospels by casting ballots![10]

In this study we assume the reliability of the Gospel accounts. These documents were all written in the first century, and Matthew, Mark and Luke circulated when many contemporaries of Jesus were still alive to refute or correct them if they had been built on myth.

As we work through the Gospels with an eye for the influence of Jesus, we see in each a portrayal of a mass movement centered in

Galilee. Jesus was a populist leader who attracted large crowds wherever He went and whose influence led to growing concern on the part of the religious establishment. The authorities fairly soon came to regard Jesus as a threat to their power and tried to find ways to thwart His movement; eventually they concluded that the only way His influence could be controlled was to eliminate Him.

Mark's Gospel is the shortest and most direct of the four canonical accounts because it focuses on the acts of Jesus with relatively little space given to His teachings. It may also have been the first of the four to be written, although that idea cannot be established conclusively and is debated by scholars. Mark provides us with the logical place to start as we explore the influence of Jesus' public ministry, leaving until later consideration of the events of the final week of His life.

Mark begins the ministry with the calling of the first disciples (1:14-20). The account is crisp and moves at a fast clip: Jesus walks beside the Lake of Galilee, sees Simon and Andrew casting a net into the water, and bids them: "Come, follow me, and I will make you fishers of men." At once they leave their nets and follow Him. He walks on a little further, meets the brothers James and John, and likewise calls them. They too leave everything to become disciples.

Much is left unsaid in this brief telling. What did Simon and Andrew, then James and John say to Jesus—or did they say anything at all? What motivated them to make a decision, seemingly on the spot, that would radically change their future?

Mark does not let us in on this play and counter play of emotions and reasonings. He simply gives the minimum facts, and these facts leave us with a first impression of Jesus as a dynamic personality for whom people are ready to renounce their livelihood.

Now follows an account of Jesus' exorcism in the synagogue at Capernaum (1:21-28). Mark records that Jesus began to teach, but he doesn't tell us what He was teaching. Instead, he emphasizes the impression Jesus' teachings made on the assembled hearers—they are "amazed," because He taught as one who had authority. But Jesus' instruction is suddenly interrupted by a shriek from a demon-possessed man who identifies Jesus as "the Holy One of God." Jesus commands the demon to be silent and to come out of him, and the demon does so. And, says Mark, the people now are even more amazed, and word about Jesus quickly spreads over the whole region of Galilee.

Then Jesus and His disciples leave the synagogue and go to the home of Simon and Andrew. Simon's mother-in-law is lying in bed with a fever; but Jesus takes her hand, the fever leaves her, and she gets up. That evening, after the Sabbath, the whole town gathers at the door. They bring the sick and the demon-possessed, and Jesus heals them (1:29-34).

Early the next morning Jesus is up and out of the house, praying alone in a solitary place. Simon and his companions seek Him out and exclaim: "Everyone is looking for you!" But Jesus refuses to stay in Capernaum; He commences an itinerant ministry of preaching and exorcisms throughout Galilee.

We have only begun the Gospel, but Mark has yet another incident for the reader to notice (1:40-45). A leper comes to Jesus, falls on his knees, and begs for cleansing. Jesus, filled with compassion, reaches out His hand, touches him, and says, "Be clean!" And, relates Mark, "immediately" the leprosy leaves him, and he is cured. Jesus tells the man to keep the news to himself, but he tells everyone he meets. As a result Jesus can no longer go about in public. He stays outside the towns, but even so people come to Him from everywhere.

All this in only two pages of Mark's Gospel! Mark has succeeded in conveying a powerful impression of Jesus as a dynamic, charismatic figure whose acts amaze the populace, set them talking, and have them flocking to hear and see Him.

The subsequent chapters merely fill out this portrait. Jesus is beset by crowds everywhere He goes. People come to hear Him from Judea, Jerusalem, Idumea, and the regions across the Jordan and around Tyre and Sidon (3:8). Because of the press Jesus has to teach from a boat in the water (v. 9). He is so busy that He doesn't have time even to eat (3:20; 6:31), and His family thinks He is losing His balance (3:21). He feeds large crowds—5,000 men on one occasion (6:44), 4,000 on another (8:9). And everywhere He goes the people are "overwhelmed with amazement" (7:37).

But the religious leaders are not impressed. They accuse Him of blasphemy (2:6, 7); of casting out demons by Beelzebub, prince of demons (3:22); of disregard for the Sabbath (2:24; 3:2). And they begin to plot His demise (3:6).

Mark's portrait of Jesus, graphic and compelling, rings with verisimilitude. We see Jesus as leader of a people movement that sweeps Galilee and attracts many from the surrounding regions.

The other three biblical accounts lead to similar conclusions concerning the influence of Jesus during His lifetime. Although each Gospel is shaped differently with particular concerns and emphases, we see the same factors: large crowds, amazement and wonder at Jesus' deeds, speculation as to who He is, hostility from the religious establishment until it determines to have Him put to death. And Jesus, predicting that betrayal, mocking, scourging and death await Him at Jerusalem, eventually sets out to observe the Passover in the city that will bring His ministry and life to an end.

John's Gospel, obviously written after the others, adds a significant element. All four writers record the miracle of the feeding of the 5,000, but only John tells us: "After the people saw the miraculous sign that Jesus did, they began to say, 'Surely this is the Prophet who is to come into the world.' Jesus, knowing they intended to come and make him king by force, withdrew again to a mountain by himself" (John 6:14, 15).

For the people of Galilee, then, Jesus was not merely a messianic figure but *the* Messiah, the one long awaited who would bring deliverance to the nation. "All day the conviction has strengthened. That crowning act is assurance that the long-looked-for Deliverer is among them. The hopes of the people rise higher and higher. This is He who will make Judea an earthly paradise, a land flowing with milk and honey. He can satisfy every desire. He can break the power of the hated Romans. He can deliver Judah and Jerusalem. He can heal the soldiers who are wounded in battle. He can supply whole armies with food. He can conquer the nations, and give to Israel the long-sought dominion."[11]

But Jesus refused to be the king they wanted. At last He set out on His final journey to Jerusalem. He entered the city on the Sunday before Passover as a popular hero, riding on a donkey as the Scriptures had foretold (Zech. 9:9), with crowds lining the route, laying down palm branches and garments, and shouting "Hosanna! Blessed is he who comes in the name of the Lord! Blessed is the King of Israel!" (John 12:12, 13).

Before the week was over He hung dying on a Roman cross. The crowds who hailed Him on Sunday as their King cried out on Friday: "Crucify Him!"

Over His head an inscription was nailed to the cross. The Gospel writers record it differently:

> Matthew: "This is Jesus, the King of the Jews" (27:37).
> Mark: "The King of the Jews" (15:26).
> Luke: "This is the King of the Jews" (23:38).
> John: "Jesus of Nazareth, the King of the Jews" (19:19).

The differences are intriguing, but ultimately of small consequence. What counts is the phrase common to all: "The King of the Jews." That speaks volumes about the perception of Jesus on the part of both Jewish and Roman authorities—He was a threat. Each group no doubt perceived Him differently, but for each He was a challenge that could be removed only by execution.

The Influence of Jesus After His Lifetime

If the enemies of Jesus thought they could crush the populist movement in His name by putting Him to death, they met with a rude shock. The events surrounding His crucifixion would propel His person and teachings onto a global arena; a Jewish affair would become a world religion. His followers would not attempt to cover up or explain away the crucifixion; rather, the cross—His cross—would become the symbol of the new faith.

The Gospel writers let us in on a curious bit of history: whereas the followers of Jesus were crushed by His death, the religious authorities remained apprehensive. The former entertained no hope that anything good would come from Jesus' tomb; the latter feared that something might happen, and set a guard to keep Jesus sealed shut forever.

But their plans were thwarted. The tomb that they planned to be the burial place of the Jesus movement became its motivating power. Despite the guard, despite precautions, the body of Jesus vanished. Jesus the crucified appeared to His followers alive from the dead, Lord of life and conqueror of the grave. It was a message that would touch the existential longings of humanity in all ages; it was unstoppable.

That Jesus of Nazareth rose from the dead is a confession of faith. "He was not seen by all the people, but by witnesses whom God had already chosen—by us who ate and drank with him after he rose from the dead," affirmed the apostle Peter (Acts 10:41). Nevertheless, the resurrection happened within history and, if true, is the most amazing event in human experience and the capstone of Christianity. It, more than any other fact or teaching associated with this remarkable individual called Jesus, is the reason for His vast and continuing influence.

Not surprisingly, those not of faith dispute His resurrection. The theories and efforts began very early with the story that His disciples stole the body and spread false reports that they had seen him alive (Matt. 28:11-15). Subsequent attempts to rebut Christianity would allege that He did not really die, that His "appearances" to the disciples resulted from their "wish fulfillment" state of mind, and so on.[12]

Two facts, indisputable and irrefutable, confront both the historian and the religious seeker—the empty tomb and the rise of the new religion.

The body disappeared: this is fact. Enemies of Christianity could have made hay of the new faith if they could have produced Jesus' remains. But they could not. Given that fact, the claims of Jesus' followers that He had risen from the dead demanded—and demand—consideration.

Out of the ashes of disappointment and blasted dreams a new, confident, joyous faith emerged: this is fact. Defeat became victory. A little band of dispirited commoners became apostles of hope. Their message spread on the wings of the wind, flooding over the regions where Jesus lived and died, pouring into lands far beyond until it reached Rome, capital of the empire whose governor had issued the death order for Jesus. Within a generation—by the time of Paul—it had won converts within the imperial court (Phil. 1:13). And still it rolled on—west, and east, and north, and south, unstoppable, dynamic. It spread among slaves and soldiers; it penetrated at last the household of Caesar himself.[13] The old order opposed it, fought it—and finally succumbed.

"Christ is risen!" "Jesus is Lord!"—was ever religion planted in less promising soil? A crucified Messiah?—what nonsense! No wonder Paul wrote that the idea was offensive to the Jews and foolishness to the Greeks (1 Cor. 1:23). But it was the genius of the new, unstoppable faith.

On a transatlantic flight I found myself seated next to a woman who spends much of her life fighting injustice and discrimination. We talked for hours in a frank exchange of views and experiences, and then she let drop the $64,000 question: "Please help me understand how a person with your values can be part of a religious organization when religion has been used to crush the weak and helpless."

How true! That is the other side, the dark side of the influence of Jesus.

The gentle Jesus eschewed violence; His followers went marching to battle with the cross as their emblem.

The poor man Jesus did not have a place to lay His head; His followers built palaces and cathedrals lined with gold.

The humble Jesus owned but one garment of any worth; His followers donned the finest and the costliest.

The just man Jesus identified with the poor; His followers lived luxuriously on the backs of the poor.

The righteous man Jesus opened the gates of the kingdom to the dispossessed, the outcasts, the marginalized; His followers threw up barriers of social standing, caste, and gender.

We can live with the pain of this history—and the history continues in the slick, polished appearances of televangelists and other distortions—only by drawing a line between Jesus and those who claimed to be His followers. Let us confess it: in His name evil, even diabolical deeds have been perpetuated; but Jesus would have been horrified by them. The dark side of the influence of Jesus has not been that of Jesus Himself but of those who took His name and abused it.

In any religion, where church joins with state, the mix is unholy. ?

In the name of God fearsome deeds—of torture, persecution, cruelty—find justification. And Christianity was not immune from the corrupting influence of power.

But that is not the whole story. A fair reading of that same history of Christianity must acknowledge that the influence of Jesus has been a continuing power for good.

For more than a thousand years He was the central and decisive figure in Western civilization, inspiring its art, music, and literature, focusing its energies and sculpture in cathedrals erected to His glory over long periods. The high moral values that flowed from His life—the dignity of each person as a child of God, purity, family, justice, truth, honesty—shaped society profoundly. The influence of Jesus led to noble lives: to men and women who devoted themselves to serve the sick, the maimed, the dying; to courage and bravery in bringing hope and healing to people in darkness; to hospitals and hospices, to schools and universities to improve the lot of humanity because this man Jesus who died on the cross died for every person and thereby showed that every person is precious in the eyes of the one God.

Among the multitude who have enriched humanity by lives of loving service, none shines brighter than Albert Schweitzer. This brilliant theologian and philosopher, exponent of the music of Johann Sebastian Bach, holder of triple doctorates (in Theology, Philosophy, and Medicine), winner of the Nobel Peace Prize, gave up a glowing career to found a mission hospital in French Equatorial Africa.

Schweitzer's study of the historical Jesus remains the definitive volume on the subject, but at the end of his penetrating account Schweitzer takes the reader beyond historical analysis: "Jesus means something to our world because a mighty spiritual force streams from Him and flows through our time also. This fact can neither be shaken nor confirmed by any historical discovery. It is the solid foundation of Christianity."[14] Schweitzer closes his epic work with these haunting words: "He comes to us as One unknown, without a name, as of old, by the lake-side, He came to those men who knew Him not. He speaks to us the same word: 'Follow thou me!' and sets us to the tasks which He has to fulfill for our time. He commands. And to those who obey Him, whether they be wise or simple, He will reveal Himself in the toils, the conflicts, the sufferings which they shall pass through in His fellowship, and, as an ineffable mystery, they shall learn in their own experience Who He is."[15]

Schweitzer's volume was published originally in German in 1906, at the height of his fame. His gripping final paragraph invites the reader to know Jesus—not by historical study—but by following Him in obedience. Which was what Schweitzer was about to do: he would go back to school, earn yet another doctorate (Medicine) and forsake Europe for a life among the poor of Africa.

There is one more fact we should take note of, one that affects all people, whether believers or agnostics. From what towering event is all history reckoned? Dr. W. H. Fitchett replies: "From the birth of a Jew, who, on the skeptical theory, if He ever existed, was a peasant in an obscure province in a far-off age; who wrote no book, made no discovery, invented no philosophy, built no temple; a peasant who died when, as men count years, He had scarcely reached His prime, and died the death of a criminal. . . Yet civilized time is dated from the birth of this Jew! The centuries carry His signature, and the years of the modern world are labeled by universal consent the 'years of our Lord.' . . .

"Every morning all the newspapers of the civilized world . . . readjust their date to His cradle. Each year as it arrives, is baptized with His name. Calendars and acts of Parliament, business, and politics, and literature—the very dates on our checks and letters— all are thus unconsciously adjusted to the chronology of Christ's life. To write a human signature on Time itself, to put a human name on the brow of the hurrying centuries—this is a marvelous achievement: Caesar has not done it, nor Shakespeare, nor Newton. Genius is vain to accomplish such a task; the sword is vain; wealth is vain. But this Jew has done it . . . .

"No conqueror's sword has ever cut deeply enough on Time to leave an enduring mark . . . . Only one name survived; only one figure was visible across wide spaces of perished time.

"The incarnate Son of God, the Word made flesh, who has come into the world's history to shape it to a new pattern—it is fitting that to Him all the years should pay the unconscious homage of bearing His name. The Christianized calendar represents the seal of Christ's kingship on Time itself. But to believe that a remote impostor, in a forgotten province of a perished empire, stamped Himself so deeply on Time as to compel all the centuries to bear His name, is to believe that a child, with its box of colors, could changed the tint of all the oceans!"[16]

Jesus of Nazareth lived and died long ago, but His influence lives on. Uncounted thousands of men and women, young people, and boys and girls along the shores of the Galilee of daily living hear His call, "Follow me!" and, like vast numbers over the course of the centuries, leave their all to follow Him. In Him alone they find peace, fulfillment, meaning and joy; and they rise with Him to a new and better life that brings the kingdom of God down on earth.

The Influence of Jesus in Our Day

The twentieth century produced a quantum shift in thinking, values and behavior. So far the impact has been less obvious in North America than in other Western societies, but that will change. The world our children and grandchildren will grow up in, the world that must hear the good news about Jesus, will be more alien to the Man of Galilee than in any period since He first appeared.

It is a world of meaningless death and therefore meaningless life. Death strikes savagely, suddenly, randomly, and there is no point in trying to find any meaning in existence. Already the forces that shape culture—movies, television, music, radio, books—convey the message that life is a "dirty joke," as Hemingway put it. That theme will dominate.

It is a world without God. Many people cling to the trappings of Christianity, but God is less and less a motivating force in their lives; on the practical level they are atheists. And intellectuals unleash an aggressive atheism, challenging people to face the consequences of a universe where everything can be accounted for by natural means—a world where we no longer *need* God.

It is a world without good or evil. Without God, good and evil, right and wrong, truth and error cease to have meaning. What is right is what is *right for me*—there can be no absolute standard.

The implications of such thinking are horrendous. Christian apologist Ravi Zacharias recounts an experience at Oxford University. After Zacharias' presentation, "a student came up along with others, to challenge the possibility of God's existence. He went on to say that God did not exist, good and evil did not exist, and that we had just created these categories to control people and put fear into people's lives. I asked him a question: 'If I brought a baby to you, and then took a knife and cut that baby up into pieces, would you think I have done something immoral?' He did not even pause, and answered, 'I would not like it, but I would not think you have done anything immoral.' "[17]

It is a world where Eastern religions replace Christianity. Once Christian missionaries went out from the West to lands abroad; now disciples of Krishna, Buddha, and Mohammed propagate their religions in the West. Ideas such as reincarnation and self-deification (I am god!) infiltrate the media and permeate the culture.

It is a world where visual images dominate. They bombard us on every side, profoundly influencing perception and decisions. Feeling takes precedence to reason—if it *feels* right, it is right—and fantasy merges with reality.

It is a world surfeiting in pleasure. Pleasure becomes the goal of life. The excitement of an "affair," the sensory rush of alcohol or other drugs, the thrill of high-risk sports and adventures—these seek to capture the flying moment and give meaning to life.

Zacharias sums up the thinking that will dominate the twenty-first century: "Philosophically, you can believe anything, so long as you do not claim it to be true. Morally, you can practice anything, so long as you do not claim that it is a 'better way.' Religiously, you can hold to anything, so long as you do not bring Jesus Christ into it. If a spiritual idea is eastern, it is granted critical immunity; if western, it is thoroughly criticized."[18]

Jesus: He is the one who does not fit in this picture. He makes people uncomfortable, so they look the other way. When they do allow Him into the conversation, they make clear that, if He is a god, He is but one among many gods.

Yet His name is uttered a billion times or more every day. Most often the use is profane, without thought. Even in a secular age Jesus is somehow never far away.

That name is also uttered by many millions of people in reverent tones. These people state without hesitation that Jesus indeed is alive, because they know Him intimately as Saviour, Lord, and Friend. Across nearly 2,000 years they find a bridge of shared experience with the Christians of the first century: "Though you have not seen him, you love him; and even though you do not see him now, you believe in him and are filled with an inexpressible and glorious joy" (1 Pet. 1:8).

The influence of Jesus still reaches out and calls people from all walks of life. Not only the nameless faces in the crowd, those who are never featured on the evening news or in the pages of *People Magazine*—no, men and women in public life, prominent scholars, writers, and artists still hear his call. Some, like Albert Schweitzer, obey; and an agnostic Oxford don becomes the Christian apologist C. S. Lewis. A Cambridge scientist Prof. John Polkinghorne becomes a Christian and enters the Anglican priesthood. And a skeptical and curmudgeonly journalist, Malcolm Muggeridge, ends up writing *Jesus Rediscovered*.

"*Fiat lux*! Let there be light!" he writes. "So everything began at God's majestic command; so it might have continued till the end of time—history unending—except that You intervened, shining another light into the innermost recesses of the human will, where the ego reigns and reaches out in tentacles of dark desire. Having seen this other light, I turn to it, striving and growing toward it as plants do toward the sun. The light of love, abolishing the darkness of hate; the light of peace, abolishing the darkness of strife and confusion; the light of life, abolishing the darkness of death; the light of creativity, abolishing the darkness of destruction. Though, in terms of history, the darkness falls, blacking out us and our world, You have overcome history. You came as light into the world in order that whoever believed in You should not remain in darkness. Your light shines in the darkness, and the darkness has not overcome it. Nor ever will."[19]

Nor are Seventh-day Adventists lacking among prominent people of our day for whom Jesus is the motivating force in life and profession. Any list will perforce be long, so a few examples must suffice: Dr. Benjamin Carson, world-renowned neurosurgeon, rated by *Time* magazine among "the best;" Dr. Leonard Bailey, of infant heart-transplant fame at Loma Linda University; Herbert Blomstedt, world acclaimed conductor of symphony orchestras; Wintley Phipps, singer at prayer breakfasts through a series of United States Presidents; Dr. Samson Kisekka, first prime minister of free Uganda; and so on.

Is this why Jesus won't go away? So long as men and women find in Him peace, joy, hope and strength for their day-by-day lives, Jesus' influence will never wane. So long as multitudes can rise up and declare that through Him and in Him they find power for new and better living—power that is strong enough to break the chains of debasing and debilitating habits—the world that would shrug Him off or curse Him away will have to deal with Jesus.

Without Jesus, we are alone in a vast, cold universe. Without Jesus, we are mere specks, meaningless creatures in a meaningless existence. Without Jesus, kindness, purity, nobility, truth, justice, and even love have no moral value, because the universe is amoral. Without Jesus, life is empty: this is all there is, we only come around once, and then it is all over.

But if Jesus is alive, we are not alone. God has come close, is with us. We are special, valued, loved, even with an everlasting love that empties heaven. We have dignity because we are sons and daughters of the King who plans for us an eternal future in his presence. Life throbs with purpose as we follow in the footsteps of the Man of Galilee, carrying onward His loving ministry of hope, healing, forgiveness, and new life.

Jesus won't go away. People can try , as some have done, to argue that He never existed, that the whole story is a myth, a legend. When that fails, they can deny that we have reliable sources and so deny His miracles and resurrection. When the Gospels are shown to withstand scrutiny, they can deny that Jesus was anything more than a man, or thought of Himself so. When they are forced to accept that He made amazing claims about Himself and His relationship to God, their final tack is to reason that He was crazy.

Would to God that the world had more such crazy people!

At the end of the day, Jesus is still here. He won't go away. After all the scholarship, the books, the articles, the songs, the plays, the movies, He is still alive.

Like those in His own time, people today give various answers when He asks, "Who do they say I am?" But then He turns the question around, speaking to us with existential force: "But what about *you*? Who do *you* say I am?" (Matt. 16:13–15).

That question, and the answer the followers of Jesus have given and still give, sets apart Christianity among the world's religions. Christianity is bound up in a person in a manner totally different from Buddhism, Hinduism, Islam, Sikhism, Shintoism, Zoroastrianism, or whatever. Not teachings, not ethics, not lifestyle but *Jesus*—that is the difference.

This question haunts our secular, materialistic twenty-first century. We can reject Jesus, but we can never forget Him. Like Charles Templeton, we will always miss Him.

But those who answer with Peter: "You are the Christ, the son of the living God" (Matt. 16:16) find that their leap of faith has a soft landing. "We accept man's testimony, but God's testimony is greater because it is the testimony of God, which he has given about his Son. Anyone who believes in the Son of God has this testimony in his heart. Anyone who does not believe God has made him out to be a liar, because he has not believed the testimony God has given about his Son. And this is the testimony: God has given us eternal life, and this life is in his Son. He who has the Son has life; he who does not have the Son of God does not have life" (1 John 5:9-12).

For Further Reading
Roy Franklin Cottrell, *The Wonderful Christ*. Nashville, TN: Southern Publishing, 1947.
Malcolm Muggeridge, *Jesus Rediscovered.* New York: Doubleday, 1969.
Lee Strobel, *The Case for Christ*. Grand Rapids, MI: Zondervan, 1998.
_____, *The Case for Faith*. Grand Rapids, MI: Zondervan, 2000.
Ravi Zacharias, *Jesus Among Other Gods*. Nashville, TN: Word, 2000.

Notes

1. Lee Strobel, *The Case for Faith: A Journalist Investigates the Toughest Objections to Christianity* (Grand Rapids, MI.: Zondervan, 2000)
2. Strobel, pp. 17–18.
3. *Time*, Dec. 6, 1999.
4. Josephus, *The Antiquities*, 20.200, 18.63–64.
5. Tacitus, *Annals* 15.44.
6. The extra–biblical sources for Jesus are dealt with elsewhere in this book.
7. John 20:30, 31.
8. Ellen G. White, *Selected Messages*, Book One (Washington, D.C.: Review and Herald, 1958), pp. 21, 22.
9. Albert Schweitzer, *The Quest of the Historical Jesus: A Critical Study of Its Progress from Reimarus to Wrede* (New York: Macmillan, 1969).
10. The work of the Jesus Seminar has been called "a self–indulgent charade" by New Testament scholar Dr. Luke Timothy Johnson and "an academic disgrace" by Dr. Howard Clark Lee. Cited, with other criticisms, in Lee Strobel, *The Case for Christ: A Journalist's Personal Investigation of the Evidence for Jesus* (Grand Rapids, MI: Zondervan,1998), p. 127.
11. Ellen G. White, *The Desire of Ages* (Mountain View, CA: Pacific Press, 1940), p. 377.
12. See the essay by David Marshall, "The Risen Jesus," elsewhere in this book.
13. F. F. Bruce, *The Spreading Flame* (Grand Rapids, MI:Eerdmans, 1958), pp. 161–164.
14. Schweitzer, p. 399.
15. Schweitzer, p. 403.
16. W. H. Fitchett, *The Unrealized Logic of Religion* (London: Epworth Press, 1922), pp. 16–26. Quoted by Roy Franklin Cottrell, *The Wonderful Christ* (Nashville, TN: Southern Publishing Association, 1947), pp. 39, 40.
17. In an address to the Billy Graham Evangelistic Association conference, Amsterdam, July 3, 2000.
18. Ravi Zacharias, *Jesus Among Other Gods* (Nashville, TN: Word Publishing, 2000), vii.
19. Malcolm Muggeridge, *Jesus Rediscovered*, (New York: Doubleday & Company, Inc., 1969), p. 51.

The Jesus of History
Nancy J. Vyhmeister

As far as the apostles and first-century Christians were concerned, the Jesus of history and the Jesus of faith were one and the same. Opponents of the faith did not attack Christians for believing in a nonexistent Jesus; they ridiculed Christians for other reasons. Not many centuries went by, however, before doubts about Jesus crept in, among Christians as well as their enemies. With the advent of modern thinking, questions about the historicity of Jesus increased. In the late twentieth century they became full blown with the high-profiled Jesus Seminar.

The purpose of this chapter is to examine the Jesus of history. Was He real? Is He believable? The first section will trace the quest for the historical Jesus as it has been undertaken largely by those skeptical of traditional views; the second examines extra-biblical sources on the historical Jesus; the third speaks to the reliability of the New Testament as a source of information on Jesus.

The Quest for the Historical Jesus

The Pre-Quest

While the modern quest for "the historical Jesus" began with the Enlightenment of the eighteenth century, there is evidence that doubts and questions arose about the life of Christ long before then. The proliferation of apocryphal gospels in the early centuries of the Christian era suggests that writers—orthodox and heretical—had more to say about Jesus than they found in the four canonical Gospels.[1]

In the late second century A.D. Tatian produced the *Diatessaron*, a life of Jesus that drew on the four Gospels. It was widely used in Syriac-speaking churches into the fifth century and was translated into several other languages. In the early fifth century Augustine, aware of criticism of discrepancies among the Gospels, prepared *The Harmony of the Gospels* in order to "prove that the writers in question do not stand in any antagonism to each other." While he defended the Gospel writers from charges "of absolute unveracity,"[2] Augustine admitted that the order of events could have been reconstructed on the basis of recollection rather than history, that the conversations recorded the sense rather than the precise words, and that details were supplementary and not contradictory.

What we may consider as the pre-quest for the historical Jesus continued in later times. For example, the thirteenth century saw the production of several lives of Christ, not in opposition to the canonical Gospels, but as chronological or thematic presentations. In the sixteenth century harmonies of the Gospels flourished for the edification of believers and defense of the faith. One scholar suggests that this indicated a renewed interest in historical questions.[3] However, the real quest for the historical Jesus, as it has come to be known, began more recently.

The Quest Proper

According to John Meier, one of many contemporary writers on this question, the real Jesus is a person who can be recovered and examined only "by using the scientific tools of modern historical research."[4] The quest for such a person began with Hermann Reimarus (1694-1768), professor of oriental languages in Hamburg and quietly a believer in the ideas proposed by English deists of the late seventeenth and early eighteenth centuries. Shortly after the death of Reimarus, G. E. Lessing published fragments from his work without giving the author's name, his identity only becoming known in 1814. Reimarus proposed to find the Jesus who had existed before the church had smothered Him in dogma—to find the real Jesus.[5] To do so, he distinguished between what the apostles preached and what Jesus had actually said. Jesus was to be understood in terms of Judaism, while Christianity was the creation of the apostles.[6] Reimarus contended that Christianity had perpetuated itself by the misuse of the prophets' writings, by the invention of the resurrection story by disciples who did not want to return to fishing, and by the narration of miracles that never happened.[7] His *Fragments* caused consternation and controversy among believers and interest among scholars.

In the nineteenth century there was optimism that the quest for the historical Jesus could, using historical criticism, reconstruct the authentic person of Jesus and His history. The purpose was to renew Christian faith, leaving dogma behind. Scholars such as F. C. Baur (1792-1860) of the Tübingen school applied the historical critical methodology to the study of Jesus. After considering the moral teachings of Jesus and the messianic convictions of Jesus and the disciples, he concluded that "the view we take of the resurrection is of minor importance for history." What mattered was that the apostles believed that it had taken place.[8] Many others during the late nineteenth and early twentieth centuries came forward with similar views. It was believed that the biblical Jesus was untenable.

Albert Schweitzer's 1910 work, *The Quest of the Historical Jesus*, critiqued the work of scholars who had studied Jesus and the Gospels from Reimarus onward. Concluding that "there is nothing more negative than the result of the critical study of the Life of Jesus," he showed how the Jesus portrayed by the scholars was "a figure designed by rationalism, endowed with life by liberalism, and clothed by modern theology in an historical garb," as writer after writer portrayed Jesus in his own image. Schweitzer's own Jesus derived from the biblical accounts was a radically apocalyptic figure who was a stranger to his own time and to ours. Schweitzer concluded that the "historical foundation of Christianity . . . no longer exists; but that does not mean that Christianity has lost its historical foundation," for "the real immovable historical foundation" is "independent of any historical confirmation or justification."[9] For Schweitzer and many of those who followed him, it was "not Jesus as historically known, but Jesus as spiritually arisen within men,"[10] who was ultimately decisive.

The work of these scholars prepared the way for the writings of Rudolf Bultmann (1884-1976), whose *Jesus* (1926) was a landmark publication. In the introduction he affirmed that "we can know almost nothing concerning the life and personality of Jesus, since the early Christian sources show no interest in either, are moreover fragmentary and often legendary; and other sources about Jesus do not exist."[11] Bultmann's skepticism responded to the liberalism in which he had been trained. For Bultmann what Jesus is reported to have said is not authentic, only "characteristic;" His miracles are "legends." Furthermore, the church attached what Jesus had said about forgiveness to His death; Jesus did not speak of it. Bultmann's book ends with no mention of the resurrection.[12]

Twentieth-century thinking about Jesus has largely been dominated by Bultmann and his disciples, culminating in the pronouncements of the so-called Jesus Seminar during the late 1980s and the 1990s. A group of seventy-four scholars from different seminaries and universities, mainly in the United States, met over six years to prepare the Scholars Version of the four canonical Gospels and the apocryphal Gospel of Thomas. After analyzing 1,500 sayings of Jesus, they cast their vote on the perceived authenticity of each. Their verdict was that "eighty-two percent of the words ascribed to Jesus in the Gospels were not actually spoken by him." The Jesus Seminar has taken a position similar to that of Bultmann on the impossibility of miracles. "The Christ of creed and dogma . . . can no longer command the assent of those who have seen the heavens through Galileo's telescope."[13] Seminar cofounder John Dominic Crossan has stated that Jesus "did not and could not cure" diseases and that no one ever "brings dead people back to life."[14]

The crucifixion is accepted as fact, yet the Gospel story of His burial is set aside. Crossan believes that Jesus was not buried in Joseph's tomb; He could have been left on the cross, but more likely was torn and eaten by wild beasts.[15] For Crossan the resurrection could have involved "trances and visions" rather than reality.[16] From 1 Corinthians 15:1-11 he derives that Paul is not talking about an actual appearance of Jesus to three different groups, but to the precedence of one group over the other.[17] In fact, the resurrection story tells us more about the origin of Christian authority than the origin of Christian faith.[18]

For Marcus Borg—a member of the seminar—"the story of the historical Jesus ends with his death on a Friday in A.D. 30, [yet] the story of Jesus does not end there." The Lord appeared to His followers "in a new way beginning on Easter Sunday" and from then on they experienced Him "as a living reality."[19] These appearances were not "straightforward events" but signified the continuing presence of Jesus in the lives of Christians.[20]

It is important to understand that the work of the Jesus Seminar and those who preceded it with similar convictions has been based on the premises of rationalism, naturalism, and criticism. Beginning with the presupposition that miracles do not happen, questers have concluded that much of what Jesus is recorded as having said and done is largely fictitious. Perhaps they should note what Philip Schaff says: "The purpose of the historian is not to construct a history from preconceived notions and to adjust it to his own liking, but to reproduce it from the best evidence and to let it speak for itself."[21]

Those who believe in the essential accuracy of the scriptural record have been unable to accept the results of this research, noting its doubtful presuppositions. They note also the biblical and extra-biblical evidences for the historicity of Jesus, treating the documents as any other historical documents, and allowing the evidence to speak for itself.

References to Jesus in Early Non-Christian Writings

There are relatively few references to Jesus in non-Christian materials of the first and second centuries. According to Meier, the reason for this comparative silence is that "Jesus was a marginal Jew leading a marginal movement in a marginal province of the vast Roman empire."[22] However, both Jewish and pagan literature contain significant statements of considerable value in substantiating the veracity of the biblical record of Jesus' existence.

Jewish Sources

Josephus

Joseph ben Matthias—a Jewish patriot and turncoat, Pharisee

and historian, who lived from A.D. 37 to about A.D. 100, and who is better known as Flavius Josephus—clearly refers to Jesus in two passages. A third reference to Jesus (though He is not mentioned by name) is found only in the Slavonic version of *Jewish War* 2.9.2. In a section on Pilate, the Slavonic (Old Russian) inserts what Meier calls "a wildly garbled condensation of Gospel events."[23] Given that this addition does not appear in any other version and that the claims made for Jesus are extreme, this passage is generally considered spurious.

James, the Brother of Jesus

In his *Jewish Antiquities*, a history of the Jews from creation until his own time, Josephus wrote around A.D. 90-95 in Book 20 of how Ananus (Ananiah), the high priest, a Sadducee, a "bold man in his temper and very insolent," took the opportunity to exercise his authority shortly after Festus died in A.D. 62:

> He [Ananus] assembled the sanhedrin of the judges, and brought before them the brother of Jesus, who was called Christ, whose name was James, and some others [or some of his companions], and when he had formed an accusation against them as breakers of the law, he delivered them to be stoned.[24]

Josephus was not writing about Jesus or Christians; he was merely setting the stage for the story of the deposition of Ananus. James, or Jacob, was a common Jewish name. Some identification was needed; thus Josephus designated him as the brother of Jesus who was also called Christ.

Some have argued that the mention of Christ is a later Christian interpolation. It should be noted, however, that Josephus did not say that James' brother *was* Christ, but that he was *called* Christ, suggesting his own unbelief. Christian sources call James the "brother of the Lord."[25] Here he is the "brother of Jesus," indicating a less worshipful, probably non-Christian point of view. This passage is intact in all Greek sources, giving no room to suspect textual amendment. Today virtually all scholars agree that this mention of the historical Jesus is authentic to Josephus.

Testimonium Flavianum

In his *Antiquities*, Book 18, Josephus writes about Pilate, the procurator of Judea. In Whiston's translation of Josephus it is recorded:

> Now, there was about this time Jesus, a wise man, if it be lawful to call him a man; for he was a doer of wonderful works, a teacher of such men as receive the truth with pleasure. He drew over to him both many of the Jews, and many of the Gentiles. He was [the] Christ. And when Pilate, at the suggestion of the principal men amongst us, had condemned him to the cross, those that loved him at the first did not forsake him; for he appeared to them alive again the third day; as the divine prophets had foretold these and ten thousand other wonderful things concerning him; and the tribe of Christians, so named from him, are not extinct at this day.[26]

For centuries scholars have debated the authenticity of this passage, resulting in four divergent positions suggesting that the paragraph: (1) is entirely a Christian interpolation; (2) shows heavy Christian editing, with possibly a pejorative mention of Jesus by Josephus; (3) includes slight Christian editing which can be isolated from Josephus' writing; (4) is entirely Josephus' own account. Current scholars tend to locate themselves somewhere in the middle, between positions two and three.

Three elements are seen as Christian interpolations: (1) "If it be lawful to call him a man;" (2) "He was [the] Christ;" and (3) "For he appeared to them alive again the third day, as the divine prophets had foretold these and ten thousand other wonderful things concerning him." Removing these three phrases or sentences does not interrupt the flow of the passage. The so-called interpolations agree with New Testament vocabulary and thinking, while the remaining description of Jesus contains grammar and vocabulary that fit well with Josephus. In fact, the text without the so-called interpolations fits a first-century Jew better than a medieval Christian who might be thought to have written the additions.

Other factors suggest that Josephus was the core author. That Jesus, brother of James and called Christ in Book 20 of the *Antiquities,* does not require further identification here could indicate that Josephus recalled that he had already mentioned Him in book 18. A Christian would hardly consider Jesus merely as a wise man. For a non-Christian this would make perfect sense. Josephus speaks of a Gentile following. This does not fit the Gospels but does reflect the situation in Rome at the end of the first century. The surprise Josephus seems to express, that the "tribe" of Christians has not disappeared, does not sit well with the idea of a Christian writer.

There are only three Greek manuscripts of book 18 of the *Antiquities*, the earliest coming from the eleventh century. However, Eusebius quotes the passage as it is known today.[27] An Arabic version of the *Testimonium*, recorded by Agapius, bishop of Hierapolis (tenth century) in his church history, became part of the discussion when Shlomo Pines published it in 1971. It differs from the passage quoted above, but provides evidence for a version other than the one handed down through the Greek. Charlesworth gives it as follows:

> At this time there was a wise man who was called Jesus. His conduct was good and [he] was known to be virtuous. And many people from among the Jews and the other nations became his disciples. Pilate condemned him to be crucified and to die. But those who had become his disciples did not abandon his discipleship. They reported that he had appeared to them three days after his crucifixion, and that he was alive; accordingly he was perhaps the Messiah, concerning whom the prophets have recounted wonders.[28]

In summarizing his discussion of the authenticity of this passage, Charlesworth admits there may be some subtle Christian alterations. However, he affirms: "We can now be as certain as historical research will presently allow that Josephus did refer to Jesus," thus providing "corroboration of the gospel account."[29]

An analysis of the two *Antiquities* passages indicates that Josephus did mention Jesus. He did so in passing, but clearly acknowledged His historicity. Asked about the significance of Josephus' mention of Jesus, Edwin Yamauchi responded: "Highly significant,. . . since his accounts of the Jewish War have proved to be very accurate; for example, they've been corroborated through archaeological excavations at Masada as well as by historians like Tacitus. He's considered to be a pretty reliable historian, and his mentioning of Jesus is considered extremely important."[30]

The Talmud

The Jewish Talmud, based on the earlier Mishnah (completed around A.D. 200, with no mention of Jesus), was produced in both its forms, the Babylonian and the Palestinian, during the fifth century A.D. It contains vast amounts of oral tradition handed down from rabbi to rabbi. Jewish scholar Joseph Klausner finds that the few mentions of Jesus in the Talmud are not historically important, "since they partake rather of the nature of vituperation and polemic against the founder of a hated party."[31] However, one statement, recorded in *Sanhedrin* 43a, deserves attention.

> On the eve of the Passover Yeshu was hanged. For forty days before the execution took place, a herald went forth and cried, "He is going forth to be stoned because he has practiced sorcery and enticed Israel to apostasy. Any one who can say anything in his favour, let him come forward and plead on his behalf." But since nothing was brought forward in his favour he was hanged on the eve of Passover.[32]

While this passage agrees with the Gospel account of the death of Jesus at the time of the Passover, it also presents difficulties. The first is that Jesus was hanged rather than crucified, as in the Gospels. However, Paul has Jesus "hanged" in Galatians 3:13, and the two thieves were "hanged" on either side of Jesus (Luke 23:39). Second, the herald announces that Yeshu will be stoned, not crucified or hanged. This would be in harmony with Jewish custom, and the Gospels report that Jesus was threatened with stoning (John 8:58, 59; 10:31-33, 39). No information is given on why stoning was announced but Yeshu was hanged; perhaps Roman authorities were involved in the change of plans. Finally, there is a forty-day period during which witnesses could "plead on his behalf." No such period is recorded in the Gospels; perhaps it was a response to accusations of a hasty trial. In any case, Jesus is depicted unfavorably, as one who deceives and leads astray. He is, however, depicted as an historical person who marginally impacted Jewish history.

Pagan Sources

Mara bar Sarapion

Written by a Syrian Stoic held in a Roman prison, this letter encourages his son Sarapion to pursue wisdom. The letter is in the British Museum and is dated A.D. 73. As examples of the value of wisdom, Mara mentions three wise men:

> What good did it do the Athenians to kill Socrates, for which deed they were punished with famine and pestilence? What did it avail the

Samians to burn Pythagoras, since their country was entirely buried under sand in one moment? Or what did it avail the Jews to kill their wise king, since their kingdom was taken away from them from that time on?

God justly avenged these three wise men. The Athenians died of famine, the Samians were flooded by the sea, the Jews were slaughtered and driven from their kingdom, everywhere living in the dispersion.

Socrates is not dead, thanks to Plato; nor Pythagoras, because of Hera's statue. Nor is the wise king, because of the new law he has given.[33]

Although Mara does not mention Jesus by name, there is little doubt that he had Him in mind. It would also seem that his information came from Christian sources such as the synoptic Gospels.

Pliny the Younger

Shortly after the beginning of the second century Pliny, a member of the Roman nobility, became governor of the province of Bithynia and Pontus. Pliny was engaged in extensive correspondence with Rome regarding the problems he faced. One of these was what to do with Christians. He wrote:

In investigations of Christians I have never taken part; hence I do not know what is the crime usually punished or investigated, or what allowances are made.. . . I have asked them if they are Christians, and if they admit it, I repeat the question a second or third time, with a warning of the punishment awaiting them.[34]

While Pliny often uses the word Christians, he uses *Christus* only twice. Pliny wrote that anyone accused of being a Christian could refute the charges by offering incense to the gods and the emperor, and blaspheming *Christus*. He also pointed out that Christians assembled before daylight and recited "by turns a form of words to *Christ* as a god; and that they bound themselves with an oath, not for any crime, but not to commit theft or robbery or adultery, nor to break their word, and not to deny a deposit when demanded."

This letter, written c. A.D. 112, adds little to our knowledge of Christian beliefs and practices in the early second century. It does, however, corroborate the existence of Christians whose faith was in Christ.

Tacitus

A Roman historian, Cornelius Tacitus (c. A.D. 55-c.117) lived under several Roman emperors. His *Annals* and *Histories* filled thirty books and covered the period between A.D. 14 and A.D. 96. Some books have been lost; unfortunately those covering the period from A.D. 29 to 32 are among those missing. His account of the great fire in Rome, A.D. 64, for which Nero was blamed, contains reference to Christians and to Christ.

> Consequently, to get rid of the report, Nero fastened the guilt and inflicted the most exquisite tortures on a class hated for their abominations, called Christians by the populace. Christus, from whom the name had its origin, suffered the extreme penalty during the reign of Tiberius at the hands of one of our procurators, Pontius Pilatus, and a most mischievous superstition, thus checked for the moment, again broke out not only in Judaea, the first source of the evil, but even in Rome, where all things hideous and shameful from every part of the world find their centre and become popular.[35]

The naming of Tiberius and Pontius Pilate in this passage shows that Tacitus had his chronology clear. Christ was for Tacitus a historical person, albeit misguided and superstitious. The anti-Christian tone of the report precludes the possibility of a Christian interpolation. Although there is no reference to sources, Tacitus had been governor in the province of Asia, where there were many Christians. He was also a close friend of Pliny, from whom he could have heard other information on Christ and the Christians. Yamauchi comments, "He was also aware that the movement, temporarily 'checked' by Jesus' death, had spread from Judea to Rome, where an 'immense multitude' professed its faith and were willing to die rather than recant."[36]

Suetonius

In his *Life of Claudius* (25.4) Suetonius, chief secretary of the Roman emperor Hadrian, writing around A.D. 125, tells of the expulsion of the Jews from Rome under Claudius (A.D. 49): "Since the Jews were constantly causing disturbances at the instigation of Chrestus, he [Claudius] expelled them from Rome." This banishment is the same one that is noted in Acts 18:2, and Chrestus may be a variant of Christus.

It is entirely possible that reference is made here to upheavals in the Jewish community due to Christian missionary work. Many scholars have concluded that the disturbances were caused by the preaching of the Christian message by converted Jews. We may suppose that Suetonius, who may or may not have read Josephus or Tacitus, in referring even obliquely to Christians, pre-supposes Christ.

Lucian of Samosata

A second-century satirist, Lucian, derides Christians and their founder. In the *Death of Peregrine* he provides information on what seems to have been a common understanding regarding Christians in those times.

> The Christians, you know, worship a man to this day—the distinguished personage who introduced their novel rites, and was crucified on that account. . . . You see, these misguided creatures start with the general conviction that they are immortal for all time, which explains the contempt of death and voluntary self-devotion which are so common among them; and then it was impressed on them by their original lawgiver that they are all brothers, from the moment that they are converted, and deny the gods of Greece, and worship the crucified sage, and live after his laws.[37]

Lucian does not use the usual word for "crucified;" instead he uses *anaskolopisthenta,* meaning "impaled." Perhaps this is because crucifixion derived from impalement; perhaps he is simply ridiculing Christ and Christians. Lucian never mentions the name of the "impaled one," but calls Him a sage (sophist in some translations) and a lawgiver. Another section of *Peregrine* gives Palestine as the location where this man was crucified. In spite of his satirical approach, Lucian never suggests that the Palestinian sage did not really exist.

Thus from Jewish and pagan sources there exist enough references of varying strength to substantiate the New Testament witness to the existence of Jesus as an historical person, if indeed His existence was ever really in doubt.

The Reliability of the Biblical Sources

Obviously, the clearest and most important sources of information on Jesus are found in the New Testament. The Gospels are evidently faith documents, written from a Christian viewpoint to create faith. But are they reliable historical documents? Believers would answer with a resounding Yes! For Christians the Gospels speak not only of Jesus as Lord and Saviour, but also of Jesus as an historical person.

In any discussion of the historical reliability of New Testament materials, one's own "personal stance, one's own point of view and background," is of utmost importance. Meier also points out that "there is no neutral Switzerland of the mind in the world of Jesus research."[38] While I value careful analysis of the biblical sources and recognize the difficulties involved in Jesus research, my own view would easily be considered conservative, favorable to the reliability of the history given in the New Testament.

I find several reasons to consider the New Testament sources as historically reliable, as well as designed to build faith. The biblical sources are close in time to the life of Christ; ancient manuscripts are abundant; chronological information in Luke further indicates historical accuracy; archaeological discoveries corroborate information provided in the Gospels. And finally, the effects of the Gospels must also be considered.

Proximity of Biblical Documents to the Events

The texts of Matthew, Mark, and Luke do not name their authors. John 21:24 suggests that the author of the fourth Gospel was John the beloved disciple. Matthew and John were disciples, eyewitnesses to the events narrated. Mark and Luke were observers once removed. Mark may have been the young man who fled naked the night Jesus was arrested (Mark 14:51, 52); he was later involved in the missionary enterprise, together with Paul (Acts 15:37; 2 Tim. 4:11), Barnabas (Acts 15:39), and Peter (1 Pet. 5:13). Luke was Paul's traveling companion (Col. 4:14; 2 Tim. 4:11) and the generally accepted author of Acts.

Earliest tradition vouches for Matthew, Mark, Luke, and John as the authors of the Gospels. For Matthew, information comes from Papias of Hierapolis around A.D. 140. About Mark, Papias notes that he was "Peter's interpreter," who wrote down Peter's story of Jesus, not necessarily in the order events happened, but with the greatest accuracy possible.[39] About A.D. 185 Irenaeus wrote that Luke, Paul's fellow apostle, had written a Gospel which provided details of the story of Jesus not given in the other three Gospels.[40] While there is debate regarding the chronology of the production of the Gospels, there is no doubt that these are ancient documents, written within a generation of the events. By way of contrast, Plutarch's biography of Alexander the Great, considered by historians to be trustworthy, was written more than four centuries after his death.

References to the life, death, and resurrection of Jesus occur frequently in the New Testament epistles. They appear in Pauline epistles that can be dated with a fair amount of precision to the middle of the first century and may be earlier than the Gospels themselves. For example, in 1 Corinthians 11:23-26, Paul passes on a "tradition" he has received—the celebration of the Lord's Supper. This letter was written from Ephesus (1 Cor. 16:8), toward the end of Paul's third journey (vs. 5-8; cf. Acts 19:21-20:3). The generally accepted date is A.D. 57. In the same epistle we read of another "tradition" that Paul passes on—the death and resurrection of Christ (1 Cor. 15:3-9). Here he includes a list of the people who had seen Jesus after His resurrection, most of whom he claimed were still alive at the time he wrote the epistle. The survival of eye witnesses some twenty-five years after the events was, for Paul, clear evidence that Jesus had indeed died and come back to life. Many scholars consider Romans 1:3, 4 and 10:9, 10 to be parts of Christian creeds. These must have been early, since they appear in a letter written in A.D. 58. Perhaps the best known example of Paul's use of early Christian materials is the description of Christ's abasement in Philippians 2:6-11. These verses have the form of a hymn and were known to Paul when he wrote the letter from prison in Rome about A.D. 63.

The Manuscripts

The manuscript evidence is another important consideration in defense of the reliability of the Gospels. The John Rylands papyrus is the oldest extant fragment of the Gospel of John. Found in Egypt, it dates from the first half of the second century, thus confirming the composition of the Gospel of John by the end of the first century A.D. Most of the Gospel of John appears in the Bodmer Papyrus II (P66), from the same period . The Chester Beatty papyri, also found in Egypt, are a collection of codices, three of which contain major portions of the New Testament. Of the discovery of these papyri in 1930, Sir Frederic Kenyon wrote: "The net result of this discovery . . . is, in fact, to reduce the gap between the earlier manuscripts and the traditional dates of the New Testament books so far that it becomes negligible in any discussion of their authenticity. No other ancient book has anything like such early and plentiful testimony to its text, and no unbiased scholar would deny that the text that has come down to us is substantially sound."[41]

No other extant manuscripts of ancient works come from so near the time of their original writing. For example, the oldest and only extant manuscript of the first six books of the *Annals* of Tacitus, written in the early second century, dates from about A.D. 1100. The oldest manuscript of Homer's *Iliad* comes from some 400 years after the epic poem was written. The earliest existing manuscript of the *Gallic Wars* of Julius Caesar was copied about A.D. 900, nearly 1,000 years after the report was written.

The number of ancient New Testament manuscripts is also remarkable. In Greek alone there are at least 5,686.[42] Because Christianity was, from the beginning, a missionary religion, the New Testament soon began to be translated into other languages. The first of these translations was into Syriac, some time in the second century; the oldest extant manuscripts come from the fourth century. Latin versions followed soon after, culminating in the Vulgate, translated by Jerome in the second half of the fourth century. Coptic (or Egyptian) manuscripts come from the third century, whereas Armenian and Ethiopic versions are from the fifth and sixth centuries. In all, more than 19,000 manuscripts in other languages survive. By comparison, the number of manuscripts of other ancient works is minimal. For example, there are only eight manuscripts of the *History* of Herodotus and twenty ancient manuscripts of the *Annals* of Tacitus.

Not only do many manuscripts exist, but the writings of the New Testament are well attested in the works of the Church Fathers. The writings of Justin Martyr (died c. A.D. 165), Irenaeus (c. A.D. 130-c. 202), Clement of Alexandria (c. A.D. 150-c. 215), Origen (c. A.D. 185-c. 254), Tertullian (c. A.D. 160-c. 225), Hippolytus (c. A.D. 170-c. 236), and Eusebius (c. A.D. 260-c. 340)[43] contain 19,368 quotations and citations from the Gospels.[44] So much of the New Testament appears in the Church Fathers that, had we no ancient manuscripts, the greater part of the New Testament could be reconstructed from their writings.

While there are minor variations among these manuscripts, scholars agree that there is no modification in the basic message they transmit. About two-thirds of New Testament verses are totally variant free. Some hand-copied manuscripts on leather or papyrus may contain scribal errors, but the entire collection of Greek manuscripts shows how few minor variations there are. No other collection of ancient manuscripts is so large or agrees to such an extent as do the New Testament manuscripts.

Luke's Chronology

In ancient times dates seem to have been less important than they are to us today; birth dates of Roman emperors and Church Fathers are often unknown. Given the primary purpose of the Gospels—to build faith in Jesus as Messiah—it is not strange that there is little reference to chronology. In the Gospels, only Luke gives specific chronological data.

The census, when Joseph and Mary went to Bethlehem (Luke 2:1, 2), is said to have taken place throughout the Roman Empire, when Quirinius (Cyrenius) was governor of Syria. A papyrus published by the British museum shows that the Roman census took place every fourteen years, with one beginning in 8 B.C.[45] In addition, an archaeological find from Egypt shows that it was customary for people to return to their city of birth "in order that they may complete the family registration of the enrollment."[46] The question of the identification of Quirinius, known from Josephus to have been governor in Syria from A.D. 6 onward, has been answered by an inscription from Antioch, according to which Quirinius was proconsul in Syria from 11 B.C. until after the death of Herod the Great (4 B.C.).

In Luke 3:1-3 we find historian Luke using a Greco-Roman

style, clearly intended to show the historicity of his Gospel. According to Meier, he also wants to impress on his readers "that the seemingly paltry events of Jesus' public ministry belong to the sweep and indeed the pivotal moment of history."[47] Even considering the complications of calculating the "fifteenth year of Tiberius," there is little doubt that this year fell between A.D. 27 and 29.[48] This would fit with Pilate's tenure, from about A.D. 26 to 36. It also fits the reigns of Herod Antipas (4 B.C.-A.D. 39) and Philip (4 B.C.-A.D. 33/34). Although Caiaphas was the official high priest (A.D. 18/19-36), his father-in-law Annas, deposed from his position as high priest around A.D. 15, is prominent in the trial of Jesus (John 18:13) and is still called high priest in Acts 4:6. The inclusion of Lysanias in the date was worrisome, since the only Lysanias known from ancient history was the ruler of Chalcis, half a century later. An inscription from the reign of Tiberius (A.D. 14-37) has now shown that one called Lysanias was indeed tetrarch in Abila, near Damascus. This carefully crafted synchronism of dates gives confidence in the historicity of the events narrated.

Archaeology

The inscription naming Lysanias as tetrarch of Abila, just as Luke pointed out, is but one of the archaeological evidences for the accuracy of the Gospel stories. In fact, Luke's mention of geographical sites—thirty-two countries, fifty-four cities, and nine islands—has proved to be totally accurate.[49] New Testament archaeology has not yet corroborated where Jesus lived; it has, however, shown clearly that there was a synagogue in Capernaum in the first century A.D.[50] Thus it might be said that the role of archaeology has been to illuminate, and in some cases to confirm, the existence of people, places, and cultural factors relevant to the historical Jesus.

Because Nazareth was not mentioned by Paul or Josephus and did not appear in the Talmud, some had thought that the town came into being decades or even centuries after Christ. Archaeologists have found lists of priests who, after the destruction of the temple, were sent from Jerusalem to other places; included is Nazareth. Furthermore, first-century tombs have been discovered, as well as remains of three stone watch towers, irrigation trenches, and agricultural terraces. There is agreement that a village with eighty to a hundred houses existed there in the first century A.D.[51] The study of first-century ports surrounding the Sea of Galilea—Capernaum, Gergesa, Magdala, and Tiberias—was made possible by a modern drought. A well-preserved first-century fishing boat found near Magdala adds to the information on fishing in the Sea of Galilee.[52]

John's affirmation that the Pool of Bethesda—called Bethzatha and other variations in ancient manuscripts—had five porticos or covered porches (John 5:2) accurately describes the double pool whose ruins are located north of the temple area. Interestingly, Eusebius and the Pilgrim of Bordeaux (both in the fourth century) speak of twin pools at Bethesda. The ruins show two rectangular pools with a portico between them and four porticos on the perimeter. While there has been some discussion on the identification of this pool, the evidence in favor of its being the pool with five porches, where the paralytic was healed, is solid.[53]

Pontius Pilate is known from several sources to have been prefect (later called procurator) of Judea. Philo described him as being "by nature rigid and stubbornly harsh" and speaks of "the bribes, the acts of pride, the acts of violence, the outrages, the cases of spiteful treatment, the constant murders without trial, the ceaseless and most grievous brutality" of which the Jews accused him.[54] Coins dated between A.D. 29 and 31 show Pilate's name as well as Roman religious symbols, corroborating his ill will towards the Jews.[55] An inscription bearing his name was discovered in Caesarea in 1961. The Gospel record and extra-biblical material agree that Pontius Pilate was in Jerusalem as prefect (procurator) at the time of the crucifixion of Jesus.

Archaeological discoveries have provided information on life in the first century A.D. For example, the so-called "Burnt House" in Jerusalem shows the elegance in which the priestly class lived. Their expensive stone cups and dishes could be purified, unlike pottery which had to be broken when it was ritually contaminated. The ritual baths that formed part of the house speak of obsession with purification, as noted in Matthew 15:2.

Archaeology has also corroborated the Gospels' references to coins—Jewish, Greek, and Roman. The widow's "mite" or "copper coin" (Gk. *lepton*; Luke 21:2, KJV) was a Jewish coin worth half a *kodrantes* (Mark 12:42). Matthew 10:29 tells us that two sparrows were sold for a Roman *assarion* (worth four *kodrantes*). The Roman *denarius* (equivalent to the Greek *drachma*) was a small silver coin considered normal wages for a day's labor (Matt. 20:2, 9, 10). Excavations have found all of these coins, dated from the time of Jesus and the Gospels.[56]

An ossuary found in Jerusalem contained the skeletal remains of Yehohanan, a young man who had died by crucifixion, probably in the year A.D. 7. One seven-inch iron nail pierced his two ankle bones and penetrated a knotty piece of olive wood. Just above the wrist, the radius of his right arm showed a scratch where a nail had been driven into the cross. His legs had been broken. Although the evidence suggests a position other than the one shown in Christian art, the manner of crucifixion clearly agrees with the Gospel narrative.[57]

Archaeology has shown that Christian symbols and prayers to Jesus can be dated to less than a quarter century after Christ's death. In 1945 E. L. Sukenik discovered two ossuaries in a tomb in the vicinity of Jerusalem. Sukenik dated the find to A.D. 50. Most interesting were the charcoal graffiti on them: four crosses and the phrases *Iesous iou* and *Iesous aloth*. The first is understood as a prayer to Jesus for help, the second as a request that Jesus would raise the person whose bones occupied the ossuary. These graffiti are perhaps the earliest Christian inscriptions.[58]

The Effects of the Gospel Records

The foregoing has far-reaching implications. A thorough and objective search for the historical Jesus leads us back to the historically reliable documents that constitute the New Testament record of His life and teachings. It is not acceptable to admit the historical reliability of the Gospels and dismiss the claims of Christ contained therein, His existence, His teachings, or the profound impact He has made on human history. While we are not sure of the exact date of Jesus' birth, that event has divided history, B.C., before Christ, and A.D., *Anno Domini,* "in the year of our Lord." Such a clear demarcation would hardly have been made were there no historical basis for the life of Jesus in Palestine in the early years of what we now call the first century A.D.[59]

The change in Peter, from a coward who denied Jesus (Luke 22:60, 61) to a passionate proclaimer of the resurrected Jesus, only fifty days after the event (Acts 2), is remarkable. His ardor continued until he was crucified for proclaiming that same message. Much the same could be said for the other disciples and early Christians, many of whom were willing to die for the veracity of their message. For example, Ignatius wrote to the Trallians of his certainty regarding Christ's death and resurrection, even as he made his way to martyrdom in Rome in A.D. 115.

Throughout nearly 2,000 years, Christians have obeyed the gospel commission (Matt. 28:18-20), traveling far from home, living in difficult lands, dying as martyrs—all for their certainty in the historicity of the Gospel narratives. It is unlikely that the devotion so many have displayed through the centuries could have been aroused by an inconsequential Jew who only lived a good life and died in Jerusalem early in the first century. Christian devotion flows from the resurrected Christ. That resurrection is basic to the life of the church. And the church, in spite of her faults, has changed the world significantly.

Christian faith is thus more than merely believing. The story of Jesus is a matter of "knowing"—of facts and certainty. The Gospel of John uses forms of the verb "to know" 109 times, more than the three Synoptic Gospels together. In John, Jesus knows the Father (John 10:15); He also knows His flock (v. 27). Jesus wants His disciples to know Him, to know the Father (10:38; 17:3). Throughout the Gospel, different ones know Jesus in a special sense: Nicodemus knows Him as a teacher sent from God (3:2); the Samaritans know that Jesus is the Christ (4:42); Martha knows that whatever she asks of God is possible (11:22). In His sacerdotal prayer Jesus purposes that all the world should know Him and know that He was sent by God; such knowledge is eternal life (17:3). The author of the Gospel, presumably the beloved disciple John, was totally sure of his record: "The man who saw it has given testimony, and his testimony is true" (19:35). At the end of his

Gospel, he penned the following: "This is the disciple who testifies to these things and who wrote them down. We know that his testimony is true" (21:24). We who did not see can still know and believe; in fact, Jesus pronounced a blessing on such as would believe without seeing (20:29).

The record of the birth, life, death, and resurrection of Jesus is a sure foundation for the faith that will make us free (John 8:32, 36). The Jesus of faith, who still calls us to believe, emerges from the historical Jesus, without whom such faith is little more than wishful thinking.

For Further Reading

C. Brown, *Jesus in European Protestant Thought*, 1788-1860. Grand Rapids, MI: Baker, 1988.

G. Habermas, *The Historical Jesus: Ancient Evidence for the Life of Christ.* Joplin, MO: College Press, 1988.

J. McDowell, *New Evidence that Demands a Verdict.* Nashville, TN: Thomas Nelson, 1999.

J. P. Meier, *A Marginal Jew.* New York: Doubleday, 1991.

Lee Strobel, *The Case for Christ.* Grand Rapids, MI: Zondervan, 1988.

G. Thiessen and A. Merz, *The Historical Jesus: A Comprehensive Guide.* Minneapolis, MN: Fortress, 1996.

B. Witherington III, *The Jesus Quest: The Third Search for the Jew of Nazareth.* Downers Grove, IL: InterVarsity. 1995.

Notes

1. See nearly four hundred pages of text and commentary in Wilhelm Schneemelcher, *New Testament Apocrypha*, vol. 1, *Gospels and Related Writings*, rev. ed. (Louisville, KY: Westminster/John Knox, 1991).
2. Augustine, *The Harmony of the Gospels* 1.7; 2.12.
3. Harvey K. McArthur, *The Quest Through the Centuries* (Philadelphia, PA: Fortress, 1966), p. 93.
4. John P. Meier, *A Marginal Jew* (New York: Doubleday, 1991), 1:25.
5. Archibald M. Hunter, *Bible and Gospel* (Philadelphia, PA: Westminster, 1969), pp. 119, 120.
6. Hermann Reimarus, *On the Goal of Jesus and His Disciples* (Leiden: Brill, 1970), p. 41.
7. Colin Brown, *Jesus in European Protestant Thought, 1788-1860* (Grand Rapids, MI: Baker, 1988), pp. 5, 6.
8. F. C. Baur, *The Church History of the First Three Centuries* (London: Williams and Norgate, 1878), 1:42, 43.

9. Albert Schweitzer, *The Quest of the Historical Jesus* (New York: Macmillan, 1959), p. 398.
10. *Ibid.*, p. 401.
11. Rudolf Bultmann, *Jesus and the Word* (New York: Scribner's, 1958), p. 8.
12. *Ibid.*, pp. 107, 108.
13. Robert W. Funk, Roy W. Hoover, and the Jesus Seminar, *The Five Gospels: The Search for the Authentic Words of Jesus* (New York: McMillan, 1993), p. 5.
14. John Dominic Crossan, *Jesus: A Revolutionary Biography* (San Francisco, CA: Harper San Francisco, 1994), pp. 82, 95.
15. *Ibid.*, p. 154.
16. *Ibid.*, p. 190.
17. *Ibid.*, pp.169, 170.
18. *Ibid.*, p. 190.
19. Marcus J. Borg, *Jesus: A New Vision: Spirit, Culture, and the Life of Discipleship* (San Francisco, CA: Harper Collins, 1987), pp. 184, 185.
20. Marcus J. Borg, "Thinking about Easter," *Bible Review* 10 (April 1994), p. 49.
21. Philip Schaff, *History of the Christian Church* (Grand Rapids, MI: Eerdmans, 1962), p. 175.
22. Meier, 1:56.
23. *Ibid.*, 1:57.
24. Flavius Josephus, *Antiquities* 20.9.1 (text taken from William Whiston's translation).
25. Paul in Gal. 1:19; Hegesippus, as quoted in Eusebius, *Ecclesiastical History* 2.23.4.
26. Flavius Josephus, *Antiquities* 18.3.3.
27. Eusebius, *Ecclesiastical History* 1.11.
28. Shlomo Pines, *An Arabic Version of the Testimonium Flavianum and Its Implications* (Jerusalem: Israel Academy of Sciences and Humanities, 1971); text taken from Charlesworth, *Jesus within Judaism: New Light from Exciting Archaeological Discoveries* (New York: Doubleday, 1988), p.95.
29. Charlesworth pp. 96, 97.
30. Lee Strobel, *The Case for Christ* (Grand Rapids, MI: Zondervan, 1998), p. 81.
31. Joseph Klausner, *Jesus of Nazareth* (New York: Macmillan, 1925), pp.18, 19; see also Meier, 1:93-111.
32. *The Babylonian Talmud*, trans. I. Epstein (London: Soncino, 1935), 27:281.
33. Meier, 1:76-78.
34. Pliny, *Letters* 10.96.
35. Tacitus, *Annals* 15.44.
36. Edwin M. Yamauchi, "Jesus Outside the New Testament: What is the Evidence?", Michael Wilkins and J.P.Moreland, eds., *Jesus Under Fire* (Grand Rapids, MI: Zondervan, 1995), p. 216.
37. Lucian, *The Death of Peregrine* 11-13, in *The Works of Lucian of Samosata*, trans. H. W. Fowler and F. G. Fowler, 4 vols. (Oxford: Clarendon, 1905), 4:82, 83.

38. Meier, 1:5.
39. Cited in Eusebius, *Church History* 3.39.
40. Irenaeus, *Against Heresies* 3.14.1-3.
41. Frederic Kenyon, *The Bible and Modern Scholarship* (London: John Murray, 1948), p. 20.
42. These are 109 papyri, 307 uncials, 2860 minuscules, and 2410 lectionaries. Josh McDowell, *The New Evidence That Demands a Verdict* (Nashville, TN: Thomas Nelson, 1999), p. 34.
43. Dates for these Church Fathers are taken from E. A. Livingstone, editor, *The Oxford Dictionary of the Christian Church* (third ed., Oxford: Oxford University Press, 1997).
44. *Ibid.*, p. 43.
45. Gonzalo Báez-Camargo, *Archaeological Commentary on the Bible* (New York: Doubleday, 1984), p. 218.
46. F. F. Bruce, *Jesus and Christian Origins Outside the New Testament* (Grand Rapids, MI: Eerdmans, 1974), p. 194; see also McDowell, p. 63.
47. Meier,1: 383.
48. Meier, 1:383-386; see also *Seventh-day Adventist Bible Commentary* (Washington, DC: Review and Herald, 1953-1957), 5:242-247.
49. Norman Geisler and Thomas Howe, *When Critics Ask: A Popular Handbook on Bible Difficulties* (Wheaton, IL: Victor, 1992), p. 385.
50. James E. Strange and Hershel Shanks, "Synagogue Where Jesus Preached Found at Capernaum," *Biblical Archaeology Review* 9 (November-December 1983): pp. 24-31.
51. "Resurrecting Nazareth," *Biblical Archaeology Review* 25 (May-June 1999), p.14.
52. Mendel Nun, "Ports of Galilee," *Biblical Archaeology Review* 25 (July-August 1999), pp. 18-31.
53. Báez-Camargo, pp. 227, 228; for a model of the twin pool, see D. F. Payne, "Bethesda, Bethzatha," *The Illustrated Bible Dictionary* (Wheaton, IL: Tyndale, 1980), pp. 187, 188.
54. Philo, *De legatione ad Gaium,* 301.
55. D. H. Wheaton, "Pilate," *The Illustrated Bible Dictionary* (Wheaton, IL: Tyndale, 1980), pp. 1229, 1230.
56. *The Illustrated Bible Dictionary* (Wheaton, IL: Tyndale, 1980), s.v. "money."
57. *The New International Dictionary of Biblical Archaeology*, ed. E. M. Blaicklock and R.. Harrison (Grand Rapids, MI: Regency, 1983), s.v. "crucifixion."
58. F. F. Bruce, "Archaeological Confirmation of the New Testament," *Revelation and the Bible*, ed. Carl F. Henry (Grand Rapids, MI: Baker, 1958), pp. 327, 328.
59. The designations "CE" for "common era" and "BCE" for "before the common era" are relatively recent and to a great extent intended to diminish the figure of Christ among non-Christians.

C H A P T E R

The Coming of Jesus Anticipated

Laurence A. Turner

In order to understand Jesus as we meet Him in the New Testament, we must first meet Him in the Old Testament. Unfortunately, many people come to the Gospels with only the haziest understanding of the Old Testament. Yet the very fact that the opening chapter of the New Testament contains Jesus' genealogy (Matt.1:1-17), which amounts to a reprise of Old Testament history, demonstrates that the story that follows cannot be understood without first understanding the story that has gone before. In a similar way, the opening words of John's Gospel, "In the beginning was the Word" (John 1:1), consciously echo the opening words of the Old Testament, "In the beginning God created" (Gen.1:1). Indeed, there is no better place to go in order to understand the reason for the Gospels at the beginning of the New Testament than the beginning of the Old Testament, the book of Genesis.

Jesus in Genesis

Without the first eleven chapters of Genesis, or the primeval history as it is often called, what follows in Scripture would make little sense. The major theme of this introduction is how God deals with order and disorder in His world. He does so in two ways. First, at the physical level, God effortlessly creates "the heavens and the earth" (Gen.1:1). He does so by transforming the initial disorder, described as being "formless and empty" (v. 2), into an ordered and coherent world which is judged to be "very good" (v. 31). God's sovereignty over the physical world is clearly demonstrated here, as it is also in the story of the flood (Gen.6-9), where once again an ordered and blessed world emerges from a watery chaos, as it did at creation.

Second, God's actions at the physical level are reproduced when He turns His attention to the problems caused by disorder at the spiritual level. When God originally created human beings they not only had a harmonious relationship with Him (Gen.2:15-17), but also with each other (vs. 23-25). However, this moral and spiritual harmony soon deteriorated to the point where the man and woman blamed each other and God (3:12), found themselves on a collision course with the rest of God's creation (vs.15, 17-19), and discovered that their relationship with each other involved pain and conflict (v. 16). This tragic degeneration, which changed spiritual order into spiritual disorder, demanded a response from God. In order to understand what God did, why He had to do it, and how all of that relates to Jesus as we meet Him in the Gospels, we need to look more closely at that most calamitous of all biblical stories, found in Genesis 3.

The first thing to notice is that the story conceals more than it reveals. For example, the serpent who enters the scene, questions God's motives, and seduces the woman into eating the fruit from the tree (Gen.3:1-6) is a mysterious character. The account spends no time telling us what his motivation is, why he should question God's goodness, or how he knows what God has said to the human pair concerning the tree. Similarly, the man and the woman are questioned by God, and we hear their excuses (vs. 9-13), but the serpent is never questioned and so has no opportunity to explain his actions. While we might learn his identity later in Scripture (e.g. Rev.12:9; 20:2), it is important to see that none of that is revealed in Genesis. Why? Because we are intended to realize that we will never understand everything about the origin of human sin. Ultimately, it is a mystery. But not so much of a mystery that we cannot understand what the human temptation was, what its consequences were, and what God's solution is.

The serpent's enticement was that if Eve would only eat from the tree, she would "be like God, knowing good and evil" (Gen.3:5). Clearly the man and woman were already "like God"—they had been created in His image (1:27). So what, exactly, does the serpent mean when he says that in becoming like God they would know "good and evil"? The Old Testament frequently expresses totality by using a figure of speech in which direct opposites are placed together. For example, the phrase "from Dan to Beersheba" is used to denote the whole country of Israel. Dan is in the far north, and Beersheba in the far south (e.g. Judg. 20:1; 1 Kgs. 4:25). The two opposites include everything in between. Similarly, when the people of Jerusalem say that "the Lord will not do good, neither will he do evil" (Zeph.1:12, KJV), they clearly believe that "the Lord will do nothing" (as in NIV). When the serpent uses the two opposite terms "good" and "evil," he employs an idiom expressing the whole of human experience. The serpent's temptation, therefore, is that they will be able to experience everything and in that sense be "like God," who has no one to restrict His freedom. He appeals directly to their pride and self-centeredness. That proves to be a temptation too great for the human pair to resist.

The consequences of siding with the serpent shatter the moral and spiritual harmony of God's creation. The man's answer to God's question, "Have you eaten from the tree. . .?" (Gen.3:11), sums up the human dilemma. He replies, "The woman you put here. . ." (v. 12). In the same breath he blames both his wife and God. The man and woman might well have sinned together, but it did not keep them together, for the essence of their sin was selfishness or self-centeredness.

Faced by such a temptation and its consequences, what is God's solution? The answer to this question will take us on a road that ends with Jesus at Calvary. The first hint of what that solution might be is found in God's words to the serpent, "I will put enmity between you and the woman, and between your offspring [literally, "seed"] and hers; he will crush your head, and you will strike his heel" (v.15). As we mentioned previously, several aspects of this story are enigmatic, and this divine promise is no less so. But some aspects are clear enough. The agent who brought sin into human experience is the serpent. So God forewarns that the conflict between humanity and the serpent that began in the garden of Eden will continue through the generations until the serpent is finally defeated. There are those who read this account purely at the surface level, arguing that Genesis is concerned solely with the fear that humans have for snakes.[1] But in an account that is concerned with the creation of the heavens and the earth, the origins of life and the human dilemma of alienation from God, such a perspective seems banal in the extreme.

In this record, the serpent introduces sin into God's good world. The crushing of his head must therefore be a future judgement on what he has done, though how and when this will be accomplished is left unexplained at this point. It is not surprising, therefore, that this verse has been called the *protevangelium* (first gospel), enigmatically stated—the first glimmer of how God intends to tackle the problem of moral and spiritual disorder. Such an understanding of this promise goes back not only to early Christian times but also to the Septuagint (a pre-Christian Greek translation of the Old Testament),[2] and to early Jewish paraphrases of the Bible, written in Aramaic, known as the Targums.[3]

With this backdrop, we can now read the rest of Genesis, and indeed the rest of Scripture, with a sense of where it is heading. And where it heads, first of all, is in a downward spiral in which human sin and alienation causes ever-increasing havoc in God's creation. Human life becomes increasingly chaotic. We move to Cain's murder of his brother Abel (Gen.4:8), which results in a life of aimless wandering (vs.12-16), and on to Lamech's boast about his unethical life (vs. 23, 24). However, matters come to a climax when human depravity results in the assessment that, "the Lord saw how great man's wickedness on the earth had become, and that every inclination of the thoughts of his heart was only evil all the time" (6:5). Such a state of affairs results in God's judgment, the flood, from which only a faithful remnant survives. However, this judgment on human sin does not provide a lasting solution to the human dilemma, for after the flood, sin continues much as it did before. So, the defeat of the serpent's work and the crushing of his head will require more than just divine judgment on human depravity. We will need to look elsewhere for victory over sin.

Exactly where we need to look becomes clearer as we come to the story of Babel and its sequel, the call of Abraham, which introduces the next section of Genesis, often called the ancestral history. At Babel, humanity once again rebels against God (Gen. 4), and God judges it by throwing it into confusion—hence its name Babel, a play on the Hebrew word *balal,* meaning "to confuse" (v. 9). And on that note, the primeval history ends.

We noted earlier that this first section of Genesis started with chaos (Gen.1:2), and it now concludes with chaos (11:9). The physical chaos which existed at the beginning was easily reversed by God's command as He created the heavens and the earth. However, the work of the serpent has now resulted in moral and spiritual chaos, which has climaxed at "Babel." But as the primeval history of Genesis concludes, there is no explicit indication of how this moral chaos will be overcome, no hint of how the serpent's head will be "crushed."

This situation is soon clarified, however. God speaks to a man called Abraham, who proves to be a key figure in the Old Testament revelation. God will bless Abraham, and from him will come "a great nation", with the final outcome that "all peoples on earth will be blessed" through him (Gen.12:3). This call of Abraham comes hot on the heels of the story of Babel's chaos, where all peoples of the earth, "the whole world" (11:1), have been judged. God's promise to Abraham reveals something of the solution to their dilemma. The answer to the problem of the human race, arising from the work of the serpent in the garden and highlighted again at Babel, will come from the line of Abraham. As we shall see, the rest of the Old Testament fills in many of the details.

Messianic Prophecies

An awareness of the opening chapters of Genesis is essential for appreciating how the rest of the Bible presents the great hope of the One who shall come. Yet these introductory stories present the origins of sin and its resolution in veiled and enigmatic ways. Thus we shouldn't expect the work of Christ to be presented so plainly in the Old Testament that it amounts to a Gospel account written centuries before the event. It is much more subtle than that. The Old Testament weaves through its narratives of ancient Israel, and in its presentations of its institutions, a whole array of anticipations of the future figure who will bring God's plan to completion. Occasionally this is done through direct and explicit predictions, but more often through hints and allusions. While we might wish for something more straightforward, this is the consistent approach of Scripture. Whether before Christ's arrival, during His ministry, or after His death and resurrection, the acceptance of Jesus as Messiah (or "Anointed One") and Saviour, must ultimately be a matter of faith, not irrefutable scientific evidence in the form of rational argument, fulfilled predictions, or historical and archaeological data.

We may begin by looking at a representative sample of the numerous "messianic" prophecies in the Old Testament. This will give us an indication of *how* the Scriptures anticipated the One who was to come and *what* they expected Him to achieve.

One of the most significant passages is found in 2 Samuel 7. King David wanted to build a permanent dwelling place for God. However, the prophet Nathan told him that this was not to be. Rather than David building a house for God, God will make a "house" for David (v. 11). That is to say, from David will come a line of kings who will be blessed by God. But on closer inspection it becomes clear that this is more than a promise about the future of the monarchy in Israel. It is part and parcel of God's plan to reverse the inroads of sin in the world. This message forms a direct link with God's promise given at the call of Abraham. For despite David's disappointment at not achieving his heart's desire, God promises, "I will make your name great" (v. 9). There is only one other verse in the Old Testament that speaks of God giving someone a great name, and that is God's promise to Abraham. So this promise to David builds on the one given previously to Abraham that through his "seed" all the nations of the world would be blessed (Gen.12:3).

This can be seen when we look at how the "seed" of David is presented in this passage. Walter Kaiser lists five main characteristics:

He will be a direct descendant of David (2 Sam.7:12).
He will be David's heir (2 Sam.7:12).

He will be God's son (2 Sam.7:14).

His kingdom and His rule over it will be eternal (2 Sam.7:16).

His appearance in the future is guaranteed by God Himself.[4]
So, the promise initiated back in the earlier chapters of Genesis in the promise to the woman and continued by the promises given to Abraham is reiterated again in this promise given to David. The future king who will one day arrive will be of the line of David.

Another instance may be found in Isaiah. The prophet Isaiah spoke during a period when the promise seemed to be under threat. Isaiah lived during the eighth century B.C., when the Assyrian empire was expanding with terrifying ruthlessness, led by one of the world's greatest military strategists, King Tiglath-pileser III. He swept down from his capital in Nineveh and took the land of Israel. Despite the seemingly hopeless situation, God promises a wonderful future for His people: "The people walking in darkness have seen a great light; on those living in the land of the shadow of death a light has dawned" (Isa. 9:2). He continues with a promise of a kingly figure, in line with his earlier promise to David in 2 Samuel 7. "For to us a child is born, to us a son is given, and the government will be on his shoulders. And he will be called Wonderful Counselor, Mighty God, Everlasting Father, Prince of Peace. Of the increase of his government and peace there will be no end. He will reign on David's throne and over his kingdom, establishing and upholding it with justice and righteousness from that time on and forever. The zeal of the Lord Almighty will accomplish this" (Isa. 9:6, 7).

Once again his name is not given, nor the time of his arrival stated, but his coming is assured because it is part of God's purposes. And clearly, he will be more than a human king. The titles "Mighty God" and "Everlasting Father" indicate his status. The fact that he will inaugurate justice and righteousness "from that time on and forever," indicates that he will transcend mere human expectations. He will not be simply a king par excellence, but God's agent to inaugurate a new age in which the human condition will be effectively dealt with.

Yet this image of the coming king is not the only one painted by the Old Testament, nor even by the prophet Isaiah himself. He presents a number of images of hope for the future. In the first half of his book, chapters 1-39, the picture of the messianic king dominates—the king of Isaiah 9 being one example. However, in the second half of Isaiah the mood shifts, and the most striking image here is that of the "servant" of the Lord. Both the messianic king and the servant are presented as ideal representatives of God and effective agents of His purpose, but the emphasis is radically different.

There are a number of "servant songs" in Isaiah 40-55. Some of them refer to the nation Israel as being the servant. For example, Isaiah 41:8, 9. "But you, O Israel, my servant, Jacob, whom I have chosen, you descendants of Abraham my friend, I took you from the ends of the earth, from its farthest corners I called you. I said, 'You are my servant;' I have chosen you and have not rejected you." So Israel is a servant of the Lord. But it is quite clear that the servant Isaiah has in mind is not simply Israel, for some of the "servant" songs speak of the servant's mission not only to the nations but also to Israel itself. For example, Isaiah 49:5, 6, "And now the Lord says—he who formed me in the womb to be his servant to bring Jacob back to him and gather Israel to himself, for I am honored in the eyes of the Lord and my God has been my strength—he says: 'It is too small a thing for you to be my servant to restore the tribes of Jacob and bring back those of Israel I have kept. I will also make you a light for the Gentiles, that you may bring my salvation to the ends of the earth.' "

So the purpose of Israel's election—to bless all the nations of the world, as we saw in the call of Abraham—will be achieved through the work of a particular servant who will also bless Israel. The "servant" songs climax in the most famous of all (Isa.52:13-53:12) in which the servant is clearly an individual.

It is the mission of this servant that is of greatest interest, for it focuses upon the solution to the human dilemma caused by sin. Of this servant it is said predictively, "Surely he took up our infirmities and carried our sorrows, yet we considered him stricken by God, smitten by him, and afflicted. But he was pierced for our transgressions, he was crushed for our iniquities; the punishment that brought us peace was upon him, and by his wounds we are healed" (Isa. 53:4, 5). The mission of this servant includes "healing" human transgressions and bringing peace through being punished, not for his own "transgressions" and "iniquities," but for those of others. Yet strangely, despite this selfless attitude, his work is not appreciated by those he helps, for he "was despised, and we esteemed him not" (v. 3).

Again, as in other passages, exactly how and when such healing and peace will happen is not stated. The prophecy conceals as much as it reveals. Yet it clearly promises a future figure who, through his own suffering, will solve the human predicament caused by sin. In the words of one Old Testament scholar:

> The restoration of Israel, God's servant, is the task of the Servant himself. Yet at another level, the Servant is identified with Israel and similar language is used of both. This is because, in the surprising purposes of God, the Servant enables the original mission of Israel to be fulfilled. That is, through him God's justice, liberation and salvation will be extended to the nations. The universal purpose of the election of Israel is to be achieved through the mission of the Servant.[5]

We may turn for a third example to Daniel. One of the most striking Old Testament passages concerning the One who will deal with the consequences of human transgression is found in Daniel 9. This chapter begins with the prophet Daniel, who is living in exile in Babylon, reflecting on the prophecy of Jeremiah, who had predicted that Judah would spend seventy years in exile (Jer. 25:11, 12; 29:10). It is easy to understand why Daniel's mind should go to this prophecy, given that he was living toward the end of that seventy-year period. However, God uses this opportunity to make a further revelation to Daniel, one which has even more far-reaching consequences than Jeremiah's prediction of Judah's release from exile. This new prediction introduces the "famous prophecy of the 'seventy weeks,'" to use the words of one Old Testament scholar.[6] The text focuses on a time period of "seventy 'sevens'" or "seventy weeks" (Dan.9:24, NKJV). So as Daniel is thinking about Jeremiah's seventy years, God speaks of a period of 490 (seventy times seven) years. What is the significance of these numbers?

In ancient Israel there was a cycle of sabbatical years, in which agricultural land would lie fallow every seventh year (Exod. 23:10, 11; Lev. 25:1-7; Deut.15:1, 2, 11, 12). Jeremiah's prophecy was based on this principle, as shown in 2 Chronicles, "The land enjoyed its sabbath rests; all the time of its desolation it rested, until the seventy years were completed in fulfillment of the word of the Lord spoken by Jeremiah" (36:21). So Jeremiah's seventy years should be seen as a cycle of ten sabbatical years. In addition to this system of sabbatical years, there was a cycle of jubilee years, calculated as occurring every seventh sabbatical year, "Count off seven Sabbaths of years—seven times seven years—so that the seven Sabbaths of years amount to a period of forty-nine years" (Lev. 25:8). This cycle of seven sabbatical years, or forty-nine years, inaugurated a "jubilee" in the fiftieth year (v. 10). In the "jubilee" year all property reverted to its original owner, slaves were freed, and agricultural land lay fallow, freed from its cycle of production.

The prophecy in Daniel 9 should be read with these matters as a backdrop. The chapter begins with his contemplation of Jeremiah's prediction that Judah would be in exile for seventy years, that is *ten sabbatical years*, and concludes with a new prophecy concerning 490 years, or *ten jubilee cycles*. Just as the jubilee year was more wide-ranging and of greater significance than the sabbatical year, so Daniel's prophecy of the 490 years has broader scope than Jeremiah's prophecy of the seventy years.[7] Jeremiah's ten sabbatical years would result in Judah being released from exile. But Gabriel's prophetic word to Daniel of the 490 years specifies a time "to finish transgression, to put an end to sin, to atone for wickedness, to bring in everlasting righteousness," and points to the arrival of "the Anointed One" or Messiah (Dan. 9:24, 25).

Given the Old Testament's general reluctance to spell out specific details concerning the One who is to come, Daniel's prophecy is remarkable for its detail and candor. What is more, it provides a strong indication of the time when this figure is to arrive, "Know and understand this: From the issuing of the decree to restore and rebuild Jerusalem until the Anointed One [Messiah], the ruler, comes, there will be seven 'sevens,' and sixty-two 'sevens' "(v. 25). That is to say, there will be a period of 69 x 7 years (483 years) between the decree to restore Jerusalem and the advent of the "Anointed One." None of the official Persian decrees concerning

Jerusalem expressly mention the restoration of the city, but the one promulgated in 457 B.C. is of particular interest, for it seems to have been understood as allowing this (see Ezra 7). If we use this date as our starting point and count forward 483 years we come to A.D. 27. The prophecy confirms that "in the middle of the [seventieth] 'seven' he will put an end to sacrifice and offering" (Dan. 9:27). The seventieth period of seven years concludes in A.D. 34. Thus this climactic act of the Anointed One would occur during the period A.D. 27-34.

These, of course, were the years in which the ministry of Christ occurred, including His crucifixion, by which He brought to an end the need for "sacrifice and offering" (v. 27), inaugurating the Christian era and the promulgation of the Christian message, atonement for human sin, and the provision of an "everlasting righteousness" for human redemption. Young says quite explicitly that Christ "alone can be described as the Anointed One" of this chapter.[8]

The Sacrificial System

Yet the Old Testament's anticipation of the One who is to come is not confined to prediction, direct or indirect. It is also woven throughout its presentation of ancient Israel's life and institutions. For many readers, the strangest aspect of the Old Testament is its system of sacrifices. However, a little reflection on the principles underlying these sacrifices will show their true essence. When we read the first enigmatic prediction concerning the "seed" of the woman (Gen.3:15), who would overturn the work of the serpent, we saw the first indication of how God would tackle the forces and consequences of sin. In the sacrifices required of ancient Israel we see in symbolic form some of the principles involved in doing just that. So while the biblical texts themselves do not say so explicitly, the Old Testament sacrifices fill in some of the details of the work of the One who was to come to solve the human predicament as promised in the Garden of Eden.

We should note in passing that there have been a number of unsatisfactory and potentially misleading suggestions made over the years as to the significance of Old Testament sacrifice. These can be quickly dismissed. Some have proposed that sacrifice is nothing more than a gift given to an angry God in order to appease him. However, no Old Testament texts support this idea. Also, the Bible is consistent in declaring that God does not *need* any such gift. Others have seen sacrifices as meals presented to a God who, just like a human being, needs to eat. While this is certainly true of Mesopotamian gods, the Bible rejects any notion that sacrifices are God's meals—except in a symbolic sense. The rhetorical question of Psalm 50:13 summarizes the biblical position, "Do I eat the flesh of bulls or drink the blood of goats?" (see also, for example, Judg.13:15-20).[9]

What, then, is the meaning of the sacrificial system? The Old Testament material on animal sacrifices is so complex that we can only deal here with some basic principles. First, it is through sacrifices that human sin is forgiven (Exod.29:36; Lev.9:7). Second, only "clean" and unblemished animals could be used (Gen. 8:20; Lev.1:3). Third, sacrifice in the Old Testament is an act of worship by the person who brings the sacrifice, though on occasions it might also be offered on behalf of the whole community (Lev.16:11; cf 6:15). Fourth, sacrifices could ratify treaties or covenants between parties (Gen.15:9, 10, 18).

In addition, there are distinct types of sacrifices, each of them underlining different elements or intending to emphasize different truths. So, while God does not *need* any gift, sacrifices are gifts from worshipers who recognize that all of their possessions come from God. Worshipers offer sacrifices partly to show that they acknowledge God as their Lord, like paying tribute to a king. And the gifts they offer are those items used to support human life. So sacrifices, especially the whole burnt offerings in which the entire sacrifice was consumed, were the surrender to God of something valuable (2 Sam. 24:24). They are the ultimate gift, with no thought of reciprocation.

Second, the offering of some sacrifices, such as "peace offerings" involved sharing the sacrifice. Part was offered on the altar, and part was eaten by the worshiper. So symbolically the sacrifice represented a meal. Just as human contracts or treaties were sealed or strengthened by sharing a meal together (Gen. 26:28-30), so such a sacrifice was intended to enhance the communion between God and the worshiper.

Third, the sin and guilt offerings, which were explained in great detail at the time of the giving of the law at Sinai and make up about half of the legislation on sacrifice, are of particular significance. What is especially emphasized here is the use of blood. The priest collected the blood from the sacrifice, sprinkling some on the veil that divided the holy place from the most holy place in the sanctuary. He then placed some blood on the corners of the altar of incense and poured the rest around the foot of the altar of burnt offering. While forgiveness of sin was a feature of many sacrifices, it is especially emphasized in these particular offerings, together with the great importance of blood (e.g. Lev.17:11). Briefly summarized, then, the various types of sacrifices are acts of worship in which God's lordship is recognized, communion with God is achieved, and sin is forgiven. How all this relates to Jesus we will deal with shortly.

If we quickly review what the Old Testament says about the solution to sin and its consequences in human experience, we see that it is not a complete or accomplished solution in itself, but looks forward to acts of God that will occur in the future. In a number of different ways, occasionally explicit but more often suggestive and enigmatic, it anticipates how the human predicament will be dealt with decisively. So, coming to the New Testament, it is quite clear that Jesus Christ is God's fulfillment of the anticipations we find in the Old Testament. The early Christian's experience of Jesus forced them to reread the Scriptures, which they now read with a new vision, influenced by their convictions about who Jesus was. They found that some aspects of the Old Testament that were not absolutely clear when *looking forward*, now made perfect sense when *looking back*.

A good example of this is found in Acts 8. Philip, one of the early Christian evangelists, met an important official from the Ethiopian court. This African man was either a convert to Judaism or a God-fearing Gentile, that is, a person attracted to the Hebrew religion. Philip met him after the man had worshiped in the Jerusalem temple and was on his way home to Ethiopia. He was sitting in his chariot reading this passage from the prophet Isaiah: "He was led like a sheep to the slaughter, and as a lamb before the shearer is silent, so he did not open his mouth. In his humiliation he was deprived of justice. Who can speak of his descendants? For his life was taken from the earth" (Acts 8:32, 33). These words come from the "Suffering Servant" passage in Isaiah 53:7, 8. The ensuing discussion between Philip and the Ethiopian illustrates the difference between looking forward and looking back in respect of the messianic message of the Old Testament. The man asked Philip, "Who is the prophet talking about, himself or someone else?" (Acts 8:34). He had clearly seen the significance of the words, but was unclear about who would fulfill the prophecy because he knew nothing about the ministry of Jesus. Philip had the advantage of being able to read Isaiah from the hindsight provided by Jesus and he "began with that very passage of Scripture and told him the good news about Jesus" (v.35), with the result that the Ethiopian came to believe and was baptized as a Christian. There must have been many people like the Ethiopian, who knew in principle the Old Testament Scriptures, with their anticipations—some transparent, some opaque—of how God would deal with the problem of sin. But it was only when Jesus actually arrived on the scene that the whole picture came into sharp focus, sometimes in surprising ways.

The Relationship Between Old and New Testaments

At the beginning of this chapter we suggested that one of the best places to go in order to understand the beginning of the New Testament was the beginning of the Old Testament. Conversely, one of the best places to go to understand the hope expressed in the Old Testament, and how the first Christians understood it, is the beginning of the New Testament.[10] Matthew begins his Gospel with the genealogy of Jesus, tracing His ancestry back to Abraham. Many of the great figures of the Old Testament are included in this genealogy. As Matthew looks back to the Old Testament, he makes a strong connection between its story and the story he is about to tell. Matthew underlines those links by quoting a number of Old Testament texts that he claims are "fulfilled" by Christ (Matt. 2:15, 17, 23).

On closer inspection, however, some of the texts he chooses are surprising—so surprising, in fact, that some have accused Matthew of wrenching texts out of context in order to invent fulfillments. However, as Christopher Wright and others have pointed out, if Matthew had wanted to engage in such an underhanded ploy, why did he choose relatively obscure passages, rather than messianic texts well known to all? Second, one wonders whether Matthew saw the passages he quotes as being predictions that had been fulfilled, because only one of the many passages he quotes—that concerning Bethlehem as the birthplace of the One who shall come (Matt. 2:5, 6 quoting Mic. 5:2)—is in fact a messianic prediction. If Matthew was inventing fulfillments to fit predictions he could surely have done better than to use Isaiah 7:14 (Matt.1:23) concerning King Ahaz in the eighth century B.C.; Hosea 11:1 (Matt. 2:15), referring to the exodus from Egypt hundreds of years earlier; Jeremiah 31:15 (Matt. 2:17, 18), describing the mourning caused by the Babylonian exile, or a prophecy that the Messiah would come from Nazareth (Matt. 2:23) that is found nowhere in the Old Testament! As Wright says, "Matthew is. . . working back from actual events which happened in the early life of Jesus to certain Hebrew scriptures in which he now sees a deeper significance than they could have had before."[11] So Matthew views many passages in the Old Testament as being promises rather than direct predictions. And he is able to see some things looking back that might not have been seen by those looking forward.

Matthew's approach becomes more understandable if we consider what he meant by the word "fulfill." It is clear that much of the time he is not working with a direct prediction-fulfillment model, such as would be the case with the prophecy of the "seventy sevens" (Dan. 9:24-27). For example, after describing how Jesus and His parents fled to Egypt to escape King Herod and how the family then left Egypt and returned home, Matthew says, "And so was fulfilled what the Lord had said through the prophet: 'Out of Egypt I called my son' "(Matt. 2:15, citing Hos.11:1). In context, however, the prophet Hosea is clearly talking about how God brought Israel out of Egypt in the exodus. How does Christ fulfill this?

The Greek word Matthew uses for fulfill, *pleroun*, is used frequently in the Greek translation of the Old Testament, the Septuagint, to translate the Hebrew word *male*. This Hebrew word is used to describe how both space (Isa.6:1) and time (Num.6:13) can be filled up or completed.[12] The great majority of its uses are not related to the fulfillment of a prediction. Thus when one is aware of Jesus and then reads the Old Testament, it is not merely "fulfilled" in the sense of having come to pass, but whole areas are "filled full" with new meaning. So, just as the exodus from Egypt was the decisive act of God's salvation in the Old Testament, so now God is working in an even more significant way through the life of His Son. Just as Jesus goes to, and returns from, the west (Egypt), so the wise men arrive from, and return to, the east (Matt. 2:1, 12). In other words, this is a story of significance for the whole world, just as God promised to Abraham way back in the early chapters of Genesis (Gen.12:3). So it can be said:

> Matthew clearly wants his readers to see that Jesus was not only the *completion* of the Old Testament story at a historical level, as his genealogy portrays, but that he was in a deeper sense its fulfillment. This gives us another way of looking at the Old Testament in relation to Jesus. Not only does the Old Testament *tell the story which Jesus completes, it also declares the promise which Jesus fulfills.*[13]

Also, looking back on such matters as the sacrifices from the perspective of Christ's death, the early Christians were able to see their deeper significance. The Old Testament sacrifices certainly anticipated ways in which God would deal with sin, but the life and death of Jesus now filled them with greater meaning. As the followers of Jesus contemplated His death and how it related to God's purposes presented in the Old Testament, they realized that His death was a perfect sacrifice. Unlike the animal sacrifices in the temple, Jesus offered Himself of His own free will (Heb.7:27). As we saw earlier, animal sacrifices had to be physically perfect, but Jesus was morally perfect (9:14). Some sacrifices sealed covenants or new relationships, and Christ's death brought about a new covenant more significant and intimate than before (1 Cor.11:25, cf. Exod. 24:8). Sin offerings and other sacrifices brought forgiveness for sins, but Christ's death brought forgiveness not only for the individual Israelite or for the nation, but for the *world* (1 John 2:2).

One writer comments, "Precisely because it was a perfect sacrifice which at one stroke exhausted all the possible aspects of sacrifice, it is unique."[14] So, rather than providing direct predictions of the work of Jesus,

> the OT sacrifices provide providential categories for the interpretation of Christ's sacrifice, but it everywhere transcends those categories. For the blood of animals, we have the blood of the man Christ Jesus (Heb.10:4). For spotlessness, we have sinlessness (Heb. 9:14; 1 Pet.1:19). For a sweet smelling odor, we have true acceptability (Eph. 5:2). For the sprinkling of our bodies with blood, we have forgiveness (Heb. 9:13, 14, 19-22; 1 Pet.1:2). For symbolic atonement, endlessly repeated we have real atonement, once for all (Heb.10:1-10).[15]

While prediction is part of the Old Testament anticipation, fulfillment is altogether richer and deeper.

The first chapters of the Old Testament show how sin and self-centeredness damage the relationship between people and God. Then, in suggestive and sometimes veiled ways, the Scriptures look forward to and present a number of images of a figure who will come to reverse the trends started by that tragic beginning. He is variously described as the "seed" of the woman (Gen.3:15, KJV), the "son" of David (2 Sam.7), the "Mighty God" and "Everlasting father" (Isa. 9:6), the suffering servant (Isa.52:13-53:12), the "Anointed One" (Dan. 9:25), and a host of other titles. Additionally, the Old Testament sacrificial system illustrates how God deals with the problem of sin, providing broad hints about how the coming One will act decisively to save humanity from its hopeless dilemma.

However, it is only after Jesus Christ has been born, lived His life, died, and has been raised from the dead that His followers fully realize the meaning of those anticipations. More importantly, in looking back they saw how the whole of the Scriptures, not simply messianic prophecies and direct predictions, were given new meaning, enriched and expanded in scope, when read from the position faith in Jesus.

This process can be illustrated by a story in the Gospel of Luke (Luke 24:25-27). On the day of Christ's resurrection two followers return from Jerusalem to their home in the nearby village of Emmaus. As they walk along the road, the resurrected Christ joins them, but they do not recognize Him. He engages them in Bible study, drawing on well-known passages from the Old Testament concerning the Messiah. But they still do not recognize Him. It is only when they invite Him to be a guest in their home, that they at last recognize who He really is. That is to say, the truth about Jesus can be anticipated, illustrated and demonstrated from Scripture. But now, as well as then, He must be encountered personally if we are to know who He really is.

For Further Reading

W. C. Kaiser, Jr., *The Messiah in the Old Testament.* Grand Rapids, MI: Zondervan,1995.

A. Motyer, *Look to the Rock: An Old Testament Background to our Understanding of Christ.* Leicester: InterVarsity Press, 1996.

P. E. Satterthwaite, R. S. Hess, and G. T. Wenham (eds.), *The Lord's Anointed: Interpretation of Old Testament Messianic Texts.* Carlisle and Grand Rapids, MI: Paternoster/Baker, 1995.

C. Wright, *Knowing Jesus through the Old Testament.* London: Marshall Pickering, 1992.

Notes

1. For a brief survey of suggested identifications for the serpent, see Gordon J. Wenham, *Genesis 1-15*, Word Biblical Commentary (Waco, TX: Word Books, 1987), pp. 72, 73.
2. R. A. Martin, "The Earliest Messianic Interpretation of Gen. 3:15," *Journal of Biblical Literature* 84 (1965), pp. 425-427.
3. For more detail see T. Desmond Alexander, "Messianic Ideology in the Book of Genesis," in Philip E Satterthwaite, Richard S. Hess, and Gordon J. Wenham (eds.), *The Lord's Anointed: Interpretation of Old Testament Messianic Texts* (Carlisle: Paternoster Press and Grand Rapids, MI: Baker Books, 1995), pp. 19-39 (27).
4. Walter C. Kaiser Jr., *The Messiah in the Old Testament* (Grand Rapids, MI: Zondervan, 1995), p. 83.
5. Christopher J. H. Wright, *Knowing Jesus Through the Old Testament* (London: Marshall Pickering, 1992), pp. 162, 163.
6. E. J. Young, *An Introduction to the Old Testament* (London: Tyndale Press, 1964), p. 374.
7. Jacques Doukhan, "The Seventy Weeks of Dan 9: An Exegetical Study,"

Andrews University Seminary Studies 17 (1979), pp. 1-22.

8. Young, p. 375.

9. For a more complete treatment of these and other theories, see Roland de Vaux, *Ancient Israel: Its Life and Institutions,* 2d ed., trans. John McHugh (London: Darton, Longman, and Todd, 1961), pp. 447-456.

10. For more detail on the section that follows, see Wright, pp. 55-63, 112-116.

11. *Ibid.*, p. 9.

12. See Brevard S. Childs, "Prophecy and Fulfillment: A Study of Contemporary Hermeneutics," *Interpretation* 12 (1958), pp. 259, 271.

13. Wright, p. 56.

14. de Vaux, p. 456.

15. R. T. Beckwith, "Sacrifice," in T. D. Alexander and Brian S. Rosner (eds.), *New Dictionary of Biblical Theology* (Leicester: InterVarsity Press and Downers Grove, IL: InterVarsity Press, 2000), p. 761.

The Birth of Jesus
Bryan W. Ball

"Now the birth of Jesus Christ was on this wise." These words with which Matthew opens his account of Jesus' birth (1:18, KJV) are beguilingly simple. They conjure up memories of Christmases past, images of the infant Jesus, and events associated with His birth that may, or may not, be completely accurate. But we must not allow ourselves to be beguiled. The question of who Jesus was is crucial to the theme of this book, and crucial to that question is the prior and related issue of His origins. Traditional Christian belief has held that Jesus existed before His life on earth began and that the babe who was born in Bethlehem c. 5 B.C. was God incarnate. Any adequate examination of Jesus' birth must therefore take into account His preexistence, the nature and meaning of the incarnation, the circumstances surrounding His birth, including the claim that He was born of a virgin mother, and at least some of the unusual features surrounding the nativity.

Pre-existence and Incarnation

The respected Scottish theologian, D. M. Baillie, described the birth of Jesus as "the coming into history of the eternally pre-existent Son of God."[1] It is a representative statement of the early and sustained Christian belief that Jesus had existed in another form before human history began and prior to His birth in Bethlehem. This understanding is foundational to the wider concept of incarnation and is based principally on two sources: Jesus' own claims and the testimony concerning Him in other New Testament writings, which this chapter, as all the others in this book, assumes to be textually reliable and authoritative.

The clearest and most consistent affirmations of Jesus' own understanding are found in recurring statements in the Gospel of John. Six times in the well-known passage in which Jesus describes Himself as the "bread of life" or "the bread from heaven" He asserts that He had come "down" to earth from heaven. For example: "I am the living bread that came down from heaven" (John 6: 51) and "I have come down from heaven not to do my will but to do the will of him who sent me" (v. 38; cf. also vs. 33, 41, 50, 58). In the same chapter Jesus referred to the possibility that in the future some of His wavering disciples might see Him ascend "to where he was before" (v. 62).

In a subsequent confrontation with a group of Pharisees who were challenging the validity of His claims, Jesus pointed to the essential distinction between them and Himself, saying, "You are from below: I am from above. You are of the world; I am not of this world" (8:23). In the same exchange the Pharisees' claim to orthodoxy and correctness on the grounds of their descent from Abraham was countered by Jesus' greater claim, "Before Abraham was born, I am" (v. 58). This is clearly an intentional declaration of His self-understanding. It reechoed God's great affirmation of self-existence to Moses in Exodus 3:14, "I am who I am. This is what you are to say to the Israelites: 'I AM has sent me to you.'" In Hebrew, as in English, this name is a form of the verb "to be" implying that the one so designated is the eternal, self-existent One. In identifying Himself with the name by which God had said He wished to be known, Jesus here expresses His own eternal being in terms that the Pharisees could not fail to understand.

What Jesus said and did not say in this respect is important. It should be noted that Jesus did not say to the Pharisees, "Before Abraham was born, I was." The tense of the verb Jesus used is significant. To have said "I was" would have been true to a limited extent, but it would have said only that Jesus' existence antedated the time of Abraham, thus leaving open the question as to whether at some point Jesus had had a beginning as Abraham had. But what Jesus declares by saying "I am" is that although His earthly life could be measured in terms of years, His existence as a person "is constant and independent of any beginning in time as was that of Abraham."[2] "I am" equates with "I always exist."

As His earthly life began to draw to a close, Jesus again reaffirmed His pre-existent relationship with the Father. "I came from the Father and entered the world; now I am leaving the world and going back to the Father" (John 16:28). Jesus' high-priestly prayer in John 17 reemphasizes this position by referring to the glory which He had shared with His Father "before the world began" (vs. 5, 24) and by praying that this glory would be restored. Lenski says, "It is the glory of the Godhead, the eternal, divine glory that extends back into all eternity, before the cosmos or any creature or created thing existed."[3] It is impossible to avoid the conclusion that Jesus knew and understood that He had existed in heaven before His life on earth began in the stable at Bethlehem.

In addition to Jesus' own claims there are a number of other important New Testament passages that testify to His preexistence. Probably the most well-known of these is found in the prologue to John's Gospel, so often associated with Christmas services celebrating the incarnation. These verses are crucial to a correct analysis of the New Testament data concerning Jesus' identity. John declares that the divine Word, which "became flesh" and dwelt among men, thereby revealed "the glory of the One and Only, who came from the Father" and who had been "with God in the beginning" (1:14, 2). In fact, the entire Gospel of John may be said to be predicated on its declarative opening sentence: "In the beginning was the Word" (v. 1). Even the life said to be inherent in this Word (v. 4; cf. 5:26), which was the light of humankind, speaks of his eternal preexistence: "In him was life original, unborrowed, underived."[4]

Perhaps equally well-known and significant are the majestic verses of Paul to the Philippians in what is generally regarded as an early Christian hymn, possibly modified by Paul in order to express adequately his deep convictions about the Jesus whom he is recommending to his readers as a model in humility. The pastoral concern of this passage does not mitigate its christological affirmation of Jesus' pre-existent being and subsequent condescension. Indeed, the latter is essential to sustain the strength of the argument in the former. Jesus, who was "in very nature God," did not consider that exalted status something to be held on to, "but made himself nothing, taking the very nature of a servant, being made in human likeness" (Phil. 2:6, 7). While this passage is usually quoted, quite correctly, in support of the incarnation itself, it also underlines Christ's pre-existent being. It is indeed one of the key New Testament passages that makes it possible for Baillie to discuss what "the church has always believed about the preexistence of Christ as the eternal Son of God."[5]

Other statements that lend support to the fact of Christ's preexistence are: "He is before all things" (Col. 1:17), "That which was from the beginning. . . we proclaim" (1 John 1:1), and Revelation 1:8 where Christ is recorded as saying, "I am the Alpha and the Omega, who is, and who was, and who is to come." In the face of the widespread and consistent textual evidence, it is difficult to avoid the conclusion that Jesus' preexistence was regarded by the early church and by Himself as an important element in understanding who He was. It has thus justifiably been said, "He existed when time commenced. There was a time when He was not flesh; but there never was a time when He was not God. He always was."[6] The force of the textual evidence has not been diminished by the passing of time.

An important aspect of Christ's preexistence is the role He played in creation. If Jesus is co-eternal and co-equal with the Father and the Holy Spirit, it is only to be expected that His role would be significant. In fact, the New Testament presents Christ as the principal creative agent within the eternal Trinity. "In the beginning was the Word . . . . Through him all things were made; without him nothing was made that has been made" (John 1:1, 2). God "has spoken to us by his Son. . . through whom he made the universe" (Heb. 1:2). "For by him all things were created: things in heaven and on earth; visible and invisible, . . . all things were created by him and for him" (Col. 1:16). Jesus, the divine, eternally pre-existent Word, who for the sake of the entire human race became flesh, was Creator as well as Redeemer. Human existence and human redemption, creation and re-creation, begin and center in Him.

From a careful reading of the foregoing texts, particularly when read in context, it would seem that Christ's role in creation was intentionally determined in the secret counsels of eternity and with the full participation of the Father. Hence it can even be said of Him, the pre-existent Word, that

> He is "before," the "prius," and therefore agent of creation itself, for it was only by means of him that the Father chose to move outside of himself, bringing into being that which is not God. It is through the Son that the Father relates himself to what is made. The eternal Son and the eternal Son alone expresses, stands for, and represents the Father.[7]

Perhaps it is even better to say, not that the pre-existent Christ was the agent in creation, but that He was the Creator. In his significant work, *Christ and Time,* Oscar Cullmann speaks of the "Christ-process," meaning that "creation and redemption appear as a single process" in God's revelatory activity. Christ is both the revealed and the revealer—the Creator and the Redeemer—in a continuing process in which God's redemptive purposes are being worked out in human history. Moreover, this divine Word, this Creator-Redeemer, entered human history at a given point in time "so completely. . . that this unique entrance can be designated by dates just as can every other historical event; it occurred under Emperor Augustus (Luke 2:1); under Emperor Tiberius (Luke 3:1)."[8]

We have now come specifically to the incarnation. If Christ's preexistence, including His role in creation, is important to Christian belief, even more so is His incarnation for it flows not only from preexistence but also, and more significantly, from deity—His total oneness with the Father. It will be recognized, of course, that traditional Christian belief has never proposed His humanity as having had a heavenly preexistence. His existence in heaven prior to Bethlehem was that of the eternal, divine Logos,[9] coequal with the Father, "very God of very God." It was this divine, eternal being who, through the mystery of the incarnation, became human. Baillie says that Christ's human life on earth inevitably leads us back "to its divine origin and eternal background in heaven, on which it all depended."[10] He who was in due time "born of a woman, born under law" (Gal. 4:4) was originally the eternal, pre-existent Word.

The word "incarnation" derives from two Latin words, *in* and *carnis*, the latter meaning "flesh," which together with the prefix *in* signifies "embodiment in human flesh." Paul says of Jesus in 1 Timothy 3:16 that He "was God manifested in the flesh" (NKJV) or "he appeared in a body" (NIV). A relatively recent defense of the incarnation explains:

> The Christian doctrine of the incarnation expresses the conviction . . . that this God has made himself known fully, specifically and personally, by taking our human nature into himself, by coming amongst us as a particular man, without in any way ceasing to be the eternal and infinite God.[11]

The same writer says that "Jesus is the human face of God."[12] All the New Testament writers came to this same conclusion—that God was in Christ. This conclusion was not exaggerated, forced, unnatural, or derived from mythology. "They meant it to be taken with the utmost seriousness."[13]

The incarnation is, at the same time, both one of the central truths of the Christian faith and a great mystery. It is no less true, no less significant, no less essential, because it is a mystery that transcends the limits of human understanding, commending itself to faith as well as to argument. And here we need to ask ourselves two pertinent questions: Is it really a mark of superior intelligence to reject something that cannot be wholly understood because it transcends human experience? And would Christianity be more likely to survive or prosper without the doctrine of the incarnation or with a modified version of it such as has been frequently proposed in recent times? The answer to both questions clearly appears to be No.

The Virgin Birth

Two things need to be understood at the outset regarding the virgin birth of Jesus. First, the virgin birth is one of the two elements in traditional Christian belief (the other being the bodily resurrection of Christ) that over that the past century or so—and again more recently—has particularly attracted the attention of critics, thus leading to escalating doubt, if not actual disbelief, in the factual nature of these events. It is, therefore, an aspect of the story of Jesus that demands consideration. Second, it needs to be said again that the term "virgin birth" is misleading. As far as can be known, the actual *birth* of Jesus was as normal as the birth of any other baby. What is really in contention is the manner of His conception which, as we shall see shortly, is the focus of the textual evidence in the New Testament. Jesus' birth came about as the result of a virginal conception. In attempting to reevaluate the basis of traditional belief in the virgin conception in the face of contemporary doubt, two fundamental questions arise: Could it have happened? And did it happen?

With regard to the first of these questions, the issue is not really confined to the virgin conception at all. The real issue is whether or not miracles can occur—naturalism as opposed to supernaturalism. Yet supernaturalism is evident throughout the New Testament, indeed throughout the entire Bible. It lies at the heart of the Christian faith. To dismiss supernaturalism is to dismiss God, or at least to relegate Him to the company of the competing heathen deities in Old Testament times whose impotence was frequently contrasted with the omnipotence of the one true God. To believe in the biblical God is to accept the possibility of the miraculous. To reject the virgin birth on the grounds that it is a violation of natural law is to reject the possibility of the miraculous altogether and therefore to challenge the nature of the Judaeo-Christian God and ultimately to deny the credibility, even the possibility, of authentic Christian faith per se.

The remainder of this section will examine the evidence that has traditionally provided the answer to the second question, Did it happen? What follows explains why Christians have believed for the best part of two millennia that it *did* happen, that Jesus *was* born of a young woman named Mary who had had no prior sexual encounter with a man. Moreover it explains why the presence of the virgin birth in the earliest creeds of the church, to use the words of

J. Gresham Machen, "shows that it was regarded as one of the essentials, like the death and resurrection."[14]

Certainly it was an early and well-established belief in the Christian church, held with equal conviction and on the same basis as every other major tenet of the faith. It is so attested in the writings of the Apostolic Fathers and others. Ignatius (c. A.D. 110), Justyn Martyr (c. A.D. 110), Irenaeus (c. A.D. 175), and Tertullian (c. A.D. 210) all assert the doctrine of the virgin birth. So does the earliest form of the *Apostles' Creed*. Although often critical of traditional Christian dogma, Adolf Harnack, the most outstanding patristic scholar of his generation, wrote "It is certain that already in the middle of the second century, and probably soon after its beginning, the birth of Jesus from the Holy Ghost and the Virgin Mary formed an established part of the Church tradition."[15] This early conviction flowed principally, if not entirely, as it still does today, from the New Testament itself, notably from the accounts in the Gospels of Matthew and Luke.

Matthew's Testimony

Both Matthew and Luke affirm unambiguously that Mary conceived Jesus, not as a result of intercourse with Joseph, but through the supernatural operation of the Holy Spirit. Matthew is quite categorical: "She was found to be with child through the Holy Spirit" (Matt. 1:18) and "What is conceived in her is from the Holy Spirit" (v. 20). The text says that Mary and Joseph were "pledged to be married." A Jewish betrothal was much more binding than a modern engagement. It carried the obligations of marriage without sexual relationships. It could be broken only by a process similar to divorce. Matthew uses the terms "husband" (v. 19) and "wife" (v. 24) of Joseph and Mary even though they were only betrothed. In these circumstances Joseph became aware of Mary's pregnancy and knew that the child she was carrying was not his. Because he was "a righteous man" and did not want to disgrace her "he had in mind to divorce her quietly" (v.19). He would also have known that under Jewish custom, Mary, so disgraced, could have been subject to harsh discipline, perhaps even death. The record states that in this context Joseph was assured, "Do not be afraid to take Mary home as your wife, because what is conceived in her is from the Holy Spirit" (v. 20). Joseph already knew that he was not the father of Mary's coming child. Now he knew the truth. What did he do? He "took Mary home as his wife. But he had no union with her until she gave birth to a son. And he gave him the name Jesus" (vs. 24, 25).

On the basis of the authority inherent in Scripture, the evident historical nature of the narrative and its accordance with known customs and procedures within the Jewish community of the time, and openness to the real possibility of divine intervention in human affairs, it is not difficult to understand why the early church came to accept the virgin birth of Jesus as fact.

Given the importance of lineage in general and the lineage of Jesus in particular, the genealogy of Christ in the opening verses of Matthew is also enlightening. Matthew begins with Abraham and proceeds "Abraham was the father of Isaac, Isaac the father of Jacob, Jacob the father of Judah and his brothers" and so on down through the successive generations until he comes to "Jacob the father of Joseph" (v. 16). There the patri-lineal account of Jesus' ancestry ends, and Joseph is described simply as "the husband of Mary." Jacob was the father of Joseph, but Joseph was not the father of Jesus. Clearly, Matthew believed that Joseph was not Jesus' natural father. Further, when he wrote of Mary, "of whom was born Jesus" (v.16), he used the genitive, feminine, singular pronoun *hes* thereby designating that the grammatical antecedent could be only the female Mary and not the male Joseph. Gromacki comments, "These abrupt changes definitely show that Joseph did not beget Jesus, but that he was simply the husband of Mary."[16]

Matthew's account also sees the birth of Jesus as a fulfillment of the prophecy in Isaiah 7:14. Isaiah had foretold, "Therefore the Lord himself will give you a sign: The virgin will be with child and will give birth to a son, and will call him Immanuel." The Hebrew word used here for virgin is *almah*. It is not the normal Hebrew word for "virgin" and is used only seven times in the Old

Testament: four times it designates a virgin, and elsewhere it means a young woman or a girl, usually chaste or unmarried. The Septuagint, the Greek version of the Old Testament current in New Testament times, uses the word _parthenos_ for the virgin of Isaiah 7:14. In the New Testament, _parthenos_ almost always means "a virgin." The fact that Matthew was probably quoting from the Septuagint rather than the Hebrew text does not invalidate his application of the prophecy to the birth of Jesus. Since _parthenos_ here refers to sexual virginity, it is a perfectly logical and acceptable application, particularly in the light of the accompanying genealogical and factual elements in Matthew's account.[17] Matthew believed that Isaiah's prophecy found its final and ultimate fulfillment in the child conceived of the Holy Ghost and born of Mary.

Luke's Testimony

There are some important differences in detail between the accounts given by Matthew and Luke, due largely to the differing perspectives from which they were written. Matthew presents the story from Joseph's standpoint, Luke from that of Mary. Thus it could be argued that the record would be less credible if the two accounts were more similar. Their dissimilarity, however, is complementary, not contradictory.

Despite his differing perspective, Luke is as equally emphatic about Mary's virginity as is Matthew. The annunciation of Jesus' impending birth was made, Luke says, "to a virgin pledged to be married to a man named Joseph, a descendent of David. The virgin's name was Mary" (Luke 1:27). Twice it is stated in the one verse that Mary was a virgin. The word used in both instances is _parthenos_. While _parthenos_ has various shades of meaning in nonbiblical usage, in the New Testament it has only the traditional meaning. Mary will conceive a child outside the normal process of human procreation, "exclusively by the creative act of God," a "miracle of virgin conception."[18]

The significance of Mary's forthcoming motherhood is emphasized, by contrast, through the annunciation of John the Baptist's birth in the preceding verses (vs. 5-25). Here, the announcement is made to the father, Zechariah (v.13). But in the case of Jesus' impending birth the mother is told, without any reference to the father. As Machen observes, Mary's unique place in the sequence of events requires an explanation. She is given a "prominence that would seem unnatural if the child belonged equally to Joseph and to her,"[19] particularly so in the context of the experience of Zechariah and Elizabeth. It is, moreover, a prominence that runs through the entire narrative from Luke 1:26 to 2:52. Machen continues:

> The prominence in it of Mary as compared with Joseph, which is so strikingly contrasted with the prominence of Zacharias as compared with Elizabeth, clearly points to something particularly significant in her relation to the promised child, something which Joseph did not share. In other words, it points to the supernatural conception, which is so plainly attested in Lk. i. 34, 35.[20]

Luke's account differs also in that it alone records Mary's response to the annunciation, "How will this be, since I am a virgin?" (1:34). Thus the NIV renders the more traditional "seeing I know not a man?" (KJV, from the Greek _andra ou ginosko_, literally "a man not I know"). This note of genuine surprise, perhaps even of veiled alarm, confirms the substance of the annunciation itself. The narrative reads smoothly and connectedly. Mary's own testimony to her virginity cannot be arbitrarily disregarded. It is a key factor in the unfolding narrative. It was the natural, spontaneous response of a young woman suddenly surprised by the turn of events. The reliability of the text supports the credibility of her claim. There is no valid evidence to show that Luke's narrative is nonfactual or untrustworthy. Mary's own testimony is one of the strongest arguments in support of the traditional belief.

The answer to Mary's question further confirms the miraculous nature of Jesus' conception even if it did not immediately allay Mary's fears. It also confirms Matthew's account. "The Holy Spirit will come upon you, and the power of the Most High will overshadow you" (v. 35). The result of this divine interposition over the normal human process is also stated unequivocally, "You will conceive in your womb and bring forth a son" (v. 31, NKJV). Even when Mary's time had fully come and she and Joseph arrived at

Bethlehem, the narrative reminds us that Mary was only "pledged" to be married to Joseph (2:5), even though she was "great with child" (v.5, KJV).

There is one further important consideration. Why did Luke begin his account of Christian origins and early development with a detailed description of the circumstances surrounding the birth of John the Baptist? Why, in fact, is John's birth so closely intertwined with that of Jesus, both in reality and in the narrative? Could it have been that it was to confirm Mary, the young mother-to-be, in her God-given role and to impress upon her its immense significance?

According to Jewish practices of the time it was customary for a girl to be "pledged" in her early teens[21] and married soon after she reached child-bearing age. It is quite possible, even probable, that Mary bore her firstborn, Jesus, in her mid-teens rather than her mid-twenties as would be customary today. How easy it would have been for her to be overawed by what was taking place. In fact, it is said she was "greatly troubled" (1:29). Mary received the news of her selection as the mother of Jesus when Elizabeth was already six months pregnant. She who was already well advanced in years and who had been barren all her life was also now to bear a son. It, too, was a miracle, an extraordinary event. The record states that the annunciation to Mary ended with the words, spoken in respect of Elizabeth's conception as well as Mary's, "For nothing is impossible with God" (v.37).

And that is the key, the focal point of the entire narrative from Luke 1:5 to Luke 2:40. It is a record of divine activity, the direct and specific intervention of the Almighty, a series of classic demonstrations of supernaturalism at work in the process of human history. Mary was no ordinary mother, and Jesus no ordinary child (in one sense) because His conception came about in an extraordinary manner. Luke's entire narrative substantiates the extraordinary. Not only was Elizabeth filled with the Holy Spirit (1:41) and Jesus conceived by the Holy Spirit; the primacy of the Spirit is evident throughout the early chapters of Luke. The entire narrative is bathed in the glow of the supernatural, the Spirit's presence and activity. Jesus' conception and birth are presented as part of that divine initiative and operation. Mary is comforted by her contact with Elizabeth and begins to understand the scope and the significance of her own impending pregnancy, and she declares, "From now on all generations will call me blessed, for the Mighty One has done great things for me" (v. 49). So Machen can conclude, "The story of the virgin birth is the story of a stupendous miracle, . . . it is an organic part of that majestic picture of Jesus which can be accepted most easily when it is taken as a whole."[22] It is still, by far, the most consistent and convincing interpretation of Matthew's and Luke's narratives.

Luke's account was written to confirm the faith of an educated and highly-placed official, Theophilus, in order to assure him of the "certainty" of the things he believed (1:3, 4). It is highly improbable that Luke, a physician and an historian, whose intention was to record Christian origins on the basis of careful investigation (v. 3), would begin his record with a story that was in any way doubtful. To have included anything of dubious authenticity would have been to jeopardize the entire project as well as his own credibility. Luke was as convinced of the virgin birth as he was that Herod was king of Judea (v. 5), that Mary visited Elizabeth (vs. 39 ff.), that Caesar Augustus ordered a census of the Roman world (2:1), and that Quirinius was governor of Syria (2:2).[23] On the evidence of eyewitnesses and his own investigations, Luke tells us that Jesus was conceived by the Holy Spirit and born of a virgin, Mary. It remains a testimony that cannot be summarily dismissed.

The Nativity

Whereas up to this point we have sought to establish the truth of Jesus' birth against those who detract from it, we are now concerned to recover it from those who add to it. Nothing in the accounts of Matthew and Luke has become so elaborated in the popular imagination as the actual birth of Jesus and the events associated with it. Within the constraints of this chapter it is necessary to distinguish between fact and fiction, to separate the accretions from the original. In so doing, we shall attempt to steer a middle course between two extremes—on the one hand the almost total rejection of every aspect of Matthew's and Luke's accounts, and on the other the gullible, uncritical acceptance of many aspects of the nativity as perpetuated in the popular, plastic culture of contemporary Christmas celebrations.

With regard to the first of these extremes, Paul Barnett notes the doubt existing about the traditional Christmas story in liberal academic and ecclesiastical circles, expressions of which are eagerly reflected in the media:

> Many today, including bishops of the church, have expressed skepticism about the historicity of the cluster of stories surrounding the birth of Jesus. It is fashionable to dismiss these stories as "myth" while purporting to accept the deep meaning said to be implicit in them. It has become as predictable as Christmas itself that the media will at that time report the deep reservations felt about it by noted academics or churchmen.[24]

What has already been said about the incarnation and the virgin conception of Jesus will have demonstrated that it is not at all necessary to accept the popular position in order to maintain one's own intellectual self-respect or the inherent credibility of the traditional view.

With regard to the other extreme, it is only necessary to read carefully the biblical accounts to see that what is frequently projected as fact in art, Christmas literature, advertising, sales promotion, and nativity tableaux is in fact fiction. As Barnett further states, "Much of what is believed to be in the Bible proves to be pure religious imagination."[25] It is one thing to say that there is "myth" in the popular presentation of the Christmas story, and quite another to say that "myth" persists in the story itself as recorded in scripture. For the sake of clarity, if not honesty, it is necessary to distinguish between fact and fiction, between what the text says and what it does not say.

At the heart of the nativity is the picture painted by Luke when he says that when Jesus was born Mary "wrapped him in swaddling clothes, and laid him in a manger; because there was no room for them in the inn" (Luke 2:7, KJV). There is both fact and fiction here in the popular understanding. The Greek word for "inn," *kataluma*, does not necessarily mean an hotel or a motel at all. It means simply, even principally, a "lodging place." There are at least three possibilities with regard to what Luke had in mind: (1) a private house; (2) a room in an unidentified place; (3) an inn, or more precisely the inn where travelers stayed, in or near Bethlehem, in accordance with the definite article in the Greek. The word is not sufficiently clear to be definitive. So Raymond Brown's detailed commentary on the birth narratives in Matthew and Luke intentionally uses the word "lodgings" in order to "preserve the ambiguity of the original."[26] Whatever it referred to was occupied, so Jesus was born in less comfortable surroundings.

The manger is also ambiguous. With the "lodgings" already taken, a place was needed for the baby. The manger was almost certainly not located in a wooden outhouse or a barn as frequently depicted in crib scenes. It was much more likely to have been in a space beneath a house, perhaps resembling a cave, which was normally used for animals. The manger itself may have been a movable wooden crib, or equally possibly, a cavity hollowed out of the rock wall. Both types of receptacle were used for animal food; either could have provided a bed for the infant Jesus. We must avoid the temptation to over-sentimentalize what were essentially rough and crude facilities in very basic surroundings. Oxen and donkeys may or may not have been present.

The record also states that wise men "from the east" came in search of the newborn infant (Matt.2:1, 2). But nowhere does it say that there were three of them. The traditional gifts of gold, incense, and myrrh may have given rise to the idea that there were three wise men, but in fact the record does not even say specifically that there were three gifts. It says that the wise men "opened their treasures and presented him with gifts of gold and of incense and of myrrh" (v. 11), but it does not specify how many gifts there were. It may be quite justifiable to conclude that there were three gifts, but on the other hand it may not. There may have been more, all the gifts of gold, incense, or myrrh. It is very easy to read into the text more than is there.

Similarly, these oriental visitors were not "kings." They were "magi," wise men, "educated, wealthy and influential,"[27] but not kings. They were pagans. One source says they were "possessors of special wisdom," particularly concerning "the course of the stars" and their "interconnection with world events."[28] They were probably astrologers from Mesopotamia who were deeply interested in the night skies and perhaps also in the Hebrew scriptures, particularly the messianic prophecies. They represent the best in the pagan quest for enlightenment through nature and divine revelation. Perhaps we should think carefully before singing, "We Three Kings of Orient Are"!

And then there is the star which is said to have guided them. It also has grown in magnitude since its first appearance in the eastern skies. Not too long ago it was regarded as strong evidence that much of the nativity story was mythological and historically unreliable. Today New Testament scholarship proposes at least three astronomical possibilities of varying credibility: (1) a supernova; (2) a comet; or (3) a conjunction of the planets Jupiter and Saturn which is known to have occurred c.6 or 7 B.C. [29] The possibility that any of these suggestions could be the correct understanding does not necessarily invalidate the traditional view that the star which appeared over Bethlehem was a fulfillment of Balaam's messianic prophecy, "a star will come out of Jacob; a scepter will rise out of Israel" (Num. 24:17), or that it was a "distant company of shining angels,"[30] a possibility which in some ways fits more easily with the star's later uncharacteristic meanderings. Only those convinced of the impossibility of the miraculous will *a priori* rule out the star's existence or its function.

All in all, careful scrutiny makes the biblical birth stories look stronger rather than weaker when divested of the accretions of the centuries. Having asked the question whether the original writers intended their narratives to be regarded as historically accurate or rather as "myths" bearing an edifying meaning, Barnett argues that the texts themselves indicate that they were to be taken at face value. He then concludes, "for the birth stories to be regarded as 'myth,' modern readers must arbitrarily go against the apparent intention of the original authors."[31] It is a persuasive argument.

Born to be King

It remains now to formulate an answer to the most important question of all, "Why was Jesus born?" What was the purpose of the incarnation? A careful reading of the biblical accounts in Matthew and Luke leads to what is apparently a twofold answer. We shall see, however, that it is in reality one answer, demonstrating the single-minded purpose of God in the incarnation of Himself in human form and flesh.

Matthew articulates the first answer in the announcement to Joseph regarding Mary's impending pregnancy. After reiterating the role of the Holy Spirit in the conception of Jesus, he states, "She will give birth to a son, and you are to give him the name Jesus, because he will save his people from their sins" (1:21). The name Jesus is the Greek form of the Hebrew Joshua, meaning "The Lord saves." The name Immanuel, "God with us" (v. 23), has the same implication. Jesus' mission is declared in theological terms. It specifically recalls the Davidic assertion of the Lord's unfailing love and intention to redeem His people "from all their sins" (Ps. 130:7, 8). The Hebrew word here is not the usual Old Testament word for sin. It indicates not so much an act or series of acts as a prevailing condition. It was the root of all problems. Sin was the cause of the incarnation, human sin—universal, deadly, and otherwise ineradicable. Jesus came to deal with it.

Luke reiterates the same theme. "Today in the town of David a Saviour has been born" (2:11). And the aged Simeon, "righteous and devout," "waiting for the consolation of Israel" (v.25), holding the infant Jesus in his arms, declares that he is now ready to depart, "For my eyes have seen your salvation" (v.30). The affirmations in verse 11 and verse 26, proceeding in the first instance from the angelic announcement and in the second from the Holy Spirit, were that the infant Jesus was the Christ. The name is the Greek equivalent of the Hebrew "Messiah," the long-awaited Saviour, the Lord's Anointed One. This babe was special indeed. There had never been, nor would there ever be, another like Him.

First and foremost, Jesus came to be the Saviour of His people, Jew and Gentile alike. It is a theme repeated throughout the Bible on countless occasions. It is the scarlet thread that runs throughout the New Testament. Luke himself expresses it again in Acts 4:12, "Salvation is found in no one else, for there is no other name. . . given to men by which we must be saved." Jesus was born to die, for it was on the cross, as a later chapter in this book will explain in much more detail, that His redemptive work was fully and finally accomplished. The Christmas story is much, much more than tinsel and baubles, lights and laughter, family and friends. It concerns alienation and redemption, sin and salvation. It was the beginning, in time, of a process that extends into eternity.

It is Luke who also articulates most clearly the second answer. He records the angelic affirmation of Mary and the momentous privilege and responsibility laid upon her to be the mother of "the Son of God" (1:35): "He will be great and will be called the Son of the Most High. The Lord God will give him the throne of his father David, and he will reign over the house of Jacob forever; his kingdom will never end" (vs. 32, 33). It would take volumes to explain adequately all the implications and nuances of these fundamental words. They expose the heart of Jesus' mission from another perspective altogether. Here Jesus is prefigured in regal terms as the King whose kingdom will endure forever. Jesus was born, not only to die, but also to rule.

Matthew also caught sight of the regnant Jesus when he adapted Micah's prophecy of the coming Ruler whose origins were much older that his actual arrival (Mic. 5:2) and applied it to Jesus, "But you, Bethlehem, in the land of Judah,. . . out of you will come a ruler who will be the shepherd of my people Israel" (Matt. 2:6). Jesus was in truth the babe born to be King. The context indicates that the worship of Jesus by the wise men (vs.2, 11)was the homage paid to royalty rather than to divinity, although the distinction may be tenuous since the reader already "knows that this child has been conceived by God's Holy Spirit and is God's Son."[32] Be that as it may, Jesus' mission is presented in regal and redemptive terms. His is both Saviour and King, Redeemer and Ruler, although at the time everything must still be taken on trust since it is impossible to see how this tiny, innocent, newborn babe can be either. Only the future will reveal how these divine assurances can be translated into reality.

That, indeed, is one of the enigmas of Jesus' coming into the world. How can He be both Saviour and King? How can He die in ignominy, deserted even by His closest followers, and reign in glory, attended by myriads of angels? (Rev. 5:11, 12). How can the despised, the rejected, the forsaken ever become the focus of joyful and unending adoration? The answer is contained in that understanding of Jesus' mission that sees His birth, not only as the beginning of His life on earth, but also as the beginning of something much greater, something that extends into the eternal future, even as His own existence extended back into the eternal past. It is the view that sees the incarnation as part of a greater whole, an event which took place only "when the time had fully come" (Gal.4: 4).

From that perspective some in more recent times have come to speak of the "Christ-event." They have seen the individual events that flowed from Christ's incarnation—His birth, death, resurrection, high-priestly ministry, and second coming—as, in reality, one over-arching event, the "Christ-event." The "Christ-event" is not a single event in Jesus' life, not His birth or His death; it is rather the sum total of the divine intervention effected through Jesus on behalf of the human race. It is the incarnation and all that flows from it. His birth was the beginning of a chain reaction that will eventually result in the total destruction of evil. Stephen Travis declares, "God's plan for the future is to complete what he began when Jesus came," and then he explains:

> Jesus healed, but people still suffer. He triumphed over evil, but evil's destructive power is still around and within us. He claimed to set free the oppressed, but still men are oppressed through war, hatred, prejudice and vested interests. Why? Because the new era which Jesus introduced was only the "beginning of the end." It wasn't God's *final* act of deliverance—that is still to come.[33]

The "Christ-event" began with Jesus' birth in Bethlehem as described by Matthew and Luke. It will end only when the eternal Christ Himself ceases to be. His future coming and everlasting rule will be the consummation of what began in Bethlehem more than 2,000 years ago.

The miraculous coming of Jesus into the world is both an event and a process. As an event it was unprecedented in human history. As a process it extends forward beyond time as well as back into eternity past. And without doing any damage to the continuity or the development of either, it may be said that the "Christ-event" and the "Christ-process" both hinged on the incarnation. The birth of

Jesus was the key to the outworking of both event and process, making it all possible, turning despair into hope and hope into reality. It was, and remains, the most significant event in human history. Maybe, like the wise men and the shepherds, it is time for us to worship Him again or even for the first time—Immanuel, "God with us," the infant Redeemer, the incarnate Ruler of time and the cosmos, the eternal God whose beneficence willed the recovery of a lost race and whose unfailing love still offers salvation and hope.

For Further Reading

P. Barnett, *The Truth about Jesus*. Sydney: Aquila, 1994.

M. Green, ed., *The Truth of God Incarnate*. London: Hodder and Stoughton, 1977.

R. G. Gromacki, *The Virgin Birth*. Grand Rapids, MI: Baker Book House, 1981.

E. Heppenstall, *The Man Who is God*. Washington, D.C.: Review and Herald, 1977.

J. G. Machen, *The Virgin Birth of Christ*. Philadelphia, PA: Presbyterian and Reformed, 1965.

Notes

1. D. M. Baillie, *God Was in Christ* (London: Faber and Faber, 1948), p. 150.
2. R. C. H. Lenski, *The Interpretation of St. John's Gospel* (Minneapolis, MI: Augsburg Publishing House, 1943), p. 671.
3. *Ibid.*, p. 1125.
4. *Seventh-day Adventist Bible Commentary,* 5 (1957), p. 1130.
5. Baillie, pp. 233 ff.
6. Edward Heppenstall, *The Man Who Is God* (Washington, DC: Review and Herald Publishing Assn., 1977), p. 23.
7. Henry Vander Goot, "Christ as Pattern and Agent of Creation," in F. K. Flinn, ed., *Christology: The Center and the Periphery* (New York: Paragon House,1989), p. 34.
8. Oscar Cullmann, *Christ and Time* (London: SCM Press Ltd, 2nd ed., 1951), p. 24.
9. The word signifies the very mind, will, and expression of the eternal Godhead.
10. Baillie, p. 150.
11. Michael Green (ed.), *The Truth of God Incarnate* (London:Hodder and Stoughton, 1977), p. 101.
12. *Ibid.*, p. 103.
13. Green, p. 29.
14. J. Gresham Machen, *The Virgin Birth of Christ* (Philadelphia, PA:

Presbyterian and Reformed Publishing Company, 1965), p. 4. Machen's detailed study remains the most comprehensive response to the objections brought against the virgin birth.

15. Cited in Robert G. Gromacki, *The Virgin Birth: Doctrine of Deity* (Grand Rapids, MI: Baker Book House, 1981), p. 83.
16. *Ibid.*, p. 80.
17. On the meaning of *almah* and its use in Isa. 7:14 and application in Matt. 1:23, see, for example, John Stott, *Christian Basics* (Grand Rapids, MI: Baker Book House, 1991), p. 74, and Heppenstall, pp. 64, 65.
18. G. Kittel and G. Friedrich (eds.), trans. G. W. Bromiley, *Theological Dictionary of the New Testament* (Grand Rapids, MI: Eerdmans, 1967), V, p. 835.
19. Machen, p. 161.
20. *Ibid.*, p. 162.
21. Kittel and Friedrich, V, p. 835.
22. Machen, pp. 381, 382.
23. On Quirinius see Werner Keller, *The Bible as History* (London: Book Club Associates, 2nd ed., 1980), pp. 322-324 and Paul Barnett, *The Truth about Jesus* (Sydney: Aquila, 1994), pp. 96-99.
24. Barnett, *The Truth about Jesus*, p. 86.
25. *Ibid.*
26. Raymond E. Brown, *The Birth of the Messiah: A commentary on the infancy narratives in Matthew and Luke* (London: Geoffrey Chapman,1977), p. 400.
27. *Seventh-day Adventist Bible Commentary* (Washington, D.C.: Review and Herald Publishing Assn., 1956), 5, p. 288.
28. Kittel, IV, p. 358.
29. Brown, pp. 171-173.
30. *Seventh-day Adventist Bible Commentary,* 5, p. 289.
31. Barnett, p. 87.
32. Brown, p. 174.
33. Stephen Travis, *The Jesus Hope* (Leicester: Inter-varsity Press, 1974), p. 32.

Jesus—Divinity
Revealed in Humility

Norman H. Young

In 1889 a dispute arose within a local congregation as to "whether or not Christ, when on earth, could have sinned." One member placed the question before the early Adventist scholar, E. J. Waggoner, to settle the matter. Waggoner replied that he had "not the slightest hesitation in saying that he could not [sin]." For him the question really asked: "Can God sin?"[1] Waggoner's response brought forth several letters in reply affirming the opposite. Waggoner then conceded that theoretically the sinful humanity of Jesus could sin, but since He was God, and not simply possessed of divine power, He did not sin. Waggoner confessed he no more understood this than anyone else.[2]

How God who would not sin, and a human who could sin, cohere unitedly in the one person of Jesus of Nazareth is indeed an intellectual enigma. However, such philosophical issues should not cloud the testimony of those who could say: "That which was from the beginning, which we have heard, which we have seen with our eyes, which we have looked at and our hands have touched—this we proclaim concerning the Word of life. The life appeared; we have seen it and testify to it, and we proclaim to you the eternal life, which was with the Father and has appeared to us. We proclaim to you what we have seen and heard" (1 John 1:1-3). Who Jesus was is a question, then, that only Scripture can ultimately settle.

The conviction that Jesus was fully divine did not arise primarily from His own direct claims to deity. There are many texts where Jesus speaks metaphorically of His person, for example, "I am the bread of life" (John 6:35), "I am the gate" (John 10:9), "I am the good shepherd" (v. 14), but significantly not once does He say "I am God." To have done so in a Jewish context would have caused controversy and confusion, and in a pagan one, misunderstanding.[3] Christian belief that Jesus was one with God Himself is the result of a confluence of material about Jesus that swells into an irresistible avalanche of data.

The direct verbal affirmation of Jesus' divinity came chiefly from others as they tried to express the breadth of the impact He made upon them during His brief life. It was the uniqueness of His person, the authority of His teaching, the awesomeness of His deeds, and above all, the power of His resurrection that evoked from those who knew Him personally and intimately the language of divinity in proclaiming their devotion to Him.

This is the more remarkable since the early Christian ethos and background was rooted in a strict Jewish monotheism. In their worship, both Jews and Christians would accept death rather than compromise their devotion to God by sacrificing to Caesar or to the pagan deities. Yet, amazingly, Christians from the very beginning addressed Jesus as Lord (1 Cor. 8:5, 6), and this was immediate, not the result of some long process. It was this spontaneous devotion to Jesus as Lord and Messiah that was the major cause of the ultimate rift between Christians and their Jewish parent. But before we look at worship in the early church we need to attempt to discover Jesus' own self-understanding.

"The Word Was God" (John 1:1)

There is a reserve in the New Testament about referring directly to Jesus as God. Nevertheless, despite many efforts to deny that it ever does, some texts seem to do so quite unambiguously. After a thorough study of the texts, Murray J. Harris concluded that there are seven specific references that refer to Jesus as God: John 1:1, 18; 20:28; Romans 9:5; Titus 2:13; Hebrews 1:8; 2 Peter 1:1. His conclusion is instructive: "The use of *theos* ["God"] as a christological title shows not that Jesus is God-in-action or God-in-revelation but rather that he is God-by-nature. Not only are the deeds and words of Jesus the deeds and words of God. The nature of Jesus is the nature of God; what God is, Jesus is. By nature, as well as by action, Jesus is God."[4]

However, Jesus' preferred designation for Himself was Son of Man.[5] This title has been widely researched with divergent results. Some see it as a circumlocution for the pronoun "I." Others, drawing on the phrase's frequent usage in Ezekiel, construe it as a Hebraic way of saying "the human being." A more likely background for Jesus' usage is Daniel 7:13. First-century A.D. Jewish apocalyptic writings drew on Daniel 7:9-13 to describe the coming Messiah as a pre-existent, supernatural, heavenly judge. There is no reason against Jesus making just such an application of the Danielic Son of Man figure to Himself.

Accordingly, the popular Christian view that the title Son of Man refers to Jesus' humanity would appear to be misplaced. Jesus hardly needed to convince His contemporaries of His humanity. The Danielic figure is surely supernatural. The association of the Son of Man with the Messiah makes sense then of Peter's reply to Jesus' query, and Jesus' reply to the high priest's interrogation:

Jesus: "Who do people say the Son of Man is?"

Disciples: "Some say John the Baptist; others say Elijah; and still others, Jeremiah or one of the prophets."

Jesus: "But what about you? Who do you say I am?"

Peter: "You are the Christ [Messiah], the Son of the living God" (Matt. 16:13-16).

In the case of the high priest's interrogation, Peter's answer becomes the question, and Jesus' answer is now what was formerly His question to Peter. Thus Messiah and Son of Man are being used interchangeably.

High Priest: "Are you the Christ [Messiah], the Son of the Blessed One?"

Jesus: "I am. And you will see the Son of Man sitting at the right hand of the Mighty One and coming on the clouds of heaven" (Mark 14:61, 62).

The allusion here to Daniel 7:13 would be evident to any first-century reader. We should remind ourselves of the total language of Daniel 7:13, 14. The Son of Man comes to the very presence of God (the Ancient of Days) with the clouds of heaven (a sign of a divine appearance, cf. 1 Thess. 4:17). All power, glory, authority, and sovereignty is given to Him. All the peoples of the earth worship Him and His kingdom lasts forever. But how could such an exalted figure be used to describe Jesus' humiliation, suffering and death (Luke 9:58; Mark 8:31; 9:12, 31)? It would seem that for Jesus the way to His ultimate role as universal ruler was through humility, rejection, and death.

Jesus' authority then lay with God and not with humans. Humans would condemn Him, but God would vindicate Him. In using the title Son of Man for Himself, Jesus is claiming that the eternal kingdom of God was present with Him. The eschatological reign of God had begun, "The blind receive sight, the lame walk, those who have leprosy are cured, the deaf hear, the dead are raised, and the good news is preached to the poor," demons are cast out by the power of God, the kingdom of God has come (Luke 7:22; 11:20). It may not be too much to say that the title Son of Man was a veiled claim to divinity.

We noted above that the terms "Messiah" and "Son of Man" were used in the exchanges with Peter and the high priest somewhat synonymously. Did Jesus then conceive of Himself as the Messiah of God? There is no doubt that the early church immediately accepted Him as the Messiah, so much so that the Greek form, "Christ," became virtually His name. The Messiah was a hoped-for anointed, royal Saviour of the Davidic line. Both the Hebrew "Messiah" and the Greek equivalent "Christ" refer to the use of anointing oil as part of the coronation or investiture ritual. Therefore, Jesus' application of the anointing language of Isa. 61:1 to Himself (Luke 4:18) indicates He understood His mission in terms of the divinely Anointed One.

Jesus' enemies certainly understood Him to have applied such a royal title to Himself for they condemned and executed Him for claiming to be "king of the Jews" (Mark 15:2, 9, 12, 18, 26; John 19:19, 21). Jesus does not dispute the designation, and the episode has good historical credibility since it is highly unlikely that later

Christians would have retrospectively applied such a politically sensitive term to Jesus. Though Jesus refused the many efforts to make Him king (Matt. 21:1-9; John 6:15), He nevertheless, by riding into Jerusalem on a donkey, symbolically accepted the royal claim. It is highly improbable that the early church would have embraced the title Messiah if Jesus had rejected it (for His tacit acceptance see Mark 8:29-33; 14:61, 62; John 4:25, 26; 19:33-37). Jesus' seeming reluctance to embrace the messianic title enthusiastically was no doubt due to how He understood His mission. Clearly He did not intend to establish His rule in an earthly messianic kingdom after annihilating the foreign powers. From Jesus' point of view, "Messiah" had some shortcomings as a description of His person and role. A richer category was needed to announce Jesus' relationship to the Father. Is "Son of God," along with "Son of Man," that better term?

Just as popular opinion misconstrued the meaning of Son of Man, the same is probably true of the title Son of God. The common view refers the title Son of God directly to Jesus' divinity, but the phrase itself does not demand this. To be a son of God places one in a favored or privileged relationship with God, but it does not of itself imply divinity. Contextually, however, the New Testament uses the language of "Son," "only Son" or "Son of God" to convey ideas of Jesus' divinity. John, for example, climaxes his Gospel with the confession of Thomas: "My Lord and my God!" and then he immediately states his purpose in writing: "that you may believe that Jesus is the Christ, the Son of God, and that by believing you may have life in his name" (20:28, 31). Clearly John understood "Son of God" to designate a unique and profound relationship between the Father and the Son. There are also indications of this in the Synoptic Gospels.

Jesus' use of the intimate Aramaic child's term *Abba*, "Father," (Mark 14:36) indicates that Jesus was conscious of a special filial relationship that gave Him the authority to redefine God's relationship with His followers. The declaration in Matthew 11:27 and Luke 10:22 that only the Son can reveal the Father also points to an exclusive relationship to God. The parable of the vineyard where the final messenger is the son whom the tenants slay contrasts Jesus with His Old Testament predecessors as God's final agent (Matt. 21:33-46). Thus, though Jesus never indisputably uses the title Son of God of Himself, there are indications that the free use of the term by the Gospel writers (sixteen times in the Synoptics, nine times in John), Acts (one occurrence), the Epistles (four times in Paul, four times in Hebrews, seven times in 1 John), and even Revelation (one occurrence) has its origins in Jesus' own self-understanding reflected in His calling God "my Father" (Matt. 26:39; 10:32; Luke 2:49) and Himself "the Son" (Matt. 28:19; Mark 13:32).

When the titles "Son of Man," "Messiah," and "Son of God" are read in the context of the broader teaching of the Gospel accounts, their implication becomes even more obvious. One's response to Jesus' person, not simply His words, is crucial for one's ultimate destiny (Matt. 7:21-23; Luke 12:8, 9); and this call takes precedence over family ties (Luke 14:26), even over one's duty to care for one's father's burial (Luke 9:59, 60). Jesus claimed the authority to assign roles in the future life (Matt. 19:28). He attributes to His own words the same eternal validity attached to the word of God (Mark 13:31; Isa. 40:8). Rejecting Him is tantamount to rejecting God (Matt. 10:40; Luke 10:16). Repeatedly Jesus applies to Himself images that had their background in applications to God in the Old Testament. For example, the rejected stone (Luke 20:18; Isa. 8:14, 15), the children's praise (Matt. 21:16; Ps. 8:2), and judging the nations (Matt. 25:32; Joel 3:1-12). His superiority over the Levitical priesthood is demonstrated by His offer of immediate forgiveness outside the processes of the temple. Even His contemporaries recognized this as a divine prerogative (Matt. 9:6; Mark 2:5-9; Luke 7:48-50).

His words, of course, are equally critical; to reject them would be catastrophic, like building on sand (Matt. 7:26). Jesus did not speak as a prophet on God's behalf ("The word of the Lord came unto me saying"), He spoke on His own authority, "But I say unto you" (Matt. 5:21, 22, 27, 28, etc.). He gave conclusive rulings on purity laws (Mark 7:18-23), the Sabbath (Mark 2:23-3:6), and divorce (Mark 10:2-12). Such a claim to have the definitive interpretation of the law, makes Him greater than Moses, the lawgiver (John 1:17), hence His pronouncement that the Law and the

Prophets climaxed with John the Baptist (Matt. 11:13). Such claims affirm an independence and authority unexampled among any other figure in the salvation history of Israel—greater than Abraham, Aaron, David, the prophets, and even Moses. His relationship with the Father was so profoundly intimate that it required a new understanding of monotheism to express it.

"The Word Became Flesh" (John 1:14)

The early church historian Eusebius informs us that messianic fears led first Emperor Vespasian (A.D. 69-79) and then his son Domitian (A.D. 81-96) to attempt to eliminate surviving members of the house of David. Because of their Davidic connection, the grandsons of Jude (Jesus' brother) were brought to Rome to stand before Domitian.[6] When the Emperor saw their calloused hands and peasant appearance he sent them home to their meager lands (between twelve and twenty-four acres), for he considered it unlikely that such impoverished individuals posed any threat to the mighty Roman Empire. There is no reason to believe that Jesus' worldly estate was any higher than that of His grandnephews.

Jesus' family background was thus extremely humble. They were peasant farmers with a carpentry shop to supplement their income. His clear concern for the poor (Luke 7:22) grew out of a personal awareness of poverty. There was, then, nothing make believe about Jesus' sharing in the human condition. As Hebrews says, "Both the one who makes men holy and those who are made holy are of the same family. . . . Since the children have flesh and blood, he too shared in their humanity. . . . For this reason he had to be made like his brothers in every way." (2:11, 14, 17). Hebrews proves His kinship with humanity by placing three Old Testament texts on the lips of Jesus. First, the author quotes Psalm 22:22 (Heb. 2:12). The "I" in "I will declare" and "I will sing" is Jesus. The recipients of Jesus' actions are "brothers," and the location is "in the presence of the congregation." Clearly the writer's point is Jesus' familial unity with the believers. Second, the writer quotes from Isaiah 8:17, and again Jesus is the assumed speaker (Heb. 2:13). Just as Jesus responded to abuse by putting His trust in God, the persecuted readers are here urged to do the same (cf. 1 Pet. 2:21-23). Jesus' oneness with believers included sharing in their suffering (v. 9,10). Third, Hebrews places Isaiah 8:18 in the mouth of Jesus. "The children God has given me" are believers whose close association with Jesus is emphasized. "So Jesus is not ashamed to call them brothers [siblings]" (Heb. 2:11).

That Jesus was one with the human family is the strong testimony of the New Testament, but what was the extent of that oneness? And what was its purpose? In what sense was Jesus born of the Virgin Mary "for our salvation"?[7] While these questions are all potential starting points for theological deviation, they are also crucial to our understanding of the person of Jesus.

Though one with humans, Jesus was not just another mortal. There was something disturbingly different and unique about His life as a man. Constantly His miraculous deeds and His powerful sayings confounded His audience (see Mark 1:22, 27; 2:12; 4:41; 5:20; 6:2, 51; 7:17; 9:15; 10:32, etc.). Two aspects of Jesus' humanity separated Him from His siblings: the circumstances of His birth and the sinlessness of His life.

Assertions about His sinlessness dramatically separate His human experience from that of the rest of humankind. Sinlessness was not a state He attained, but rather retained. From the beginning He was in a wholesome relationship with the Father. He did not repent, He was not reconciled to God. The rest of us do not have an angel announce our forthcoming birth and describe us as "the holy one. . . the Son of God" (Luke 1:35). What the Gospels reveal, the Epistle to the Hebrews declares, namely, that Jesus "is holy, blameless, pure, set apart from sinners, exalted above the heavens" (Heb. 7:26).

Unlike other priests, Jesus did not sacrifice first for His own sins and then for the sins of the people. He offered Himself exclusively for the sins of others (Heb. 2:17; 10:10). There is no thought of Him offering anything for Himself; rather He offered Himself (9:14). As Paul declares unequivocally, God treated Jesus who knew no sin as though He had known sin. Paul thus relates Jesus' sinlessness to His crucifixion. "Knew no sin" means not simply that He committed no overt act of sin, but that he had no inner experience of sin.

His purity was of the heart and not simply in outward conformity to the law. He had a unique and pure inner quality (1 John 3:5). Were it otherwise, He would fall under the condemnation of His own teachings about sin having its origins in the heart (Matt. 15:19).

Jesus was able to ask, "Can any of you prove me guilty of sin?" (John 8:46; 1 Pet. 2:22) and expect no one to come forward. When He challenged a crowd by suggesting only one who was himself without sin could cast the first stone, no one threw a missile at the woman. He alone could have, but He did not. Like Peter, we all feel condemned before the sinless One. "When Simon Peter saw this, he fell at Jesus' knees and said, 'Go away from me, Lord; I am a sinful man!' " (Luke 5:8). If there were not something essentially different about Jesus, neither Peter nor we would experience such discomfort in His presence. Even His judges and opponents recognized Jesus' innocence, and Luke intends his readers to understand His innocence at a level beyond the merely legal (Luke 23: 4, 14, 22, 41, 47, 48).

Mark refers to Jesus as the son of Mary (Mark 6:3), which is an unusual identification given the patrilineal bias of first-century Jewish culture. Indeed, Joseph does not feature at all in the Gospel narratives after the accounts of the birth of Jesus. Such details indicate that Jesus' origins were outside the normal. Both friend and foe recognized this; the former seeing a miraculous divine birth and the latter perceiving adultery. The nature of Jesus' birth was unusual from every angle, not least, of course, the conviction of Matthew and Luke that His mother had had no prior sexual intercourse with a man (Matt. 1:18; Luke 1:34, 35). Bockmuehl points out how Jesus' virginal conception relates to the theme of God's glory revealed in the humble circumstances of an unexpected pregnancy and single motherhood. In this, he concludes, "was seen both the utter humanity and the complete otherness of Jesus."[8] This is the paradox of the incarnation, and it cannot be resolved without distortion. To remain upright, Christian belief must hold the guy ropes of His "utter humanity" and "complete otherness" in tension.

A key passage in Paul where this tension is powerfully present is Romans 8:3. J. Zurcher rightly notes that this passage is the major text used to support the claim that Jesus triumphed over sin despite His accepting a human state that involved all the pull of a fallen condition.[9] Jesus' sinlessness then becomes a model for His followers to attain to. This triumph of Jesus, and consequently of His followers, is seen as the essence of the gospel. There can be no denying the serious emphasis in the New Testament on ethical living as the believer's indispensable response to the gift of salvation. It is equally true that this ethical demand is centered in the gospel events of the death and resurrection of Jesus. The role of the Holy Spirit in the behavioral renewal of the believer is also stressed in the New Testament.

What can be denied, however, is that Jesus' sinlessness is presented in the New Testament as an attainable state for Christians in this life, either in the last days or in any other day. The ethical demands of the New Testament are to be embraced seriously by Christians, but so too is the continuing mercy of the gospel. The reference to Jesus' death as a "sin offering" in Romans 8:3 makes it clear that the redemptive act proper occurred on the cross. As D. Moo notes, "the sacrificial allusions later in this verse [v. 3] show that, without eliminating allusion to the incarnation, Paul's application of the language [of God sending his Son] is broader, with a particular focus on the redemptive death of the Son."[10] Indeed, that the cross is the redemptive act proper and not the sinlessness of Jesus is the emphasis of the New Testament in general.[11]

The NIV translates the Greek word *sarx* in Romans. 8:3 as "sinful nature" or "sinful man." This is not helpful. "Flesh" does not necessarily involve any ideas of "sinful nature". When used by itself, it generally means no more than a human being. The qualifying genitive in v. 3b, however, certainly gives "flesh" a negative reference, that is, "flesh of sin."[12] How far should this daring language be extended?

As we have seen, the New Testament is emphatic that Jesus was innocent of any act of sin. So clearly "flesh of sin" does not extend that far. But should we go as far as C. K. Barrett and deduce that Jesus "took precisely the same fallen nature that we ourselves have, and that he remained sinless because he constantly overcame a proclivity to sin,"[13] or should we withdraw to J. R. Edwards' safe position and say that Jesus successfully resisted sin because "the Son entered humanity with a nature like Adam's before the Fall"?[14]

If Barrett goes too far, Edwards does not seem to go far enough given Paul's graphic language. At the very least the text tells us that Jesus identified with humanity in a meaningful way, and yet remained innocent of any sin. In going beyond this we are saying more than Scripture says. Jesus participated in our sin in that He entered a world alienated from God, He felt the powerful pull to abandon His oneness with the Father, and finally on the cross He completely experienced that alienation. He was not immune to such a test. He was mortal and possessed the fears that are associated with our mortality (Heb. 5:7). T. Weinandy, who argues that Jesus entered humanity in its fallen condition, describes Jesus' "sinful flesh" as experiencing "many of the effects of sin which permeate the world and plague human beings—hunger and thirst, sickness and sorrow, temptation and harassment by Satan, being hated and despised, fear and loneliness, even death and separation from God."[15]

It is not useful to say more than this. On the other hand to say less than this tends towards Docetism.[16] Notwithstanding this latter danger, to suggest that Jesus' nature, like ours, was perverted and insensitive to sin would put the fact of His sinlessness in jeopardy. Even Weinandy, despite his arguing that Jesus "assumed our sinful flesh," is obliged to exclude His having any "inner propensity to sin (concupiscence)."[17] If Jesus never sinned, not even as a child, we must ask why not? The fact that He never sinned is inexplicable unless we accept that at some point His being was different from ours. It is time to return to Romans 8:3.

The addition of "likeness" (homoioma) to the phrase "of flesh of sin" should be seen as a boundary. It is not added to compromise the reality of Jesus' human existence, nor His participation in a world vitiated and dominated by sin. Nor should it be construed to mean "mere appearance" as opposed to "very form." The latter seems to be Paul's meaning whenever he uses homoioma (see Rom. 1:23; 5:14; 6:5; Phil. 2:7). However, "likeness" does constitute a limit, so that whatever Jesus' condescension into the realm of human sin, we must not conceive of Him as altogether like the rest of humanity. Paul (with us) is traversing a fine line in maintaining Jesus' identity with us and His distinction from us. To lurch too far one way or the other is to distort the nature of Jesus' humanity.

The same is true of texts such as Hebrews 2:14-17 and 4:15. The recipients of the Epistle to the Hebrews had suffered much for their Christian faith (Heb. 10:32-34; 12:4; 13:3), and the writer encourages them to persevere in suffering in the knowledge that Jesus had also experienced suffering. Jesus too, the writer reminds his readers, knew what it was like to want to pull back (5:7-10), but He pressed on committing His ways to God. The readers are urged to follow Jesus' example and continue their Christian pilgrimage enduring the scandal of the cross (12:1, 2; 13:12-14).

The author draws on the realities of the incarnation for a pastoral purpose. Despite His exalted status (1:1-14), Jesus became a man and endured severe deprivation in order to deliver those who trusted in Him. The intent is to encourage the readers to persevere even at the peril of their lives. He was the Son of God, He was entirely human, and He did suffer for our benefit. It is not wise to venture beyond these facts.

To be like His siblings in every way (*kata panta*, Heb. 2:17) takes us no further than Jesus' sharing in like manner (*paraplesios*) in the same things (*ton auton*) as His siblings (v. 14). The "same things" are flesh and blood, that is, humanity. Jesus shared with His siblings in human life, including its suffering. Having known suffering, He is able to sympathize with those first-century Christians in particular and all Christians in general who suffer for their faith. It would be tragic to submerge this profound message in futile arguments about the niceties of the incarnation. One thing is clear: Jesus is an example for Christians to follow in His faithfulness to God in testing circumstances. On the other hand, Hebrews says nothing about Jesus providing a model of how to live without sin despite inheriting a fallen condition.

In Hebrews 4:15 the writer is again concerned to give his struggling readers confidence. They are in danger of drifting away (2:1), of failing to enter (4:1), of falling away (6:6), of spurning the Son of God (10:29), of shrinking back (10:32), of growing weary and faint-hearted (12:3), of refusing the voice of God (12:25), and of being led astray (13:9). It is a powerful encouragement for such readers to be reminded that Jesus too had felt the force of being tempted (or better "tested") to turn from the course God had set before Him. But Jesus remained faithful; He did not abandon His calling ("without sin"). "So," the writer exhorts his readers, "let us hold firmly [like Jesus did] to the faith we profess" (2:14).

The author comforts his reader with the assurance that in their Christian struggle, Jesus, their High Priest, sympathizes with the understanding gained from His own suffering. The fidelity of Jesus under stress is the limit of the author's concern to present Him as a leader worthy of emulation. We do not find Hebrews portraying Jesus' incarnational life as the exemplar for the gaining of total victory over sin. The author consistently relates Jesus' oneness with His siblings to His death, not to His being a sinless ideal for us to reproduce.

The writer's own final clauses (in bold) demonstrate where his emphasis lies. "He suffered death, **so that** by the grace of God **he might taste** death for everyone" (2:9), "**so that** by his death **he might destroy** him who holds the power of death—that is, the devil" (2:14), "**in order that he might become** a merciful and faithful high priest" (2:17a), "**that he might make** atonement for the sins of the people" (2:17b), "Christ was sacrificed...**to take away** the sins of many people" (9:28), "Jesus also suffered outside the city gate **to make** the people holy through his own blood" (13:12).

Hebrews 4:15 is another example of a pastoral concern to encourage those suffering for their faith to persevere and follow the path of submission that Jesus trod. To read more from the phrase "tempted [tested] in every way, just as we are—yet was without sin" is to entirely ignore the larger context of the Epistle. The recipients of the letter lost social status and wealth when they became Christians. Their test is to accept the social derision and ostracism of their unbelieving neighbors rather than winning back their approval by abandoning Christ.[18]

In speaking of Jesus' humanity, we often forget the specifics of His human life. Jesus was a first-century Jew living in Roman-occupied Palestine. He was born like all of us from a mother's womb, He was nurtured at her breast, brought up under the piety of the Torah (biblical Law), and lived out His life, by and large, as an observant Jew (Luke 2:7; 11:27; Gal. 4:4). Jesus ate, slept, got tired, wept, showed emotion, prayed, confessed ignorance, and matured like any other mortal. In common with the rest of humanity, He had a family and a hometown, as His contemporaries often derisively reminded Him. They knew His family connections and His family's address: "Isn't this Joseph's son?" (Luke 4:22). "'But we know where this man is from; when the Christ comes, no one will know where he is from'" (John 7:27; cf. Matt. 13:54, 55; Mark 6:3; John 6:42). Yet granting all this, He was not just another man, for through Him God was present in the world in a way never before or since experienced—He was God as a man.

"They Worshiped Him" (Luke 24:52)[19]

For any being other than God to accept worship or set themselves up as an object of worship was for Jews an abomination. This was the blasphemy of the little horn of Daniel (Dan. 8:11; 11:36, 37) and the lawless one that Paul predicted would arise (2 Thess. 2:4). It is in worship, that is, in credal statements (Rom. 1:3, 4; 10:9, 10), in church prayers (8:15; 1 Cor. 16:22; Gal. 4:6); in hymns (Phil. 2:5-11; Col. 1:15-20; 1 Tim. 3:16), that we find Christians spontaneously rethinking their understanding of the nature of God. And this initial outburst of theological energy, let us remind ourselves, occurred among converted monotheistic Jews.

Larry Hurtado sums up the historical phenomenon very well:

> Within the first two decades of Christianity, Jewish Christians gathered in Jesus' name for worship, prayed to him and sang hymns to him, regarded him as exalted to a position of heavenly rule above all angelic orders, appropriated to him titles and Old Testament passages originally referring to God, sought to bring fellow Jews as well as Gentiles to embrace him as the divinely appointed redeemer, and in general redefined their devotion to the God of their fathers so as to include the veneration of Jesus.[20]

The earliest Christian writings are not the Gospels as commonly and understandably supposed, but the letters of Paul. Paul became a Christian in the early to mid-30s A.D., and as he himself says, he was by no means the first convert (Rom. 16:5, 7). His earliest letters date around A.D. 51, and immediately we find the Son closely bracketed with the Father as of equal status (1 Thess. 1:1, 9, 10; 5:23, 28). Romans 1:1-4 is thought to preserve pre-Pauline confessional language. Here, according to Hurtado, the title "Son of God" "seems intended to convey the elevation of Jesus to a position of transcendent status and a uniquely close connection with God."[21]

The most sublime Christian theology is found in its hymns. This was true from the movement's very beginnings. The early church expressed its devotion in sacred songs (1 Cor. 14:26; Col. 3:16, 17; Eph. 5:18-20). And it is in the context of worship that the New Testament Christians directed their most profound praise to Christ. Texts that are thought to have their context in hymnic worship are John 1:1-18; Colossians 1:15-20; Philippians 2:5-11; Ephesians 5:14; 1 Peter 3:18-22; Hebrews 1:3. The hymns to Christ in the book of Revelation (5:9,10, 13, 14) probably also reflect actual Christian worship in the first century. The New Testament writers were avowedly monotheistic (1 Cor. 8.1-6; Rev. 14:6, 7), yet in their celebration of Christ they show "the binitarian shape of early Christian devotion."[22]

The Colossian Christ-hymn or poem (1:15-20) presents a torrent of exalted titles for Jesus: "image of the invisible God," "the first-born," "head . . . of the church," "the beginning," and "all his full-ness dwell[s] in him." The poem draws on the language of Proverbs 8 where "wisdom" is praised as God's agent in creation. The motifs of creation and redemption are conjoined (Col. 1: 16, 20). Both Jesus' pre-existence (vs. 16,17) and His humanness (v. 20) are affirmed. The hymn is, in Tom Wright's apt expression, an example of "*christological monotheism.*"[23] That is to say, Jewish creational monotheism is restated, but Christ is now set within the bounds of that affirmation, "for in Christ all the fullness of the Deity lives in bodily form" (Col. 2:9). He is prior to creation and exalted above it. The hymn's majestic language transcends anything ever said in Judaism about wisdom. The praise is directed to God in celebration of Jesus' lordship in creation and reconciliation.

For monotheistic Jews, prayer was directed exclusively to God, yet Jewish Christians were moved to address Jesus in prayer (Acts 7:59, 60; 2 Cor. 12:2-10). Paul's benedictions are prayers (1 Thess.

3:11-13) that implore Father and Son jointly (Rom. 16:20; Gal. 6:18; 1 Thess 5:28; 2 Cor. 13:14). Of special note is 1 Corinthians 16:22, where the Aramaic *maran* ("our Lord," for the Greek equivalent see Rev. 22:20) is preserved. The context of this prayer was likely the Lord's Supper (1 Cor. 11:26), and it goes back into the worship practice of Aramaic speaking Christian Jews, thus it is very early indeed. In the context of worship, it is impossible to restrict "Lord" to a title of respect. To address Jesus as Lord in the context of worship assumes the most awesome divine status for the One so addressed.

As well as the hymns and prayers to Christ, we can add the references to calling on the name of Jesus (Acts 9:14, 21; 22:16; Rom. 10:13; 1 Cor. 1:2, 10). For calling on the name of God (Gen. 13:4; Ps. 105:1; Jer. 10:25) and confessing Jesus (Rom. 10:9; 1 John 4:2, 3, 15) again are acts of prayer-worship, often in the context of baptism. Christians confessed Jesus as Lord (Rom. 10:9), as Son of God (1:3, 4) and as Christ (Acts 9:22). This kind of religious devotion is normally reserved for God alone. Yet immediately, not after some prolonged linear process, Jewish Christians were worshiping Jesus in these terms alongside the Father.

The early Christians did not make Jesus a second God, nor confuse Him with the Father, yet their adoration of Jesus necessitated what Hurtado deems "a noteworthy mutation in the religious practice of Jewish monotheism."[24] And such a new religious experience required a new language or theology to express it. This does not mean the worship created the idea of Christ's deity. The worship was the spontaneous reaction to the person of Jesus, as when Jesus in the Gospels accepted worship (Matt. 14:33; 28:9, 17; John 20:28). It was the phenomenon of the whole of the Christ-event that elicited the worship, not the reverse.

Word meanings are formed by their social as well as literary contexts. Many of the key Christian titles for Jesus occur in the context of the early church's religious life. Jesus is bracketed with the Father in thanksgivings (Col. 1:3), benedictions (Rom. 16:25-27), letters end with praise to God and the Lord Jesus Christ in unison (2 Cor. 13:14), and songs and music in the heart are made to the Lord (Jesus) (Eph. 5:19). Christian worship celebrated Jesus and makes sense only if He was, in the words of His brother, James, "the Lord of glory" (Jas. 2:1, KJV).

"I Am Gentle and Humble in Heart" (Matt. 11:29)

How should we conceive of God? As an awesome mountain? As a mighty storm? As a triumphant warrior? As a stern judge? As a strict father? As a slave hanging on a cross? The last mentioned may not have come readily to mind, but it is the powerful image used by Paul in what many think is a hymn to Jesus (Phil. 2:5-11). In this passage we have one of the most powerful presentations of Jesus' deity and incarnation. Attempts to exclude from these texts any reference to preexistence and to limit the language to Christ's earthly life are generally considered a failure.

The epistle dates from A.D. 62-63, and the hymn may incorporate earlier material, so again we find the exaltation of Christ very early in the Christian tradition. The opening words are sublime. Though (or perhaps "because") He was in the very form of God, He did not consider equality with God as something to be exploited for His own advantage (v. 6). To the contrary, He saw equality with God in the context of emptying Himself by taking the form of a slave at the human level (v. 7). As such He humbled himself by being an obedient slave, and His obedience was until death, even the cruel death of crucifixion.

In some five lines Paul has provided one of the most profound pictures of God ever penned. The essential deity and preexistence of Jesus is plainly declared. Even more moving is how that deity is expressed—God as revealed in Jesus is not some despotic or self-serving deity, but a God of humility and self-effacement. And Paul's purpose in reminding the Philippians of the character of God as revealed in Jesus is for their attitude to one another to "be the same as that of Christ Jesus" (v. 5).

The opening verses of chapter two indicate that Paul's desire for the Philippian church is unity, where all things are done without arguing or rancor (2:14). He anxiously desires them to be of the same mind, "having the same love," and "being in full accord, of one mind" with one another (v. 2, KJV). He urges them to eschew "selfish ambition or conceit" and instead "in humility regard others as better" than themselves (v. 3). The key is for each to consider not only their own interests, but also the interests of others (v. 4). In a word, they are to display the same attitude to one another that Jesus manifested in His incarnation and death (vs. 7, 8). Hence many of the very terms that Paul uses in his admonition to the Philippians reoccur in his hymn to Christ (vs. 6-11).

The tragedy of the devil is that his desire to be like God was potentially worthy, but foundered because he totally misconstrued the nature of God. Though he coveted the divine power, he perceived nothing of the humility of God. In human wisdom the cross is the stupidity of God, but the folly of God is wiser than human wisdom (1 Cor. 1:23-25). The wish to be like God is a good desire, but only if it includes the picture of the crucified Jesus. Furthermore, Philippians 2:2-4 reminds us that emulating the life of the One who is equal to God takes place in the interactions of everyday life. This is not to turn the gospel into some form of redemption by ethical behavior, but a reminder that humble service is an integral part of Jesus' saving mission. The call to serve one another after the example of His own role is a strong element in Jesus' own teaching (Mark 9:35; 10:43-45; Matt. 20:25, 26; Luke 22:24-27; Matt. 23:11; and especially the act of footwashing, John 13:5-17).

Does the exaltation of Jesus in Philippians 2:9-11 reverse the humiliation of verses 5-8? Was Jesus' condescension simply a temporary abdication of His throne? Not at all. God highly exalts the name of Jesus (v. 10), so that every creature confesses Him to be Lord (v. 11), because humility is the essence of divinity. This is reinforced by the fact that vs. 10, 11 are a quotation from Isa. 45:23, which originally referred to God. It is quite common in the New Testament to apply to Jesus texts that originally referred to the Father (Matt. 3:3; Isa. 40:3; Acts 2:21; Joel 2:32; Rom. 9:33; Isa. 28:16; Heb. 1:10; Ps. 102:25). God praises the servanthood of Jesus, since this is what God is like and what He values. This element again goes back deep into Jesus' own teaching where He asserts that those who humble themselves will be exalted (Matt. 18:4; 23:12; Luke 14:11; 18:14). The humiliation is the exaltation, just as the cross is His exaltation (John 3:14; 8:28; 12:32, 34). The One who now sits on the throne is still a sacrificed Lamb (Rev. 5:6, 9, 12).

In Conclusion

Jaroslav Pelikan points out that the oldest surviving liturgical prayer was a prayer addressed to Christ: "Our Lord, come" (1 Cor. 16:22 written about A.D. 40 or earlier). The oldest surviving pagan report described Christians as gathering before sunrise and "singing a hymn to Christ as though to a god" (Governor Pliny's letter to Trajan, A.D. 112). The oldest surviving Christian sermon after the New Testament opened with the words: "We ought to think of Jesus Christ as of God" (2 Clement 1.1, 2, A.D. 120-140). The oldest surviving account of a Christian martyr contained the confession: "It will be impossible for us to forsake Christ. . . or to worship any other. For him being the Son of God we adore" (Polycarp A.D. 155).[25] Clearly the early church found it entirely appropriate to ascribe the title "God" to Jesus.[26] If we have read the New Testament texts correctly, this practice is grounded in the words of the apostles and of Jesus Himself.

Scholars occasionally see the divinity of Jesus in terms of function rather than His being. But this is a false contrast. In New Testament teaching about Jesus the two are inseparable. Yet it would be just as wrong to imagine that the New Testament was consumed with theological speculation about the relationship between the divine and human in Jesus. Statements about Jesus' person came indirectly in the context of worship and pastoral exhortation. This is because the New Testament is not a theological treatise but a collection of pastoral letters, salvation history, and Gospel biographies.

The New Testament makes assertions about Jesus' divinity, pre-existence, and manhood in the context of such practical items as giving a generous offering (2 Cor. 8:9, 12); remaining a Christian despite social abuse (Heb. 2:14-16; 4:15); cultivating a concern for the well-being of others (Phil. 2:5-11); and defending the apostolic ministry (2 Cor. 5:21). The desire to be like God can be a worthy aspiration as well as a satanic delusion, depending on how we perceive the nature of God. In Christ we see the essence of God, and it is one of humble self-giving. To grasp that, or rather to be grasped by it, is the lowering of human pride and conceit in the dust.

For Further Reading

P. W. Barnett, *The Truth about Jesus: The Challenge of the Evidence.* Sydney: Aquila,1994.

J. M. Harris, *Three Crucial Questions about Jesus.* Carlisle: OM Publications: 1994.

L. T. Johnson, *The Real Jesus: The Misguided Quest for the Historical Jesus and the Truth of the Traditional Gospels.* San Francisco, CA: Harper, 1996.

N. T. Wright, *Who Was Jesus?* London: SPCK, 1992.

N. T. Wright, *The Challenge of Jesus.* London: SPCK, 1999.

Notes

1. *Signs of the Times* 15 (Dec. 23, 1889), p. 784.
2. *Ibid.,* 16 (June 9, 1890), p. 342.
3. Jews would have thought He meant He was God the Father, while pagans would have heard the claim within a polytheistic framework.
4. M. J. Harris, *Jesus as God: The New Testament Use of Theos in Reference to Jesus* (Grand Rapids, MI: Baker, 1992), p. 291.
5. The title occurs some eighty times in the Gospels and only four times outside of them. Of the eighty instances in the Gospels, nearly all of them are self-designations by Jesus (see R. E. Brown, *An Introduction to New Testament Christology* (New York: Paulist Press, 1994) p. 90.
6. Eusebius, *History of the Church,* 3.19, 20.
7. Quoting from the Chalcedon Formula (451 A.D.).
8. M. N. A. Bockmuehl, *This Jesus: Martyr, Lord, Messiah* (Edinburgh: T & T Clark, 1994), p. 34.
9. J. R. Zurcher, *Touched With Our Feelings: A Historical Survey of Adventist Thought on the Human Nature of Christ* (Hagerstown, MD: Review & Herald, 1999), p. 295.
10. D. J. Moo, *The Epistle to the Romans* (NICNT; Grand Rapids, MI: Eerdmans, 1996), p. 479. Moo, rightly in my opinion, also relates the clause "God condemned sin in the flesh" not so much to the incarnational life of Jesus, but "the atoning death of his Son," p. 481.
11. All the great redemptive words of the New Testament (in bold type below) are related to Jesus' death, not his sinless life. "In him we have **redemption** though his blood" (Eph. 1:7); We are now "**justified** by his blood" (Rom. 5:9); Jesus "suffered outside the gate in order to **set apart** the people by his blood" (Heb. 1:12); "You are not your own; you were **bought** at a price" (1 Cor. 6:19, 20); "This is my blood of the covenant which is poured out for

many for the **forgiveness** of sins" (Matt. 26:28); he has **reconciled** you in his body of flesh by his death (Col. 1.22); "Your blood did **ransom** people for God" (Rev. 5:9); "they have **washed** their robes and made them white in the blood of the Lamb" (7:14).

12. The genitive of *hamartia* is used elsewhere in Paul's writings: "the knowledge of sin" (Rom. 3:20), "the body of sin" (Rom. 6:6), "slaves of sin" (6:17, 20), "the wages of sin" (6:23), "the law of sin" (7:23, 25; 8:2), "the power of sin" (1 Cor 15:56), "a servant of sin" (Gal. 2:17). In none of these is it obvious that the genitive means "sinful."
13. C. K. Barrett, *The Epistle to the Romans* (BNTC; London: A & C Black, 1957), p. 156.
14. J. R. Edwards, *Romans* (NIBC; Peabody, MA: Hendrickson, 1992), p. 202.
15. T. Weinandy, *In the Likeness of Sinful Flesh: An Essay on the Humanity of Christ* (Edinburgh: T & T Clark, 1993), p. 18.
16. In Docetism the divinity of Christ so overwhelms the humanity that the reality of His human person is compromised.
17. Weinandy, *op. cit.*, p.18. Similarly, H. Johnson, who defines "fallen human nature" as being "open to the possibility of sin," looks to the power of Jesus' divinity as the means of living a perfect life (*The Humanity of the Saviour*, London: Epworth, 1962), pp. 22, 31.
18. D. A. de Silva, *Perseverance in Gratitude: A Socio-Rhetorical Commentary on the Epistle to the Hebrews* (Grand Rapids, MI: Eerdmans, 2000), pp. 16-20 and *passim*.
19 I am indebted to the works of L. W. Hurtado for this section, especially *One God, One Lord: Early Christian Devotion and Ancient Jewish Monotheism* (London: SCM Press, 1988).
20. Hurtado, *op. cit.*, p. 11.
21. *Ibid.*, p. 95.
22. *Ibid.*, p. 104.
23. N. T. Wright, *The Climax of the Covenant: Christ and the Law in Pauline Theology* (Edinburgh : T & T Clark, 1991), p. 114.
24. Hurtado, p. 108.
25. Stephen, the first martyr (A.D. 35), died with this prayer on his lips: "Lord Jesus, receive my spirit" (Acts 7:59).
26. Jaroslav Pelikan, *The Christian Tradition: A History of the Development of Doctrine* (5 vols.; Chicago: University Press, 1971), 1.173.

The Work and Words of Jesus

Steven A. Thompson

Jesus, according to the record, was "mighty in deeds and words" (Luke. 24:19).[1] In that light, this chapter has a dual purpose: first, to confirm that it is relevant to know what Jesus did and said, and second, to outline those deeds and sayings according to the four New Testament Gospels. For a long time students of Jesus have attempted to add to or subtract from the information about Jesus contained in these Gospels, usually by accessing either hypothetical or real documents that possibly contain isolated information about Jesus, or by omitting part or all of the information contained in one or more of the Gospels in their quest to get "behind" the New Testament to find the "historical" Jesus.[2]

What follows is based on my understanding that one cannot get "behind" the four Gospels, that they preserve Jesus as He existed in the memories of His closest followers, and that these memories give us the best access to the mighty work and words of Jesus.[3]

The Question of Relevance

To answer the question of relevance, we begin by asking why His earliest followers thought a knowledge of Jesus' work and words was relevant. Why was such knowledge important for them? The eleven disciples agreed without any hesitation that Jesus appeared to all of them after His crucifixion. At first they met reports of His appearances with some skepticism, but the reality of the risen Jesus and His continuing impact on His followers united and energized them in a new way and gave them a message that they immediately began to share with others. They sensed a continuity between Jesus the Galilean teacher and healer who had been executed by the authorities, and the risen Christ who through His Spirit was again among them, as their leader, in a new and powerful manner.

For Matthew

In the Gospel of Matthew, Jesus spends much of His time teaching. This teaching is gathered into five sections, interspersed with accounts of what Jesus and His followers did. The Gospel closes with the risen Jesus instructing His disciples to "make disciples... *teaching* them to observe all that *I have commanded you*." (28:20, emphasis supplied), suggesting that the teaching of Jesus was authoritative.

Matthew's central message about Jesus is expressed in 1:23: "his name shall be called Immanuel, which means 'God with us,'" and is repeated in the Gospel's closing words: "Lo, I am with you always, to the close of the age" (28:20). To this central teaching—that in the risen Jesus, God is with His people—Matthew adds details, reflecting two major themes: Jesus' authority, and the community established for His followers.

Authority

Authority is at issue when Jesus comments on the Torah, the source of spiritual authority for the Jews of His day[4]. Written Torah was contained in the five books of Moses, but was accompanied by generations of unwritten applications passed on from scribe to scribe. Matthew records the relation of Jesus to the Jewish religious leaders, whose task it was to interpret and apply the Torah to life. According to Matthew, Jesus, rather than other religious leaders in the community, was the only correct interpreter of the Torah. He went on to present Jesus as fulfilling the Torah, replacing it as God's Word for His followers. The area of religious authority is a minefield, and Jesus stepped into it with predictable results.

Community

Matthew recorded several of the guidelines Jesus provided for His followers regarding the building of community. For example, how should Jews who had recently converted to Christianity, relate to their fellow Jews? How should they relate to Gentiles, whether Christian or non-Christian? And, very importantly, how should Christians relate to one another? The inner life of the church includes humility and service, and sometimes rebuke, correction, and even exclusion of members. Overall, a spirit of forgiveness marks the community of Jesus' followers, according to Jesus in Matthew. Jesus' teaching about the mission of the community is also emphasized—spreading the good news which brought it into being. Its members enter the wider world to share their message, they nurture one another in faith and hope and they await the return of their Lord.

For Mark

Mark provides a less detailed account of what Jesus taught than Matthew, but he focuses more on the impact of Jesus on people whom He encountered. Mark frequently records their testimony about what Jesus did for them when they encountered Him. Jesus is a Spirit-filled healer and exorciser of evil spirits, according to Mark. He is also a teacher or rabbi, terms Mark employs frequently. Jesus' teaching manner appears sometimes abrupt, and He is inclined to call for secrecy about the source of the helpful intervention received by some to whom He ministered.

The overall message of Jesus, according to Mark, was that the rule of God over this present world has begun in a new way, demonstrated by miracles and by the formation of a core group of followers who, in spite of limited understanding, proclaim the essential truths about God's rule by means of simple personal testimony of what God has done for them through Jesus.

For Luke

Luke's Gospel, when read with the book of Acts, provides a wider viewpoint than the other Gospels of the continuity between the people of Israel, Jesus, and the church in the fulfillment of God's plan.

Jesus as Prophesied and Prophetic Messiah

Luke recognizes the role of prophecy in the ministry of Jesus.[5] Jesus Himself was a prophet, although not universally accepted— His hometown rejected His prophetic ministry (4:16-30). His prophetic ministry echoed hints of the ministries of Elijah and Elisha, which ministries sometimes extended beyond the confines of the people of Israel. Jesus' ministry also broke through the cultural confines of His own people and touched others, infrequently during His lifetime, explosively so after His resurrection.

Forming the Community

Luke's biggest section of Jesus' teaching—chapters 9 to 19—is directed at three groups: the crowds, His opponents, and His disciples. His theme: God's kingdom has come, ready or not! To the uncommitted crowds He typically spoke of kingdom growth, selection criteria for entry, and God's judgment on those who refuse to join (13:18-30;14:1-35). He warns His opponents of the risk of rejecting Him and admonishes them against abuse of spiritual authority in their leadership positions (13:31-35; 15:1-32). He instructs His disciples about possessions and support for the poor (16:1-13), how to deal with scandal and violation of group codes within the community, lack of faith among believers, and the need for humility among leaders (17:1-10).

For John

Readers of John's Gospel enter a different atmosphere. The words and work of Jesus are noticeably different. John preserves none of the parables of the first three Gospels. Jesus speaks in lengthy passages rather than in short, pithy sayings, and verbal confrontations with His opponents tend to focus not so much on the particular controversial deed done by Jesus, but rather on its spiritual significance, and His identity and relation to God. Most of the miracles of the earlier Gospels are replaced by seven "signs" or nature miracles. No exorcisms are recorded.

John's aim is expressed by his words "that you may believe that Jesus is the Christ, the Son of God, and that by believing you may have life in his name" (20:30, 31). He also included selections from what Jesus taught about community, worship, the already present resurrection life, and the deeper symbolism of Jesus' actions.⁶ John's viewpoint includes the early believers whose continued faith in Jesus is nurtured by reading John's record of what He did and said (v. 30), and whose increased insight into His person, nature, and mission is repeatedly promised (2:17-22; 12:16; 14:25, 26; 20:9). His continuing presence with His followers is the subject of several of His best-known and most-loved sayings (14:25-31; 15:1-11). It may be concluded from the foregoing that it is still relevant for Jesus' disciples to know what He did and said, largely for the same reasons that He was relevant to His earliest followers.

The Work of Jesus

Jesus' works, according to the earliest witnesses, were striking and set Him apart. The Gospels, supplemented by other New Testament passages, list a range of works performed by Jesus, but all His deeds can be summarized under the following headings: powerful works, forming God's new people, and transforming death into life.

Powerful Works, or Miracles

The attempt to define "miracle" has engaged philosophers, scientists and theologians for centuries, and this is not the place to resolve the issue. Rather, we bypass the arguments by reverting to the terms applied by those who experienced the powerful acts of Jesus firsthand—they called them "works" (*erga*), "signs" (*semeia*), or "outpourings of divine power" (*dynameis*), which brought spectacular results reported in the Gospels and summarized in Luke 24:19: "Jesus of Nazareth. . . who by deeds and words of power, proved himself a prophet in the sight of God and the whole people." Again, in Acts 10:38 ff: "God anointed Jesus of Nazareth with the Holy Spirit and with power. Because God was with him he went about doing good and healing all who were oppressed by the Devil. And we can bear witness to all that he did in the Jewish countryside and in Jerusalem."

These powerful works belong to the following categories: dra-

matic healings (leprosy, blindness, lameness, deafness, hemor-
rhage, perhaps epilepsy, physical deformity, dropsy, sword wound),
exorcisms of evil spirits, raisings of the dead, and dramatic occurrences in the natural world (stilling the storm, feeding the multitude, walking on water, the withered fig tree, the coin in a fish's
mouth, a huge catch of fish, turning water to wine).

Did these things really happen? In answer to this question, note
that the accounts of these powerful works are integrated into the
very fabric of all four Gospels, giving the impression that they
belonged from the beginning to the story of Jesus; they were not
added to the story at some later date to enhance Jesus' authority. To
tell His story without them does injustice to the message. These
miracles were not optional or peripheral; they were part and parcel
of His work. Even His opponents were forced to acknowledge His
works, which they attempted to discredit as black magic (Luke
11:20).

Works such as Jesus performed were not as common in His
times as some recent critics of the Gospels sweepingly declare.[7] If
the street corners and marketplaces of ancient cities were occupied
by those who performed the kind of works recorded in the Gospels,
and if their "everydayness" as well as their genuineness were taken
for granted by the ancients, there would be no point in attributing
them to Jesus—such would not have made Him stand out from any
other street corner wonder worker and thus would not have gained
support for His mission.

Are the Gospel records of these powerful works really objec-
tionable to contemporary people? Few people today have totally
abandoned belief in the possibility of miracles on the basis of modern scientific reasoning. People on their deathbeds still experience
unexpected recovery, which can draw from the lips of onlookers the
word "miraculous!" While most of us go a lifetime without experiencing a miracle, their possibility is still accepted, especially when
those directly involved utter their convincing firsthand testimony to
the unexpected change.

Why did Jesus perform these mighty works? A widely-held
answer to this question among previous generations of Christians
was that the miracles of Jesus provided evidence of His divine

nature. Miracles "proved" the divinity of Jesus. How does Jesus Himself explain His powerful works? On occasion He refused to perform them, particularly upon demand, refusing to use them as evidence of His divine nature (Matt. 4:5; 12:38, 39). Similarly, He refused to rescue Himself by performing a miracle (Matt. 4:1; Luke 23:25). While some works were done in public, such as the healing of a withered arm (Mark 3:1-5) and the feeding of the multitudes, He commanded secrecy in connection with others (Mark 8:26).

The works of Jesus provided dramatic confirmation of His message of God's kingdom.[8] "If I by the finger of God cast out demons, then the kingdom of God has come upon you" (Luke 11:20). In other words, He challenged His listeners to observe the powerful work, then draw their own conclusions about the source of the power. This is seen in His reply to messengers John the Baptist sent from prison to ask if Jesus was really the promised One. After having them witness a typical day in His ministry, which included healings, He sent them back to John the Baptist after telling them, "Blessed are those who do not find me an obstacle to faith" (Luke 7:23)—in other words, "The things the prophet Isaiah prophesied for the time of restoration are actually happening in my ministry. Draw your own conclusion, based on the eyewitness testimony of your followers."

Jesus' powerful works also pointed forward to the sort of world God intended, with human beings and nature redeemed from the interference of evil with its consequent disease and suffering. His works brought glimpses of that new world to many individuals, their families and villages.

Finally, powerful works rewarded faith. Jesus expected faith on the part of the beneficiaries of His works: "Daughter, your faith has made you well" (Mark 5:34); "Fear not; only believe" (v. 36); "all things are possible to him who believes" (9:23); "This kind cannot be driven out by anything but prayer" (9:29). The eyes of faith, observing the powerful works of Jesus, realized what God intended for His children and saw the beginnings of that new reality in His ministry. This is why the Gospels place His powerful works squarely in the center of the picture—Jesus would not have been Jesus without them, nor would God be God.

Forming God's New People

When John the Baptist appeared on the scene, he announced his mission in words of the prophet Isaiah:

A voice cries:
Clear a road through the wilderness for the Lord,
Prepare a highway across the desert for our God. . . .
Then will the glory of the Lord be revealed,
And all mankind together will see it.
(Isa. 40:3-5, cited in Luke 3:4-6, REV).

Jesus began His ministry in this atmosphere of expectation with a clear intention to form God's new people. His first step in forming the new people of God was to gather a group of disciples who would serve as the core of the new community. The process had two steps: first, He called people to follow Him; later, from among those who responded, He chose a smaller band who would provide the foundation of God's new people.

Calling Followers

A disciple was a learner, much like an apprentice, attached to a rabbi in the Jewish community. Rabbis had followers, much as ancient Greek wandering philosophers attracted followers. The aim was to learn the law, and his rabbi's interpretations of it, so well that the disciple in turn might become a rabbi with his own disciples. Jesus partly fit the role of rabbi and was acknowledged as such in the Gospels, so it was natural that He also had disciples. But He took the initiative in calling His disciples to join Him with the well-known invitation "Follow me" (Luke 5:1-11; Mark 1:17; John 1:43), rather than waiting for them to attach themselves to Him.

Being a disciple of Jesus differed from typical rabbinical discipleship. Instead of teaching them to interpret the Torah, Jesus called them to service. A. M. Hunter remarks, "Those so called were not invited to spend their days interpreting the Torah, but summoned to become 'apprentices' in the work of God's kingdom."[9] This was a natural extension of His own role as servant: "the Son of Man [came]. . . to serve" (Mark 10:45); "I am among you as one who serves" (Luke 22:27). Jesus' own ministry was shaped by the image of the servant of the Lord introduced by the prophet Isaiah

(42:1-4, quoted in Matt. 12:18-21) and 52:13-53:12, quoted in Matt. 8:17). He expected His disciples to assume the attitude of servants. Metaphors such as "fishers of men" (Matt. 4:19) and field hands gathering the harvest (Luke 10:2) illustrate the direction of His training. Finally, He taught them to reflect their relation to Him by the way they treated one another: "Let the greatest disciple become as the youngest; the leader as one who serves" (Luke 22:26) and taught them to state their role in God's kingdom with the words "We are unprofitable servants, only doing our duty" (Luke 17:10).

Jesus' call had an intensity and finality about it that demanded a clear decision. People were to sit down and count the cost of discipleship, just as a property owner counts the cost before starting to construct a building or a king takes stock of his fighting resources before going to war (Luke 14:28-32). The filtering process used by Jesus is glimpsed in Luke 9:57-62 where prospective disciples are rejected for such lapses of commitment as questioning the sort of accommodation on offer, expressing a wish to bury a father prior to signing up, and taking farewell of the family before hitting the road. In each case, Jesus calls for an immediate decision and is unwilling to allow other tasks to intervene.[10] This hands-on apprenticeship would prepare them for their unique role as proclaimers of the coming of God in Christ, while at the same time they would serve as the founders of the new community of Israel, God's new people.

Jesus had more than twelve followers, including females as well as males (Luke 8:2, 3; 23:49; 24:18). Luke's vocabulary indicates women responded to Jesus' call back in Galilee at the beginning of His ministry. The loyalty and service provided by these unnamed followers, male and female, was unswerving, as seen during His trial and crucifixion when the twelve temporarily abandoned Him. These disciples were first to become aware of His resurrection (Luke 24:5, 31) and, as a result, first to "preach" the resurrection of Jesus, according to 24:9, 34, 35.

Choosing the Twelve

At a point in His ministry in Galilee Jesus chose twelve men from among His followers, whose group identity remained special for the duration of His ministry. Made up of eleven Galileans and one Judean, they included a tax collector, at least four fishermen, a political zealot, and one twin. The group had an inner circle of three—Peter, James, and John—and a spokesman—Peter.

The number twelve had obvious significance for the people of Jesus' day, evoking the twelve sons of the patriarch Jacob who became the founding fathers of the people of Israel. Through these twelve men, Jesus signaled His plan to found a new Israel. The message to the people and the spiritual leaders of Jesus' day could not have been clearer—God is beginning afresh, building anew from the foundations, keeping old promises in a new way, through a new structure. The twelve received special training for their role, with intense delivery of instruction—twenty-four hours a day, day in and day out, they witnessed His ministry and learned lessons that would enable them to carry on.

During the latter part of His ministry, Jesus commenced training the twelve for harsher future conditions, reflected in His call to take up their cross and follow him (Mark 8:34). The future would get worse before getting better, and they would be subjected to severe trials. He wanted disciples to whom He could say "You are the ones who have continued with me in my trials" (Luke 22:28), who would "watch and pray" with Him. They had a reward to look forward to: "Whoever loses his life for my sake and the gospel's shall save it" (Mark 8:35); "Whoever endures to the end will be saved" (Mark 13:13). But before the end of His ministry there was a crucial task for His disciples to accomplish—a sort of solo flight that would launch them on their mission.

Sending Messengers

The mandate to the twelve was straight forward—to proclaim the good news of God's rule. They were instructed and empowered to overcome evil spirits and cure diseases. In short, God's new people were to be recruited directly from the realm of evil, to be released from spirit possession, illness and infirmity, and be given an invitation to step into God's kingdom. The choice was theirs, but those who refused it faced the unhappy prospect of being reconquered by evil forces.

Time was short, and the twelve were not to become entangled socially on their mission nor be detracted from the urgency of their message by invitations to engage in theological debate. They were to travel light and be sustained by the hospitality of their short-term village hosts. Time would run out on them, and God's new rule would dawn while they were still making their rounds of the villages (see Matt. 10 and Luke 9 for details).

Did Jesus intend to found the church? Some students of His ministry deny that founding the church was part of His plan. The French liberal scholar Alfred Loisy summed up the liberal view which dominated the twentieth century: "Jesus expected the kingdom of God—and the church came."[11] A reading of the Gospels with this question in mind can give the impression that Jesus foresaw only a brief period of time between His crucifixion and His second coming during which no particular structure or organization would be needed.

However, the Gospels contain a rich collection of church imagery that originated with Jesus. True, the Gospels include nothing like a church manual, but neither does the rest of the New Testament. Still, a community of believers with some coherence and organization is assumed to stand behind the following images of the church: a flock of sheep (Luke 12:32; Mark 14:27; Matt. 26:31ff; John 10:1-29) with a shepherd (Matt. 12:30; Luke 11:23; Matt. 15:24); a crop planted by God (Matt. 13:24-30; 15:13), a fishing net with various fish (Matt. 13:47; Mark 1:17); God's city on a hill (Matt. 5:14; Luke 16:8); God's family (this is possibly Jesus' favorite image), a substitute for an earthly family, with God as father (Matt. 23:9); Jesus as master of the house which His followers occupy (Matt. 10:25). Older women who hear His word are mothers, while men and youth are His siblings (Mark 3:34; called "little ones" in Matt. 11:25); the family appears at table fellowship (Mark 2:15-17; 6:34-42; 8:1-10). Add to these images the occasional suggestions of a delay in the return of Jesus ("My master delayeth his return" [Matt. 24:48]), and the parable of ten bridesmaids (Matt. 25) and one gains a more balanced picture. Jesus foresaw the need for a community of believers on earth awaiting His return.

Transforming Death Into Life

The third main work of Jesus was to transform death into life by undergoing death Himself. Gospel accounts of the arrest, trial, death, and resurrection of Jesus occupy a considerable amount of their total space, nearly one-third of the Gospel of Mark, for example. This was not accidental, but a deliberate indication of the centrality of the death of Jesus to the substance of the Christian faith.

The most visible restriction on the time for accomplishing the mission of the disciples was the looming threat to the life of Jesus. From the earliest days of His life and ministry, His mission had come under the scrutiny of leaders who suspected Him of plotting to usurp their authority. For some time their efforts to silence Him were stymied by divisions—Pharisees pursued one scheme while Sadducees pursued another—but once Jesus left the rural region of Galilee for Jerusalem, His opponents found it easier to unite their forces to plan His death. In the meantime He conducted His ministry in such openness that He seemed deliberately bent on provoking a response from the religious leaders.

Jesus worked with a sense of divine timing (John 2:4, 7:6) and prepared Himself and His disciples for His coming death (Matt. 20:18, 19). Through the closing stages of His ministry He took steps which would land Him in the hands of jealous authorities, who would deal with Him when His time came. Luke gives a poignant glimpse of Him striding determinedly towards Jerusalem (13:22; 18:31; 19:11, 28, 41, 45), where He would complete His work.

The main features of Jesus' death and its meaning had been outlined in the prophet Isaiah's suffering servant passage (52:13-53:12), which describes the work of the Lord's servant who would "pour out his soul unto death." The point of His death was to provide a ransom: "The Son of Man did not come to be served but to serve, and to give his life as a ransom for many" (Mark 10:45).

Jesus understood that His own death was part of the divine plan for Him, and that He could not avoid it without derailing the purpose of His ministry. This becomes clearer when we examine the nature of the three metaphors used by Jesus to describe His coming death.[12] In each metaphor, there is an obvious place for God the

Father. First, Jesus used the metaphor of "baptism" for His coming death: "Can you be baptized with the baptism I am baptized with?" (Mark 10:38). Baptism was administered by someone, so God would be administering death to His Son. The second metaphor was a cup: "Can you drink of the cup that I am drinking?" (Mark 10:38). In Gethsemane He prays, "Father, all things are possible to thee; remove this cup from me; yet not what I will, but what thou wilt" (Mark 14:36). Third, Jesus spoke of His death as a journey: "The Son of Man is going the way appointed for him in the Scriptures" (v. 21). Thus each of these three metaphors implies that the Father Himself recognized the death of Jesus as a necessity.

Finally, Jesus spoke of His death as establishing a new covenant. As the covenant at Sinai had been ratified by shedding blood, so the new covenant, promised by the prophets as inaugurating a new way of relating to God (Jer. 31:31), would be ratified by shedding blood. "This is my blood of the covenant, which is poured out for many" (Mark 14:24). Only God, the chief signatory to the covenant, could dictate its terms and conditions. By placing His death squarely within the framework of the divine covenant, Jesus showed that at the deepest level He believed His coming death to be essential in making possible the salvation not just of a particular people, but of the entire human family. God had His work, and Jesus had His; both works were essential to redemption (John 5:17).

Paradox is the ability of apparent contradictions to exist side by side. Transforming death into life is paradoxical, shocking the observer by bringing out a deeper unity from the apparent paradox. Jesus' transformation of death into life at first certainly shocked His disciples. And the message His followers in all generations have taken to the world is equally paradoxical—through the humiliating death of His Son on a cross, God was at work, reconciling the world to Himself, in order that His gift of life might be made available on the widest possible basis.

The Words of Jesus

"By word no less than deed Jesus intended to proclaim the power of God. He referred to it as 'the kingdom of God.' "[13] Like His seamless robe, the words of Jesus are interwoven into His work. After a brief observation of His teaching methods, the rest of the chapter surveys the three central themes that recur in the words of Jesus—God and His kingdom, Jesus and His place in the kingdom, and the place of His disciples in the kingdom. The section concludes with Jesus' words about the future.

Teaching Methods

There were trained teachers among the Jews of Jesus' day, but He was not one of them. Their training required a life different from the one He lived, and His townspeople in Nazareth noted the difference when they said, "Where did he get all this?. . . is he not the carpenter's son?" (Mark 6:1). This absence of formal rabbinic education did not hinder Him as a teacher, but it influenced the way He taught.

First, He rejected the extensive unwritten interpretation of Scripture that had been added by generations of rabbis. For Him, the written word of God was the Hebrew Scriptures. Second, His teaching was free from technical jargon. It is significant that Jesus taught that righteousness is the basis for our saving relation to God, yet in the Gospels He rarely employed the technical term "righteousness by faith" or "justified." Third, Jesus was able to contextualize His teaching, drawing His object lessons, for example, from the more widely-understood world of farming, rather than from carpentry.

God and His Kingdom

With their long history of belief in one, personal God, the Jewish people had a distinctive religious perspective compared to neighboring peoples, enabling them to focus on relating to the one God. However, even they had more to learn and Jesus highlighted the relation between God and persons primarily by use of the word "Father."

God as Father
The taunt "Where is your father?" (John 8:18) was probably hurled at Jesus many times from childhood until the end of His life.

From the point of view of human development it is essential that children know their father well if they are to develop into mature, functioning adults. Jesus stressed in His teaching more than any Israelite before Him the reality of God as personal father, or *Abba,* to use the colloquial word of the everyday Aramaic language of Palestinian Jews.

Jesus always used *Abba* in addressing God (sixteen times in the Gospels, see for example Mark 14:36) with one exception—His cry from the cross, when He used the opening line of Psalm 22, "My God, my God, why have you forsaken me?" This form of address, extremely rare in Jewish literature, expressed Jesus' close relationship with His heavenly Father.[14] He spoke to Him as a child speaks to its earthly father, using an intimate term to express confidence and security on one hand, obedience and submission on the other.

God's Children

Scrutiny of the sayings of Jesus reveals a surprising demarcation between God's children and other people. When Jesus spoke in the Gospels of God using the words "your Father" He always addressed His own followers. Twenty-two times Jesus calls God the Father of His followers, but He never calls God the Father of those who were not His followers, whether the Jews in general or His opponents in particular![15] God enters a new and qualitatively different relationship to individuals within the sphere of His kingdom, according to Jesus. The Father of Jesus is also, by extension, the Father of all His new children, without regard to their nation, gender, or tribe. A new reality has been introduced, an all-powerful heavenly Father who in addition to the "common generosity" expressed in His sending of the sun and rain onto the lands of all peoples, has a special new generosity for His newly-adopted children: "Don't be afraid, little flock, because your father has resolved to give you the kingdom" (Luke 12:32).

Jesus in God's Kingdom

Jesus had a central place in God's kingdom. He was both messenger and centerpiece of that kingdom, and neither can be understood without the other.

Labels and Titles

Several labels and titles appear in the pages of the Gospels, some on the lips of Jesus, applied to Himself, others on the lips of others, applied to Him. The titles Jesus used about Himself, or that His followers applied to Him, used to be a starting point for surveying His teaching. But a closer look at them indicates that their intention was not so much to provide theological meaning about the divine-human nature of Jesus during the incarnation. Rather, they were chosen because they communicated to the contemporaries of Jesus. This is seen in the fact that these labels are firmly rooted in the world of Jesus, and are not readily transferable to our world. Until we recover the key to their ancient meaning, we are likely to misinterpret them.

Messiah

The word "Christ" has become the last name of Jesus in popular usage, but the word was originally a title. In the ancient Greek world it meant "Anointed One." The Hebrew equivalent was *Mashiach* which is translated "Messiah." So a Messiah, or a Christ, was someone whose appointment to a special position was accompanied by a ceremony which included pouring olive oil over the anointee's head.

In ancient Israel, anointing was connected to celebrations of prosperity and blessing (as in Psalm 23 "Thou anointest my head with oil, my cup runneth over," KJV). Formal, public anointings were usually reserved for kings and high priests, whose anointing signaled divine appointment to office. The title took on special meaning in connection with the dynasty of king David, which was to last forever (2 Sam. 7:16). This hope survived the centuries after David's last physical descendent disappeared from the throne in 586 B.C. God was expected to make good His promise to David by restoring both throne and dynasty. For this reason "Son of David" meant nearly the same thing as "Messiah." By the time of Jesus, the royal terms "Son of David" and "Messiah" had become virtually synonymous. The Jewish people certainly looked for a royal descendant of king David who would do for his people what any good and powerful king should do—liberate them from their national enemy (Mark 12:35).

Jesus seemed reluctant to accept the title, probably because it was loaded with potential for misunderstanding, with its politicized implications. He expressed the word once in the Gospels (John 4: 15, 26), and quietly accepted it from the lips of Peter (Mark 8:29) and the high priest (Matt. 26:63, 64; Luke 22:67). In one of the most dramatic public events of His ministry Jesus accepted messiahship by entering Jerusalem on the back of a donkey, the traditional mode of entry for new kings (Matt. 21:1-12). The shouts of "Hosanna to the Son of David" from the multitude that day made clear that Jesus was Messiah. Messiahs did not last long in Jesus' day. Less than a week later Jesus was dead.

Prophet

How was Jesus regarded by His contemporaries? The unanimous verdict is that He was regarded as a prophet. The title is applied to Him directly or indirectly by the crowds (Mark 6:15), His disciples (Matt. 16:14), and the Pharisees, with some skepticism, ("If this man were a prophet, he would know. . ." Luke 7:39). Finally, it was as a false prophet the Jesus was arrested and accused, a fact not lost on His Roman guards who taunted Him to "prophesy." Jesus did not reject this label. He included Himself among the prophets (Luke 13:33, 34; Matt. 23:31, 32; Mark 6:4). Jesus claimed to possess the Spirit of God, which was the hallmark of a prophet (Mark 3:28, 29; Luke 4:18-21) This partly explains His influence among the people who had previously come under the influence of John the Baptist.

John and Jesus seem to have patterned their ministries on two of the great non-writing prophets of Israel, Elijah and Elisha. John was seen as a prophet by the masses, according to Matthew 14:5. The final prophecy of the Hebrew Scriptures included a prediction of the return of Elijah before the coming of the day of the Lord (Mal. 4:5, 6). The connection is implied in Jesus' sermon in the synagogue in Nazareth when He indirectly claimed to be a prophet by referring to Elisha's healing of Naaman the leper (2 Kgs. 4:42-44; Mark 6:35-44). John the Baptist was the elusive Elijah, suddenly appearing seemingly from nowhere with a message prior to disappearing for a time. John is the promised Elijah (Matt. 11:14), while the ministry of Jesus included episodes which resembled Elisha's, including the miraculous feeding of a multitude (2 Kgs. 4:42-44; Mark 6:35-44). Significantly, just as Elijah "baptized" his successor Elisha in the river Jordan by taking him through the parted water, so John took his successor Jesus through the same river, symbolically baptizing Him at the beginning of His ministry. It concluded with His triumphal entry into Jerusalem which was greeted by shouts "this is Jesus the prophet!" (Matt. 21:11).

But Jesus was more than a prophet. He was not only the prophetic herald of God's kingdom, He was also the prophesied agent of that kingdom.

Truth

Jesus called himself "truth" according to John 14:6, and claimed to speak the truth (8:45) and witness to the truth (5:33). Ultimate truth entered the world in a new way through Jesus of Nazareth (1:14, 17). Truth and grace were brought by Jesus and combined with the already-present Torah, which came through Moses, forming a unique triad of law, grace, and truth. John's Gospel develops the relation between Jesus and truth, and John 14:6 sums up the main points. First, it tells us that truth is revealed in the life of Jesus, the Word of God made human. It also tells us that in Him truth stands in opposition to deception and falsehood. The Jesus of the carpenter's workshop and the dusty roads of Galilee is more than virtual truth and reality; He is God's own truth and reality, packaged and delivered in the most accessible form possible for humans. Truth doesn't get more true or reality more real than in Jesus.

The Disciples in God's Kingdom

In practical terms for the person on the street, what was God's kingdom, according to Jesus? What did it offer? At heart like any kingdom, it consisted of king and subject. In the words of a leading Jesus scholar, T. W. Manson, "The Kingdom here is a personal relation between the King and the subject. The claim on God's part to rule, and the acknowledgment on man's part of that claim, together constitute the actual Kingdom."[16] God, in the guise of a magnanimous monarch, offers identity, protection, opportunity and hope to His potential subject, who responds with trust, faith, loyalty and service. All else, such as territory and boundaries, terms and conditions, numbers and size, are peripheral—at heart the kingdom of God is relationship and attitude.

Note that Jesus did not chose as a model for this relationship to God a business partnership or a democracy, although both models were surely known to Him. His choice of "kingdom" was deliberate. Monarchs are not elected leaders; they wield absolute rule and authority, and their subjects accept whatever comes from their hands with submission. While a kingdom may initially or in principle be small, at heart consisting of a king and a subject , its growth potential is unlimited, as highlighted in the parables of yeast in bread dough and the tiny mustard seed.

When Jesus issued the invitation to enter the kingdom of God, this was another way of saying "Become a disciple. Submit to the reign of God. Trust Him to reciprocate in ways appropriate to a good king." This explains why the illustrations employed by Jesus to illustrate life in the kingdom are dominated by masters, monarchs, military commanders and landlords, all of whom tend to give orders that their subjects, officers, and agents are expected to obey. These kingdom models are not easily updated, and Western contemporary readers of the Gospels sometimes fail to appreciate the significance of the social and cultural world in which the teaching of Jesus was set. There is no basis in Jesus' teaching for recasting God in the role of a modern elected leader with the need to please his electorate, with one eye on the opinion polls.

God's invitation to enter the kingdom is the greatest possible offer—a new dimension of life beginning now and reaching fulfillment in a post-resurrection world. The terms and conditions are complete and require total commitment. Count the cost before accepting the invitation.

In this light we will sample two of the many features of the teaching of Jesus that affected the day-to-day nature of the life of disciples in the kingdom.

Themes in the Teaching of Jesus

The Gospels preserve words of Jesus on a surprising range of important issues too numerous to survey here, including the following: repentance and forgiveness, law and grace, prayer, Bible study, emotions/inner life, hope, hypocrisy, recreation and entertainment, hospitality, food and drink, work and leisure, sexuality, marriage, family, parents, children, divorce, health and sickness, prosperity and economics, paying taxes, possessions, racism and discrimination, nationalism, angels and spirits, death and resurrection. Here we will survey what Jesus taught on only two themes: worship, and the future.

Worship

How does a contemporary Christian worship? Is church attendance required? A sermon? The earliest followers of Jesus faced their own serious and urgent question about worship. Had God abandoned the Jerusalem temple? If Jesus was their priest and sacrifice, what was the point of the temple, after the resurrection?

The question was already hotly debated in Jesus' day. Sectarian Jews living in Qumran, an isolated community on the shore of the Dead Sea a few miles east of Jerusalem, made a fundamental belief of their conviction that God had abandoned the temple and its priesthood. They saw themselves and their little community as both true spiritual priesthood and true spiritual temple of God. A few miles north of Jerusalem on Mount Gerazim another group, the Samaritans, maintained an alternate temple for the same belief— God had abandoned His house and His priesthood in Jerusalem.

When Jesus encountered the Samaritan woman at the well, she turned the conversation towards a debate about worship—this mountain or that mountain? Gerazim or Zion? How did Jesus respond to this burning issue? He revealed to her that the Jerusalem temple's days were numbered: "the days are coming when you will worship the Father neither on this mountain nor in Jerusalem" (John 4:21). His dramatic temple-cleansing action showed His displeasure with its corrupt priesthood. He could have encouraged His followers to abandon the temple, but He did not. On the contrary,

He encouraged regard for the legitimacy of the temple by paying the temple tax, by participating Himself in its services, and by spending time there with His followers, observing people and rituals, right up to the time of His arrest. His support for the authority of the priesthood was indicated by His instructions to a cleansed leper: "Go, show yourself to the priest" (Matt. 8:4).

However, Jesus advocated a radical re-ordering of the place of public worship compared with authentic relationship in the kingdom by His teaching: "If you are presenting your gift at the altar and suddenly remember that your brother has a grievance against you, leave your gift where it is before the altar. First go and make you peace with your brother; then come back and offer your gift" (Matt. 5:23, 24). Here Jesus insisted on the correct priority between right living and right worship, argued centuries earlier by the prophet Micah (6:6-8). Jesus went beyond the demands of the prophet when He individualized the action, saying in effect that in God's kingdom reconciliation and harmony in relationships among individuals takes priority over issues of public worship. Notice that for Jesus it was not either/or, but both/and. Reconciling relationships take priority over worship, but can never take the place of worship: "Then, come back and offer your gift." It is a principle that continues to undergird authentic worship.

The Future

The question of the future loomed large for Jesus, and He tried to prepare His followers for it.[17] In Matthew, the second longest continuous block of teaching delivered by Jesus (chaps. 24, 25) was entirely devoted to answering their questions about the future, which were prompted by His reference to the coming destruction of the Jerusalem temple, of which He predicted "not one stone will be left on another" (24:2). In response they asked questions: "When will this happen?" and "What will be the sign of your return and of the end of the world?" (v. 3).

Matthew and Mark both carefully note that Jesus answered these questions in a closed, restricted setting—according to Matthew 24:3 to the disciples "privately"; according to Mark 13:3 only Peter,

James, John and Andrew heard His answer. This suggests that Jesus respected a Jewish custom of restricting apocalyptic-type teachings to select small groups of insiders. This custom appears as early as the book of Daniel, where a group known as "the wise" figures prominently several times, entrusted with the deeper apocalyptic secrets.[18] Restricted access is explicit in the book of Revelation 13:18, which specifies that the only ones invited to calculate the number of the beast are those who have the same attributes of the select insiders named in the book of Daniel, namely wisdom and special understanding. Mark hints a second time at a restricted audience in this account when he inserts the cryptic phrase "let the reader understand" in 13:14.

In the light of this restriction, uninitiated readers of the Gospels, such as ourselves, should perhaps not expect access to the detailed teaching of the future shared by Jesus with the twelve. However, key themes emerge even for the uninitiated. First, a localized "end" consisting of the destruction of Jerusalem, bringing great suffering on the Jewish nation, followed in the longer-range future by the coming of the Son of man, bringing final judgment and the end of the world. The end of Jerusalem and its temple came just as Jesus foretold. Significantly, His followers were spared Jerusalem's destruction because they heeded His instructions to escape (see Matt. 24:15-20).

The final, worldwide events leading up to Christ's return to earth are briefly described next. Answering the question "When?" Jesus insists that no one, not even the Son, knows the day of the end (Matt. 24:36, 42; 25:13), and no attempt should be made to calculate it (Acts 1:7). In addressing whether there is a fixed or variable amount of time left, Jesus seems to suggest that time is not fixed. In the parable of the unjust judge who is gradually persuaded to intervene by the constant pleas of a poor widow (Luke 18:2-5), the point is that God, listening to the cries of His suffering children, can decide to step into the picture independently of any divine timetable. The parable of the unfruitful tree in the orchard (Luke 13:6-9) indicates that God could extend the time of mercy in response to appeals from His followers.

The most acute timing question facing believers today is the apparent delay of Christ's return. There is no saying in the Gospels that postpones His return for 2,000 years; on the contrary, the only consistent reply He gave to the question "When?" is "Soon!" However, He prepared His followers for a delay, likening their experience of waiting to that of an estate manager who, puzzled over the seeming delay of the return of the owner, has to decide whether or not to be faithful to his owner's expectations (Matt. 24:45-51). The parable of the ten bridesmaids (25:1-12) drives home the point of an unexpected delay and focuses on the attitudes and practices of the bridesmaids. Delay is the story's key theme. The coming will be delayed beyond the expectations of even the best-prepared. Nevertheless, the coming is certain.

What about signs of the end? Don't they help calculate its nearness? Jesus spoke of heavenly signs (sun, moon, stars), signs in the natural world (earthquakes), plus signs in the human realm (wars and famines). While God provides signs, they seem to recur generation after generation, hence in themselves are not specific enough to indicate the great day. The only possible exception is the sign of the Gospel preached to the entire world (Matt. 24:14; Mark 13:10); once that has been accomplished, the end will come.

A less well-known theme of Jesus about His return is that of its suddenness in the midst of daily life. Amidst a growing crescendo of images, He points out that for many people the final day will come without warning, as it did in Noah's day when people were eating and drinking and living fairly routine lives up to the day Noah entered the ark. For them the end of their world came with little warning. Two men in the field, possibly doing the day's plowing, are suddenly separated by Christ's return, as are two women grinding the grain for that day's baking (Matt. 24:37-41). In these illustrations, everyday life continues until, without significant warning, the end occurs. Notice that although one of the men and one of the women was "taken"—in other words, "ready" for Christ's return—they had no clearer idea than did their left-behind partner that this day would be their last. For both, it was an ordinary day like any other.

Since the day of Christ's return is unknowable, the only safe response of His followers is to "be ready" in the present, the only moment over which they have any control. Readiness consists of entering God's kingdom, carrying out God's commission, and living the life of faith one day at a time.[19]

In Conclusion

This chapter has surveyed what Jesus did and said according to the four Gospels, which for the vast majority of His followers have been the authoritative written record of His work and words. However, many of His followers have also been convinced that Jesus continues to meet with and guide them in more ways than just through the pages of the Gospels. Indeed, those very Gospels make clear that Jesus assured His followers that He would continue to be with them through His Spirit: "Remember, I am with you always, to the end of the age" (Matt. 28:20). Luke reports, "See, I am sending upon you what my Father promised; so stay here in the city until you have been clothed with power from on high" (Luke 24:49). John spells out even more precisely what would happen: "When he had said this, he breathed on them and said to them, 'Receive the Holy Spirit.' " (John 20:22).

The remaining documents of the New Testament record the activities of His Spirit-filled followers, conducted under the strong conviction that the risen Christ, through His Spirit, continued with them, working through them to extend and complete the work of God's kingdom begun by Jesus, and throughout remaining faithful to His own teachings, remembered and recorded in the Gospels. Jesus still continues calling people to follow Him. Those who respond experience fellowship with Him in God's kingdom, present and future, and all the other benefits and blessings of that kingdom.

For Further Reading

The best written sources are, of course, the four Gospels. Because of the scholarly trends influencing the study of the Gospels, most books published during the past fifty years cover either the life of Jesus or His teachings, but not both. Books on Jesus' life tend to be written by scholars pursuing the historical Jesus. The following can be recommended:

D. Guthrie, *A Shorter Life of Christ*. Grand Rapids, MI: Zondervan, 1970.

E. P. Sanders, *The Historical Figure of Jesus*. London: Penguin, 1993.

Jesus' teaching is typically included in books on the theology of the New Testament such as the following:
G. B. Caird, *New Testament Theology.* Oxford: Clarendon Press, 1994.
D. Guthrie, *New Testament Theology.* Downers Grove, IL: InterVarsity, 1981.
J. Jeremias, *New Testament Theology,* vol.1, *The Proclamation of Jesus.* London: SCM Press, 1971.

There are a few authors, however, who survey both the work and the teaching of Jesus:
A. M. Hunter, *The Work & Words of Jesus.* London: SCM Press, revised edition, 1973.
N. T. Wright, *Who Was Jesus?* Grand Rapids, MI: Eerdmans, 1992.
E. G. White, *The Desire of Ages.* Oakland, CA: Pacific Press, first edition, 1898.

Notes

1. Most Scripture passages quoted in this chapter are from the Revised English Bible.
2. A survey of books on the work and words of Jesus convinces the reader of the correctness of Luke's observation that many writers "have undertaken to draw up an account" (Luke 1:1) of what Jesus did and said. The literature is massive. The title of this chapter echoes that of A. M. Hunter's book, *The Work and Words of Jesus.* Donald Guthrie in *A Shorter Life of Christ* (Grand Rapids, MI: Zondervan, 1970) surveyed scholarly approaches to the life of Jesus during the previous two hundred years. For a survey and critique of more recent attempts to find Jesus "behind" the New Testament, see L. T. Johnson, *The Real Jesus* (New York: Harper Collins, 1996).
3. This view is developed by L. T. Johnson in ch. 6, "Jesus in the Memory of the Church," in *The Writings of the New Testament* (Philadelphia, PA: Fortress, 1986), and in his *The Real Jesus,* pp. 141-166.
4. See Johnson, *Writings of the New Testament,* pp. 183-190.
5. *Ibid.,* pp. 205-207.
6. *Ibid.,* p. 470.
7. This position is summarized by Joachim Jeremias in his *New Testament Theology,* vol.1, *The Proclamation of Jesus* (English translation, London : SCM, 1971), pp.88-91.
8. See Leonhard Goppelt, *Theology of the New Testament,* vol.1 (English translation, Grand Rapids, MI: Eerdmans, 1981), p. 61.
9. A. M. Hunter, *The Work and Words of Jesus* (revised edition, London : SCM, 1973), p. 69.
10. For an explanation of these sayings in their Jewish context, see Jeremias, *New Testament Theology,* p. 132.

11. Cited in Hans Conzelmann, *An Outline of the Theology of the New Testament* (English translation, London: SCM Press, 1969), p. 33.
12. I am indebted to A. M. Hunter for drawing attention to these three metaphors in *The Work and Words of Jesus,* p. 117.
13. E. P. Sanders, *The Historical Figure of Jesus* (London: Penguin, 1993), p. 169.
14. For Gospel occurrences of the word, plus discussion, see Jeremias, *New Testament Theology,* vol.1, 62f, with the corrective in Dale C. Allison, *Jesus of Nazareth: Millenarian Prophet* (Minneapolis, MN : Fortress, 1998), p. 5.
15. This remarkable observation was made by Jeremias, *Ibid.,* p. 180.
16. T. W. Manson, *The Teaching of Jesus* (2nd ed., Cambridge: University Press, 1935, reprinted 1967), p. 131.
17. Contemporary scholarly opinion on Jesus is sharply divided over the question of Jesus and the future. The main promoters of the Jesus Seminar (see ch.2, "The Jesus of History," for a critique of the Jesus Seminar), for example, deny that Jesus taught His own future return to earth. However, scholars such as E. P. Sanders and Dale C. Allison affirm the view that Jesus taught that God would soon intervene dramatically in human history.
18. This idea is developed in my article "Those Who Are Wise: the *Maskilim* in Daniel and the New Testament" in David Merling, editor, *To Understand the Scriptures: Essays in Honor of William H. Shea* (Berrien Springs, MI: Institute of Archaeology, 1997), p. 220.
19. Literature on the teaching of Jesus about the future and about His second coming is immense. Surveys include Harold Fagal, "The Advent Hope in the New Testament," in V. Norskov Olsen, editor, *The Advent Hope in Scripture and History* (Hagerstown, MD: Review and Herald, 1987), pp. 46-64; Jon Paulien, *What the Bible Says about the End-Time* (Hagerstown, MD: Review and Herald, 1994), pp. 75-83; Hans LaRondelle, *How to Understand the End-Time Prophecies of the Bible* (Sarasota, FL: First Impressions, 1997), pp. 34-58; Ben Witherington, III, *Jesus, Paul and the End of the World* (Downers Grove, IL: InterVarsity, 1992); and the works of Stephen H. Travis.

The Death of Jesus
Raoul F. Dederen

At the very heart of the Christian religion is the cross—and the resurrection—of Jesus of Nazareth. It is the high point of all four Gospels. It has been estimated that about one-third of the Gospels' narratives alludes to and focuses on the events pertaining to the last week of Jesus' ministry in Jerusalem, culminating in His death and resurrection. John's Gospel alone devotes nine of its twenty-one chapters to the long weekend extending from the night of the last supper to the resurrection.[1] The crucifixion itself is related in Matthew 27, Mark 15, Luke 23, and John 19. It is also often referred to elsewhere in the New Testament (as in Acts 2:23, 36; 4:10; 1 Cor. 2:8; Gal. 3:1; Rev. 11:8).

That the Gospels' accounts of the life and ministry of Jesus should end with a record of His death may have been unavoidable. What we are offered, however, is not just a brief statement of the facts and circumstances but a narrative the length and fullness of which is entirely out of proportion to the rest of the story. There is nothing similar in the pages recounting the lives of other prominent biblical figures such as Abraham, Moses, David, Peter, or Paul. Obviously, prompted by the Holy Spirit, the Gospel writers understood that Christ's death, not only His life and teaching, was of supreme importance. Its significance went far above and beyond the tragic ending of the life of a prophet sent by God.

Jesus' Unequivocal Testimony

During Jesus' ministry the disciples were at times bewildered by the implications of His statements on the subject. But it was their conviction that Jesus Himself was fully persuaded that the cross was His destiny. He expressed Himself clearly to Nicodemus early in His ministry (John 3:14,15) and was increasingly specific about it. There were implicit statements, such as the sufferings implied in His words about the bridegroom to be "taken from them" (Matt. 9:15; Mark 2:20; Luke 5:35); the "baptism" He was to undergo and the distress He knew until it would be accomplished (Luke 12:50); the cup He had to drink (Matt. 20:22; Mark 8:38, 39; Luke 22:42; John 18:11); Jerusalem, where the prophets "die" (literally, "perish," Luke 13:33); the murdered son (Matt. 21:39; Mark 12:8; Luke 20:15); His body anointed for burial (Matt. 26:12; Mark 14:8); the grain of wheat that must die in order to bear fruit (John 12:24); the need to be "lifted up" to draw all men to Himself (John 12:32).

There were also more explicit predictions. They all point to the inescapable finale to His mission awaiting Him in Jerusalem. Thus, following Peter's confession, Jesus "began to explain to his disciples that he must go to Jerusalem and suffer many things at the hands of the elders, chief priests and teachers of the law, and that he must be killed and on the third day be raised to life" (Matt. 16:21; cf. Mark 8:31; Luke 9:18-22). In the aftermath of the transfiguration He told His disciples that He was "to be betrayed into the hands of men" who would kill Him. Soon afterward the same specific prediction was again shared with the disciples (Matt. 17:22, 23; Mark 9:31; cf. Luke 9:44), Matthew adding that they "were filled with grief" (v. 23). Right after His interaction with a young rich ruler, Jesus once more told the twelve that they were going to Jerusalem, where He would be delivered to the chief priests and scribes who would condemn Him to death and "turn him over to the Gentiles to be mocked and flogged and crucified" (Matt. 20:18, 19; Mark 10:31, 32; Luke 18:31-33). Note the reference to what He was expecting, namely a crucifixion.

Even John's Gospel, which focuses on Christ the Revealer of God, brings to the fore the importance and necessity of Jesus' death. Thus there was "an hour" or a fixed "time" to which the movement of His whole ministry was leading. Defined several times as "not yet come" (John 2:4; 7:6, 8, 30; 8:20) its meaning is finally made plain when, with the cross only a few hours away,

Jesus declares, "The hour has come" (12:23; 17:1). John also notes that several times Jesus used the phrase "lifted up" in reference to His death. Early on He had affirmed that just as Moses had lifted up the brazen serpent on a pole in the wilderness (Num. 21:9) "so the Son of Man must be lifted up, that everyone who believes in him may have eternal life" (John 3:14, 15). The expression comes up again a few months before the end (8:28) and finally a third time less than three days before the cross: "But I, when I am lifted up from the earth, will draw all men to myself" (12:32). It is true that on the basis of the words "from the earth" some have related the statement to Jesus' ascension (cf. Acts 1:9). In the very next verse, however, John confirms the reference to be to the cross: "He said this to show the kind of death he was going to die" (v. 33).

On the Purpose of the Cross

Jesus was just as clear as to the purpose of His suffering and death. He told the disciples that He had come "to seek and to save what was lost" (Luke 19:10), to "give his life [literally, 'himself'] as a ransom for many" (Matt. 20:28; Mark 10:45). The blood He would shed would be "poured out for many" (Mark 14:24) to which Matthew adds "for the forgiveness of sins" (Matt. 26:28). And He knew He would die because that was what was written of the Messiah in the Scriptures. To the disciples, in the upper room, He made clear that "the Son of Man will go just as it is written about him" (Mark 14:21; cf. Luke 24:24-27, 44-47).

It is not possible to exaggerate the stunning nature of Jesus' testimony and the dramatic importance of Calvary. More than His teaching and His works of power, what dominated His mind was the "hour" for which He had come into the world. That "hour" was of *the* utmost importance. John Stott writes:

> And the four evangelists who bear witness to him in the Gospels, show that they understand this by the disproportionate amount of space which they give to the story of his last few days on earth, his death and resurrection. It occupies between a third and a quarter of the three Synoptic Gospels, while John's Gospel has justly been described as having two parts, "the Book of the Signs" and "the Book of the Passion," since John spends an almost equal amount of time on each.[2]

Some, to be sure, have argued that Jesus' explicit predictions about the crisis awaiting Him were not His but in fact statements written after the events, post-resurrection interpolations reflecting the early church's interpretation of our Lord's death. But for those who accept the New Testament accounts as genuine and historical the evidence is irresistible.

Like the four evangelists, the rest of the New Testament writers regard the death—and resurrection—of Jesus as the very heart and center of the Christian message. The two are not often considered apart. Yet it was the cross that tended to fix itself as the fundamental fact and the characteristic symbol of Christianity. To the Corinthians Paul wrote, "I resolved to know nothing while I was with you except Jesus Christ and him crucified" (1 Cor. 2:2). Likewise it is the figure of Him who "bore our sins in his body on the tree" which dominates the first epistle of Peter (1 Pet. 2:24). And the Epistle to the Hebrews, though it opens with one of the most significant christological passages (Heb. 1:1-13), repeatedly emphasizes the death of Jesus and its implications (1:3; 2:9; 7:27; 9:12; 12:2).

For Paul, the "glorious gospel of the blessed God" with which he had been entrusted (1 Tim. 1:11), the touchstone of all Christian preaching (Gal.1:8, 9; 1Tim. 6 :3, 4), and preached alike to Jews and Gentiles (1 Cor. 1:24), is "the word of the cross" (v. 18, RSV). Those who reject it are "enemies of the cross of Christ" (Phil. 3:18). John is in close agreement with Paul and Peter. The Apocalypse rings with the praises of the Lamb who "had been slain" and by whose blood sinners have been ransomed for God (Rev. 5:6, 9, 12,13; 7:13-17).

A Most Shocking Insistence

The persistence with which the apostles set forth a *crucified* Lord as the very foundation of the Christian faith is to say the least surprising. It must have sounded shocking, even offensive, to their contemporaries, both Jews and Gentiles. We know from contemporary evidence that death by crucifixion, generally preceded by flogging, was a widespread form of execution in the Roman Empire. It was as a rule reserved for notorious criminals, seditious slaves, and rebels against the Roman state. Its forms varied considerably, depending on the caprice and sadism of the executioners. It was a pitiless and utterly shameful form of punishment intended to subject its victims to the utmost indignity.[3]

It is not that Greeks and Romans were entirely unprepared for this strange new proclamation of a crucified Son of God. From childhood onward they had been familiar with legends, myths, parodies, and accounts of voluntary death accepted for the common good of one's city, family, or friends.[4] Such accounts had been with them from primeval times. But in the days of the apostles such archaic views could no longer be reconciled with the loftier understanding of religion, especially in educated circles. It isn't that the message of the death of Jesus of Nazareth was unintelligible to them. It simply was ethically offensive, if not repulsive, for here was a Jewish carpenter, executed on a cross as a state criminal, who claimed to be God, King of kings and Lord of lords, and to have brought atonement not just for this or that particular crime or sin, but for all sins and for all humans for all time. Nor was there need any longer to appease the wrath of God by one's actions or offerings since a gracious God Himself had provided the expiatory sacrifice that erases all guilt, once for all. Absurd, utter nonsense!

It was even more so for the Jewish people. First-century Jews generally expected a kingly, glorious Messiah. To them the message of the Messiah dying on a cross and then raised by God was senseless. It was taken for granted among them that God would bless him with victory and triumph. He was the righteous and sinless one par excellence. Any talk of a crucified Messiah would inevitably be understood as blasphemy since the Torah itself stated that a man hanging "on a tree" was "under God's curse" (Deut. 21:22, 23; cf. Gal. 3:13). There was no way for the Messiah to be at the same time Israel's Messiah and accursed by God.[5] Any such proclamation was despicable, sheer madness. How accurate was Paul's observation: "We preach Christ crucified: a stumbling block to Jews and foolishness to Gentiles" (1 Cor. 1:23).

Crying Out for Interpretation

Obviously the scandalous nature of Jesus' execution on a cross cried out for interpretation and validation. Its significance had to be made clear. And this is exactly what the early disciples did, under the guidance of the Spirit. In their eyes, the "shame" (Heb. 12:2) of the crucifixion was no despicable catastrophe. On the contrary, it was part of God's plan for human salvation. From the very start, at Pentecost, Peter asserted that the crucifixion was not the triumph of human wickedness but the consummation of a divine purpose, "God's set purpose and foreknowledge" (Acts 2:23). Nor was it just a bare historical fact but a gospel, "good news," an event whose reality and importance lay in its unique significance, a message of divine love and forgiveness. Jesus of Nazareth "died for our sins" (1 Cor. 15:3), "died for us," even while we were yet sinners (Rom. 5:8) and did so "once for all" (1 Pet. 3:18), after which "he sat down at the right hand of God" (Heb. 10:12). So deep was God's love for erring humanity! Hence there was no immorality nor defeat in His death. Jesus was never more kingly and triumphant than when He reigned on the cross.

With the Jews in mind, the apostles insisted that the cross, so fully explicable in terms of God's love and purpose, was also foretold and foreshadowed in the Old Testament Scriptures. Thus, in the New Testament writings one finds Jesus time and again portrayed in dress often borrowed from the Old Testament figure of the "suffering righteous servant." He is betrayed by a table intimate (Ps. 41:9; John 13:18) for thirty pieces of silver (Zech.11:12, 13; Matt. 26:15). He is crucified with criminals (Isa. 53:12; Matt. 27:38), mocked (Ps. 22:7; Matt. 27:39), His garments divided among evildoers (Ps. 22:18; John 19:23, 24). He cries out from the cross (Ps. 22:1; Mark 15:34) yet is vindicated by His resurrection and declared to be the Son of God (Isa. 52:13-15; 53:10-12; Rom. 1:4).

Why That Particular Cross?

But why *that* cross? There were indeed three crosses on Golgotha. Yet only one has redemptive meaning. It has atoning significance not just because He was the example of man's most noble endeavors, but because of the One who died there. His death has saving worth because of who He is. The gospel of good news is in fact the proclamation of the Word become flesh and crucified. He was "the Son of God, Jesus Christ" (2 Cor. 1:19). A genuine incarnation of the everlasting, pre-existent Son of God had occurred. For the apostles, the One who died on the cross was at the same time fully divine and fully human, the sinless God-man.[6]

They also made plain that one could not truly appreciate the significance of the Word's incarnation and crucifixion apart from a keen perception of the plight of the human race corrupted by sin. All had sinned and fallen short of the glory of God (Rom. 3:23). Sin was not just defect or ignorance, but rebellion against God's will, sheer enmity against Him. As an objective reality seeking to enslave us (John 8:34), a power reigning since the days of Adam (Rom. 5:12), it holds its captives in bondage (Rom. 6:6-11; John 8:34). It brings separation from God (Isa. 59:2; Eph. 2:12). Sin's wages is death (Rom. 6:23). It consists not simply in individual actions of sin, but in a state, a sinful condition common to all humans who by nature are children of wrath and dead in trespasses and sins (Eph. 2:1-3; Rom. 7:8, 9, 17, 20). It infects the whole human being and the entire race, leaving us helpless to help ourselves as well as others either morally or spiritually (Eph. 4:1-19). The only antidote is Jesus Christ who alone is sinless (1 John 3:5; Heb. 7:26; 1 Pet. 2:22), and who being fully divine and fully human "died for sins once for all, the righteous for the unrighteous, to bring you to God" (1 Pet. 3:18).

Scores of Images

But in what sense did Jesus' death bring us back to God? What did happen at Calvary? In their struggle to articulate meaningfully the significance of the cross and how salvation has been provided through it, the New Testament writers, Paul in particular, used a variety of expressions and images. Literally dozens of such images expose and illuminate the benefits of Jesus' death. Only a few can be mentioned here: salvation (1 Tim. 1:15), redemption (1 Pet. 3:18), adoption (Gal. 4:5), forgiveness of sins (Acts 5:30, 31), reconciliation (2 Cor. 5:14-6:2), substitution (1 Tim. 2:6), sacrifice (Heb. 9:23-26), expiation-propitiation (1 John 2:2), new creation (2 Cor. 5:17), access to God (Eph. 2:18), justification (Rom. 5:9), righteousness in the sight of God (Rom. 3:21, 22) peace with God

(Rom. 5:1, 2), assurance of God's unfailing love (1 John 4:9), grace (Eph. 2:4-5), life eternal (John 3:16, 36) and deliverance from this evil age (Gal. 1:4).

This sheer diversity of images may well demonstrate that no single figure is exhaustive in itself or sufficient to give us a comprehensive understanding of how and why Jesus died for our sins. At the same time we need to remember that whether one refers to them as images, analogies, or metaphors—the differences between those terms for Christian theology are still debated—these images are ways of speaking about God in terms rooted in human realities. When, guided by the Spirit, they used such entities, the apostles were not reducing God to the level of a created being, but merely affirming that there is a likeness or correspondence between God and the world He created. A likeness, a correspondence, but not an identity. Hence, however useful, human images break down at some point. There comes a point when they cannot be pressed further, as indicated by their use in the Scriptures themselves, where they balance and supplement one another.[7]

Theories of the Atonement

Such reflection on the meaning of the death of Christ did not come to an end with the passing of the last New Testament writer. Through the centuries, Christians in different countries and in different ages have tried to bring together the various strands of biblical teaching on the subject and work them into theories intended to help others understand how the cross relates to our salvation. These are usually referred to as theories or models of the atonement.

The term "atonement" itself is derived from the phrase "at one" and, in Christian theology, refers to the act of healing the break opened by sin between God and human beings. Atonement theories may be grouped around three or four basic models, each of which could be broken into several sub-models.[8] Certain specific features stand out in each basic approach. One perceives Jesus' atoning death as a victory over sin and Satan. Another understands it in terms of satisfaction due to the insulted majesty of God. The exemplarist or moral influence theory looks upon the death of Jesus as primarily a demonstration of the depth of God's love and as an example to His followers, and often little more. The sixteenth-century Reformers taught that, in bearing by voluntary submission the punishment due to sinners, Jesus was reckoned by God a sinner in their place. Each theory draws attention to an important aspect of God's plan of redemption, yet all four cannot simply be accepted without qualification for to some extent they come into conflict with one another.

It is our contention that the biblical theology of the cross is most evident in the vicarious, substitutionary understanding of the atonement. It maintains the valid insights of the models just mentioned. Whether it be atonement as victory over evil, atonement as an expression of God's justice and majesty, or atonement as a demonstration of God's love, it is only on the basis of the substitutionary view that these other insights hold compelling significance. It is a concept which begins its life in the Old Testament and is worked out and enriched in the New Testament theology of the cross.

A Sacrificial Death

The testimony of the apostles should be given due regard. One of the most prominent categories by which they share their comprehension of Jesus' death is that of sacrifice. Their vocabulary is rich and varied. At times the reference may be somewhat indirect as when Paul writes that Christ "gave himself for our sins" (Gal. 1:4; cf. 1 Pet. 2:24; Heb. 8:3; 10:26), at other times it is most specific: "Christ loved us and gave himself up for us, as a fragrant offering and sacrifice to God" (Eph. 5:2; 1 John 5:7; Heb. 7:27; 9:14, 23-26; 10:10,12,14). Throughout the New Testament Christ's sacrificial death is thought of as fully achieving all that the Old Testament sacrifices dimly foreshadowed (Heb. 9:23, 24; 8:1, 2; 10:14), the means as well as the condition of human salvation.[9]

In what sense? What does Christ's sacrificial death tell us? As the apostles see it, Christ's crucifixion is a manifestation of the love of God. Paul points out that "God demonstrates his own love for us in this: While we were still sinners, Christ died for us" (Rom. 5:8). This statement is particularly important. The apostle could easily have said that at the cross *Christ* showed His love for us, which He did. But Paul is making the point that the cross demonstrates just as clearly the love of the Father. The keynote is struck time and again (1 Pet. 1:2, 3; Heb. 2:9; 10:9, 10). In 1 John we find the stupendous statement that "this is love: not that we loved God, but that he loved us and sent his Son as an atoning sacrifice for our sins" (4:10). It is in God's love that the early believers saw the original motif of Christ's sacrificial death, for, as Paul put it, "All this is from God, who reconciled us to himself through Christ" (2 Cor. 5:18). We may fully agree with Charles A. Dinsmore when he concludes that "there was a cross in the heart of God before there was one planted on the green hill outside Jerusalem."[10]

But the death of Christ is not only a manifestation of the love of the Father, it is also the supreme expression of the love of Christ Himself. "For Christ's love compels us," rejoices Paul, "because we are convinced that one has died for all and therefore all died" (2 Cor. 5:14). "I live by faith in the Son of God," adds the apostle, "who loved me and gave himself for me" (Gal. 2:20). "Christ died for sins once for all, the righteous for the unrighteous, to bring you to God" insists Peter (1 Pet. 3:18), while John, years later, confesses "Jesus Christ laid down his life for us" (1 John 3:16). This was a willing sacrifice, Jesus' own deliberate choice (John 10:17, 18; Eph. 5:25; Gal. 2:20), motivated by love.

A Penal Substitutionary Sacrifice

This is only part of the picture, however. To speak of the death of Jesus as a sacrifice and a manifestation of the love of both the Father and the Son is to place a number of intimately related truths on the table. Thus, while insisting that Christ's crucifixion is closely associated with the putting away of sin (cf. Rom. 4:25; 5:8, 9; 2 Cor. 5:14; Gal. 1:4; Heb. 9:26, 28; 1 John 1:7), the apostles make plain that it was a vicarious, a substitutionary death.

So, to the Romans Paul states that sinners "are justified freely by his [God's] grace" as a gift, "through the redemption [literally, 'ransoming']" which is in Christ Jesus (Rom. 3:24, 25). As a result, "there is now no condemnation for those who are in Christ Jesus"

(Rom. 8:1). Similarly Peter reminds his readers that they "were ransomed . . . not with . . . silver or gold, but with the precious blood of Christ like that of a lamb without blemish or spot" (1 Pet. 1:18, 19, RSV). To ransom means to release on receipt of a payment, to set someone free. The term conveys the meaning of substitution.

Jesus, too, saw Himself as our substitute and His death as a ransom. He told His disciples that the Son of Man came "to serve and to give his life [literally, 'himself'] as a ransom for many" (Matt. 20:28). This notion is further affirmed by his use of the preposition *anti* ("*for* many") which essentially means "instead of," "in the place of." Whether it be Jesus', Peter's or Paul's pronouncements these are all clear statements concerning the substitutionary nature of Jesus' death. He bore our sins. They were laid on Him, transferred from us to Him. *Hyper*, another pertinent preposition, used even more frequently, adds to the substitutionary intimation of *anti* the basic meaning of "on behalf of," "in favor of." Jesus died in our place and on our behalf.[11]

The same substitutionary aspect is strongly underlined in Paul's saying that Jesus "gave himself as a ransom for all men" (1 Tim. 2:6) where the two prepositions are used, both *hyper* and *anti*, but *anti* appears in the compound noun *antilytron* (literally, "ransom-in-lieu-of"). The force of this combined word, along with the statements we just considered, attests that in Jesus' crucifixion the apostles saw a death endured by one both on behalf of and instead of others, so that in His death Christ took our place, and we no longer need to die eternally if we accept Him as our substitute. Jesus was "offered once to take away the sins of many" (Heb. 9:28), he "bore our sins in his body on the tree" (1 Pet. 2:24), and "redeemed us from the curse of the law by becoming a curse for us" (Gal. 3:13). There is no hint, however, as to the identity of the one to whom the ransom was paid. As mentioned earlier, analogies break down at some point. For the New Testament writers "ransom" means freedom, deliverance, and beyond that point the analogy breaks down.

It is on the ground of such biblical statements that a penal substitutionary understanding of the atonement is justified, even enjoined. Whatever happened, in His death on the cross Christ our substitute bore our penalty. Since the penalty has been borne in our stead, it cannot be imposed again. Jesus died our death. His cross was our cross. In spite of the protests of some we feel compelled to agree with Donald Guthrie, who points out that "even if we avoid the term 'penal,' which Paul himself does not use, there is no way of avoiding the conclusion that in his thought Christ had died the sinner's death."[12]

What About Expiation and Propitiation?

In a celebrated passage the apostle Paul explains that to redeem us God put Christ forward "as an *expiation* by his blood, to be received by faith" (Rom. 3:25, RSV; emphasis supplied), to which John adds that our Lord "is the *expiation* for our sins" and that "in this is love, not that we loved God but that he loved us and sent his Son to be the *expiation* for our sins" (1 John 2:2; 4:10, RSV; emphasis supplied). To expiate means to cancel the guilt incurred by an offense or to pay the penalty for it, just as a convict is said to have expiated his crime once he or she is set free. That's what happened at Golgotha. As Donald M. Baillie rightly observes, the sacrifice of Christ "is an expiatory sacrifice, because sin is a dreadfully real thing which love cannot tolerate or lightly pass over, and it is only out of the suffering of such inexorable love that true forgiveness, as distinct from an indulgent amnesty, could ever come. That is the objective process of atonement that goes on in the very life of God."[13]

In each of the three foregoing scriptural statements most modern versions have translated the verb *hilaskomai* and its cognates as "expiation" though it literally should be rendered "propitiation." The NIV reads "a sacrifice of atonement" (Rom. 3:25), which is even further removed from a literal translation. "Propitiation"?, some will ask. "Do you mean that the cross of Christ propitiated God, that it appeased God and changed Him from a wrathful God to a loving God?" This was indeed the prevailing sense in which the term was used among Paul's and John's contemporaries.[14] But if the atonement springs from the love of God how can we speak of propitiating Him? The argument is compelling, but only if this is the biblical definition of propitiation, which it is not.

True, few have done as much as C. H. Dodd to demonstrate that in the Septuagint, the Greek version of the Old Testament, *hilasko-mai* and its derivatives should be rendered "expiation" and that it is expiation rather than propitiation that the New Testament writers had in mind when they used those terms.[15] " 'Propitiation' is simply illegitimate and the 'wrath of God' an archaic phrase befitting 'a thoroughly archaic age.' "[16] It is agreed that the pagan concepts of wrath and propitiation are foreign to the biblical view of God. But does this mean that all ideas of wrath are absent from it? This is certainly not Paul's sentiment when he builds his case that Gentiles and Jews alike have fallen short of the glory of God and as sinners come under the wrath and judgment of God (Rom. 1:18; 2:5,8; 3:5, 6; 4:15; 5:9). And the apostle's grasp of the wrath of God is not just some inevitable concept of cause and effect in a moral world. Such a view does not do full justice to Paul's thought. To be sure, sin has its consequences (Gal. 6:7), but in these verses what is brought out is God's personal activity, the active presence of His judgment toward "all the godlessness and wickedness" (Rom. 1:18).[17]

What is being maintained in Scripture is that sin is a barrier between sinners and God (Isa. 59:1,2; Eph. 2:12; 4:17, 18). By His very nature a God of holiness can do nothing else than condemn it (Eph. 5:5, 6; Col. 3:5, 6). His wrath, however, is not an irrational outburst of uncontrolled passion, so frequently associated with our human experience. It actually discloses the reverse side of God's relentless love for sinners and His stern reaction to evil. When Paul mentions God's wrath he means God's wrath against sin. He sees no difficulty conceiving of the coexistence of perfect love and "hate." God's love is never in question (John 3:16; Rom. 5:8; 1 John 4:10). What His holiness required God's love provided. Thus on the cross Christ bore our sins (1 Pet. 2:24) in that He was condemned as a sinner and forsaken of God (Matt. 27:46; Mark 15:34). He faced God's wrath and judgment that are ours, not His. At this point Christ's obedient love and saving work may appropriately be called an expiation-propitiation of our sins. Here love and justice encountered each other. "At the cross," observes Ellen White, "justice and mercy met together, and righteousness and peace kissed each other."[18]

Reflecting on Jesus' great cry, "My God, my God, why have you forsaken me?", the same author writes: "But this great sacrifice was not made in order to create in the Father's heart a love for man, not to make Him willing to save. No, no! 'God so loved the world, that He gave His only-begotten Son.' John 3:16. The Father loves us, not because of the great propitiation, but He provided the propitiation because He loves us. Christ was the medium through which He could pour out His infinite love upon a fallen world."[19]

"Wrath" and "propitiation" may not be ideal words for our purpose, but for lack of more appropriate terms we will have to use them, with care. There is no need to rule them out. They safeguard two awesome truths: the reality of sin and of its unfathomable sinfulness as well as the unsearchable depths of God's love and holiness. To leave out either dimension from the love of God is to rob it of much of its apostolic meaning.

"A Foolishness . . . Wiser than Man's Wisdom"

As in the days of the apostles, the "word of the cross" remains a knowledge "that surpasses knowledge" (Eph. 3:19). It still is "foolishness" to some and a "stumbling block" to others (1 Cor. 1:18, 23), but to Christ's disciples, those who have come to understanding, it is "the wisdom of God" (v. 24), a wisdom whose "foolishness . . . is wiser than man's wisdom" (v. 25). The preaching of "Christ crucified for us" may not measure up to the expectations of those of our contemporaries eager to explain rationally and with finality any aspect of God's working and existence. It will always remain inadequate to its object, for the Creator and His work are inscrutable, intelligible to us only as He has disclosed them to us (Deut. 29:29; Rom 11:33). It is the kind of preaching that makes the Christian say, "Now we see in a mirror dimly . . . . Now we know in part" (1 Cor. 13:12, RSV). It is a kind of knowledge that, though genuine and trustworthy, is not full.

No single interpretation of Jesus' atoning life and death, therefore, will suffice to express the fullness of what happened at the cross. We should especially not nourish the assumption that our proclamation of Christ's work on the cross has to resolve all the "how problems," so that all puzzlement is dispelled and no mystery remains. Along with the early believers let us declare the meaning of the atonement rather than its mechanics. This meaning dominates everything the apostles wrote, and they saw it in a variety of ways. Now they see it as a divine initiative, now as a penal substitutionary sacrifice, now as reconciliation, now as redemption-deliverance, now as an act of justification, now as adoption into God's family, now as forgiveness of sin, now as a call to repentance, now as cleansing and purification, and so forth. It is not that the teaching of the New Testament is unclear. Jesus' atoning work is simply too great in extent to be described or comprehended in one single model. It is beyond even the wisest of men.

At the same time, while all theories and explanations have in them a measure of truth and none, taken separately, is adequate to contain all the evidence exhaustively, that does not give us permission to abandon part of the biblical evidence because modern minds do not appreciate it. We are concerned to contend for the fact that penal substitution is at the heart of the atonement. We do not mean to say that when we use the phrase "penal substitution" we have solved all the problems. In a sense we have only begun. But we cannot escape the idea of penal substitution if we carry our task on biblical premises. It may not be considered correct today in some quarters to call Jesus' death "penal" or to regard Him as our "substitute." But can we avoid using such terms when expressing the biblical view of the atonement, especially Paul's view? And if we cannot, as J. I. Packer asks, can we justify ourselves in holding a view of the atonement in which penal substitution has no place?[20]

Today the crucified Saviour meets us as the resurrected Lord and our heavenly high priest (Acts 5:30-31; Rom. 8:34; Heb. 6:19, 20; 7:23-25; 9:24). His death at Calvary was a perfect sacrifice. It was also the beginning of a priesthood which continues for ever, "in the sanctuary, the true tabernacle set up by the Lord" (Heb. 8:2), Himself the sacrifice and Himself the priest. There He exercises a ministry "as essential to the plan of salvation as was His death upon the cross,"[21] a ministry of mediation, applying the merits of His sinless life and substitutionary death to all who "approach the throne of grace with confidence, so that . . . [they] may receive mercy and find grace to help . . . [them] in . . . [their] time of need" (Heb. 4:16; cf. 10:19-22).[22]

"Be Reconciled to God"

In other words, everything depends on Jesus' atoning death as an objective, unique, and once-for-all sacrifice. It was something ordained by the Father, accomplished by the Son, and offered to all, long before we were born and entirely apart from our response to it. It is an objective reality. But it has also a subjective dimension. *It does require a response.* Note Paul's plea: "God was reconciling the world to himself in Christ. . . . . We implore you on Christ's behalf : Be reconciled to God" (2 Cor. 5:19, 20). The apostle is calling for a personal response, an individual appropriation of Christ's atoning death, which becomes effective for us when we claim its benefits and by faith are united with Jesus in death and resurrection, dying to sin and rising in newness of life in Him, through the ministry of the Spirit (John 3:36; Acts 3:19; Rom. 6:1-11; 13:11-14). Our faith brings the historical cross into the realm of our daily lives and regenerates them. It is true that Christ died for our sins, but He died *for* our sins so that, by His grace in us, we might die *to* our sins (Rom. 3:31; 8:13; Gal. 2:20; 5:24). His sacrifice of perfect obedience does not make my life of obedience unnecessary. It makes it possible, through a grateful response to God's gracious gift of salvation in Jesus Christ.

These two aspects of Christ's atoning life and death are not to be separated as if independent of each other. We must tenaciously reject any one-sided emphasis upon the atonement either as a once-for-all historical event apart from the response of faith or as a one-sided emphasis upon our subjective, inner experience of dying and rising with Christ without due recognition that we can die and rise with Him only because long ago on Golgotha in a unique event He died in our stead.

It has not been the intention to put forth in this chapter a detailed elaboration of the biblical theology of the cross. This could only be achieved in larger volumes. The present survey has done no more than erect signposts toward an understanding of one of the most profound biblical mysteries (cf. 1 Tim. 3:16). No essay would be able to present a total picture. But the New Testament writers give ample indication that what is necessary to know about the life and death of

Jesus can be known. This is the basic assumption that colors their entire theological and missionary task. Such understanding should motivate us as it motivated them. It should lead us to remember that not only are we to die to self that we might live unto Christ but that, grateful, we are to give ourselves in the service of others, even as Christ in the days of His flesh. Thus, through us the eternal benefits of His atoning work may be extended to the whole world.

For Further Reading

H. D. McDonald, *The Atonement of the Death of Christ, in Faith, Revelation, and History*. Grand Rapids, MI: Baker, 1985.
_____ , *The New Testament Concept of the Atonement*. Grand Rapids, MI: Baker, 1994.
A. E. McGrath, *Understanding Jesus*. Grand Rapids, MI: Zondervan, 1987.
L. Morris, *The Apostolic Preaching of the Cross*. London: Tyndale Press, 1955.
J. R. W. Stott, *The Cross of Christ*. Downers Grove, IL: InterVarsity, 1986.
E. C. Webster, *Crosscurrents in Adventist Theology*. Berrien Springs, MI: Andrews University Press, 1992.

Notes

1. Joel B. Green and Mark D. Baker, *Recovering the Scandal of the Cross* (Downers Grove, IL: InterVarsity Press, 2000), p. 16.
2. John R. W. Stott, *The Cross of Christ* (Downers Grove, IL: InterVarsity Press, 1986), p. 32.
3. On the origins, forms, and practice of crucifixion in the ancient world see Martin Hengel's landmark publication, *Crucifixion in the Ancient World and the Folly of the Message of the Cross* (Philadelphia, PA: Fortress Press, 1977), pp. 22-32, 69 ff. Hengel has provided us with another equally penetrating volume, closely related to the former, *The Atonement: the Origins of the Doctrine in the New Testament* (Philadelphia, PA: Fortress Press, 1981).
4. For details about such accounts see Hengel, *The Atonement*, pp. 4-28.
5. *Ibid.*, pp. 28-32, 39-47.
6. On the incarnation, the divinity, and humanity of Jesus, see Norman Young, "The Person of Jesus," ch. 5 in the present volume. Cf. R. Dederen, "Christ: His Person and Work," in *Handbook of Seventh-day Adventist Theology* ed. R. Dederen (Hagerstown, MD: Review and Herald, 2000), pp.161-169.
7. On the nature of the theological language, see Alister E. McGrath, *Christian Theology: An Introduction* (Oxford: Blackwell, 1994), pp.134-143.
8. The interested reader will find a detailed study of atonement theories in H. D. McDonald, *The Atonement of the Death of Christ* (Grand Rapids, MI: Baker Press, 1985), pp.115-341.

9. For a survey of the Old Testament sacrificial system, its characteristics, and foreshadowing sacrifices see Angel Rodriguez, "The Sanctuary," in *Handbook of Seventh-day Adventist Theology*, pp. 376-387; *The Sanctuary and the Atonement: Biblical, Historical, and Theological Studies*, Arnold V. Wallenkampf and W. R. Lesher, eds. (General Conference of SDAs: Biblical Research Institute, Washington, D. C., 1981), esp. pp.1-156; Roy Gane, *Altar Call* (Berrien Springs, MI: Diadem, 1999).

10. Quoted by D. M. Baillie, *God was in Christ: An Essay on Incarnation and Atonement* (New York: Charles Scribner's Sons, 1948), p. 198.

11. On the meaning of *anti* and *hyper* in secular and New Testament Greek, see *A Greek-English Lexicon of the New Testament and Other Early Church Literature*, 3rd ed., revised and edited by Frederick William Danker, based on Walter Bauer's work (Chicago, IL: University of Chicago Press, 2000), pp. 87, 88, 1030,1031.

12. Donald Guthrie, *New Testament Theology* (Downers Grove, IL: InterVarsity Press, 1981), p. 470. While not a Pauline metaphor as such, "penal substitution" is a mixing of several of them.

13. Baillie, p. 198.

14. On the meaning of *hilaskomai* in secular Greek and in the New Testament, see "Hilaskomai," "Hilasmos," "Hilasterion." in Danker, *A Greek-English Lexicon,* pp. 473, 474; J. M. Gundry-Volf, "Expiation, Propitiation, Mercy Seat," *Dictionary of Paul and His Letters*, Gerald F. Hawthorne *et al,* eds. (Downers Grove, IL: InterVarsity Press, 1993), pp. 279-284; M. A. Seifried, "Death of Christ," in *Dictionary of the Later New Testament and Its Development*, eds. Ralph P. Martin and Peter H. Davids (Downers Grove, IL: InterVarsity Press, 1997), pp. 275, 281, 282.

15. C. H. Dodd, *The Bible and the Greeks* (London: Hodder and Stoughton, 1954), pp.82-95. For an extended reaction to Dodd's view see Roger Nicole, "C. H. Dodd and the Doctrine of Propitiation," *Westminster Theological Journal*, 9 (1955), pp. 117-157.

16. Cf. C. H. Dodd, *The Epistle of Paul to the Romans* (*Moffat New Testament Commentary*, New York: Harper and Row, 1932), pp. 20-24.

17. For a detailed survey of the theme of the wrath of God in the New Testament, see Gustav Stählin, *"orge"*, in *Theological Dictionary of the New Testament*, ed. Gerhard Kittel, vol. 5 (Grand Rapids, MI: Eerdmans, 1968), pp. 422- 447.

18. E. G. White, *Review and Herald*, June 25, 1908, p. 8.

19. E. G. White, *Steps to Christ* (Mountain View, CA: Pacific Press, 1956), p. 13.

20. J. I. Packer, "What Did the Cross of Christ Achieve? The Logic of Penal Substitution," *The Tyndale Bulletin*, 25/1974, p. 45.

21. E. G. White, *The Great Controversy* (Mountain View, CA: Pacific Press, 1911), p. 489.

22. For an excellent reflection on Christ's heavenly ministry, see Frank B. Holbrook, *The Atoning Priesthood of Christ* (Berrien Springs, MI: Adventist Theological Society, 1996).

C H A P T E R

The Risen Jesus
David N. Marshall

The whole case for Christianity rests on the bodily resurrection of Jesus. Without it Christianity would have been stillborn, for a living faith cannot outlive a dead Saviour.

But as Paul, Christ's great champion, discovered the whole idea of resurrection was in head-on collision with the Greek philosophy against which Christianity had to make headway in the first century (Acts 17:18, 19, 31, 32). The Greeks believed in the immortality of the soul and, for them, that involved the total dissolution of the body.[1] It is not surprising, therefore, that less than twenty-five years after Christ's resurrection, some of the Christians in Corinth just could not grasp the concept of resurrection. It was not the resurrection of Christ that they denied, but resurrection of the dead in general. This gave Paul the opportunity to provide them with a closely-argued treatise on both.[2]

The Importance of the Resurrection

Paul began by reminding his readers of the Christian gospel. He had presented it to them earlier; they had received it; and hence it was common ground. Through the acceptance of that gospel they had been saved (1 Cor. 15:1-3). That salvation was possible because of the significance of three historical events: the death, the burial, and the resurrection of Jesus (vs. 3, 4).

Jesus died and, in demonstration of the reality of His death, He was buried. Critics of the New Testament point out that, unlike the writers of the four Gospels, Paul did not mention the empty tomb.

Clearly, however, Paul *believed* in the empty tomb. What was Jesus buried in if it was not a tomb?

Jesus was raised and, in order to demonstrate the reality of His resurrection, He was seen. And Paul gave details of the resurrection appearances (vs.5-9). His summary of Christ's redemptive act, the substance of the Christian gospel, involved four verbs: He died, was buried, was raised, and appeared. All had the same subject (Jesus), and all referred to the same person, the same body. We have no right to change either the topic or the subject mid-sentence and say that the death and burial were physical and the resurrection and appearances were, in some sense, "spiritual." Paul made no such concession to the Greeks, and so there is nothing on which modern critics can build their arguments.

The bodily, historical, third-day resurrection of Jesus is foundational to Christianity. It was the core of the argument for Christianity presented by its front runners. In their sermons and subsequent letters the death and resurrection of Jesus were indissolubly coupled. His death had represented man's verdict of rejection. His resurrection had represented God's verdict of vindication. Seven times the leading apostles, Peter and Paul, repeated the same formula: You killed Him; God raised Him; and we are witnesses (e.g., Acts 2:23-32; 3:15; 4:9,10; 5:30-32).

These witnesses of Christ's resurrection could never forget their feelings of total desolation when man's verdict—by means of pseudo-legal procedures, the baying of a mob, and the work of Roman executioners—had totally gone against Jesus. What had seemed worst of all was when He uttered the words "My God, my God, why have you forsaken me?" (Matt. 27:46), making it even appear that He was God-forsaken. His burial in a rock-hewn tomb must have seemed like the ultimate end. The verdict of rejection upon Jesus was as decisive as it could possibly have been.

The witnesses of Christ's resurrection, having spent long hours in an uncomprehending, emotional deep, would never forget the exhilaration of Easter morning's good news. Some believed it immediately; others hardly dared to; while still others had to be convinced. God had reversed man's verdict by raising Jesus to life. The human verdict on His claim to be the "Son of Man" had been "blasphemy!" But God had reversed it. As far as the messianic claims of Jesus were concerned He had been treated like a pretender; but God raised Him as Lord, Christ, and Saviour. Death and burial were verdicts in themselves, but God reversed them and raised Him the "Author of life" and guarantor of everlasting life to all who believe (Acts 3:15; 1 Cor. 15:19, 20).

Only God could have reversed the verdict. The resurrection was not just a recovery of lost morale or proof that Jesus could survive even death. It was a divine act. Further, it was an historical act— and it was public! "On the third day" was not an oft-repeated throwaway phrase; it demonstrated that the resurrection was a precise historical event. The condemnation and crucifixion of Jesus could hardly have been more public; so the reversal of the verdict had to be equally public. Eyewitnesses who could say, "We saw Him," "He appeared to us," "We talked with Him," "He ate with us," and the visible testimony of the empty tomb made it so.

"What the early church insisted about Jesus was that He had been well and truly physically resurrected and was now well and truly physically alive."[3] Nevertheless, in presenting his treatise to the Corinthians, Paul did not shrink from an examination of the implications of the opposite scenario, a denial of the resurrection (1 Cor. 15:12-19). He led into it by arguing that if Christ's resurrection was preached, what grounds could there possibly be for the case of those in the Corinthian church who denied the resurrection of the dead? If there was no resurrection, "then not even Christ" had been raised. And if Christ had not been raised then both "our preaching" and "your faith" were "useless." The apostles preached that Jesus had died, been buried, been resurrected, and been seen. If only half of this was true, then they had only half a gospel. And half a gospel would mean that Jesus was still buried—so it was no gospel at all! God would have left Him dead and buried—and not vindicated. If that were the case, the apostles were charlatans, there was no forgiveness of sins, no salvation, and Christians who had "fallen asleep" had simply perished in the ground, their lives snuffed out like candles in the wind. If Christ had not been raised, then sin, death, and Satan had been victorious.

Paul concluded the bleak scenario like this: "If all we get out of

Christ is a little inspiration for a few short years, we're a pretty sorry lot."[4] "We are to be pitied more than all men. *But Christ has indeed been raised from the dead"* (1 Cor. 15:19, 20, emphasis supplied). And *because* He has been raised we can build our faith on firm foundations:

First, Jesus is Lord.

Second, we can have faith in the witness of the apostles, the Word.

Third, salvation by grace through faith in Him is a certainty.

Fourth, Christ intercedes for us and empowers us.

Fifth, through justification we can experience the assurance of salvation and life everlasting.

While the cross is the central focus of the New Testament, it should never be viewed apart from the resurrection as though it made sufficient sense (let alone a sufficient gospel!) in and of itself. The resurrection explains and validates the cross. What the cross won for us the resurrection made available to us. Thus the resurrection is as necessary for salvation as is the cross.

Did the Resurrection Really Happen?
The Evidence Reassessed

The bodily resurrection of Jesus is a reality, a fact of history. This is Paul's central assertion in his great resurrection chapter, 1 Corinthians 15. Together with this assertion Paul presents the evidence for the resurrection, discusses the nature of Christ's resurrection body, and examines the implications of the resurrection as the conquest of death for all who believe. The resurrection issue removes the question "Is Christianity valid?" from the realm of philosophy and forces it to be an issue of history.

Those Who Have Examined the Evidence

C. S. Lewis *became* Christianity's foremost apologist in twentieth-century England. But this is not how this Fellow of Magdalen College, Oxford, and Professor of Medieval and Renaissance Literature, Cambridge, began. For years he resisted Christianity. He wrote of God as the "Adversary." What began a slow process of change was when "the hardest boiled of all the atheists I ever knew" (he doesn't name him) conceded that "the evidence for the historicity of the Gospels was really surprisingly good."[5] What brought Lewis to the point of conversion was when his close friend, Prof. J. R. R. Tolkien, a practicing Christian, presented him with further proof for the historical reliability of the Gospels and, hence, the historicity of the resurrection.[6]

Contemporary American apologist Dr. Josh McDowell who, arguably, has done more than any other in recent times to demonstrate the historicity of the resurrection, himself began as an opponent. Years of examining the evidence, however, brought him to a position in which, in answer to the question, "Professor McDowell, why can't you intellectually refute Christianity?" he could reply, "For a simple reason. I am not able to explain away an event in history—the resurrection of Jesus Christ."[7] Michael Green cites two Jewish authors—Joseph Klausner and Pinchas Lapide—who, having examined the case for and the case against the resurrection, accepted it as an "historical event."[8]

Ross Clifford has brought together the testimonies of leading lawyers who have examined the evidence for the resurrection. Prof. Simon Greenleaf (1783-1853) of Harvard Law School, whose three-volume *Treatise on the Law of Evidence* is still regarded as authoritative, wrote *The Testimony of the Evangelists Examined by the Rules of Evidence Administered in Courts of Justice*, which represented an application of the principles of his earlier work to the resurrection. Each of the four "witnesses" (the Gospel writers) passed the most rigorous tests. Their form and style were different. The minor discrepancies in their testimonies were sufficient to demonstrate that there had been no collusion and that what he was dealing with was the evidence of eyewitnesses, not apologetics. No intelligent jury would fail to bring in a verdict in favor of the resurrection.[9]

A number of contemporary legal figures, among them Charles Colson, have reached the same conclusion by the same or similar means. Lawyer Val Grieve has written: "I have carefully examined the evidence for the resurrection, the physical return from the dead of Jesus Christ. . . . Logic must point in the direction of his resurrection on an actual day and date in our history when, if you had been there, you could have touched the living Jesus and heard Him speak."[10]

Frank Morison, a rationalistic lawyer, having set out to look at the evidence in order to disprove the resurrection, ended by writing the standard work, *Who Moved the Stone?* (Faber, 1958), displaying the evidence *for* the resurrection. He had used the critical faculties of his keen, lawyer's brain to sift data and admit nothing as evidence that did not meet the stiff criteria for admission into the law courts and had become persuaded, against his will, that the bodily resurrection was fact.

Alternative Views

Joseph Ernst Renan (1823-1902), among those very much under the influence of the closed-universe philosophy . of the Enlightenment, began the resurrection chapter in his *Life of Jesus* (1863) with the words, "There is no such thing as a miracle. Therefore the resurrection did not take place." David Friedrich Strauss (1808-1874), also under the influence of the closed-universe philosophy, in his *The Life of Jesus* (1835), explained the post-resurrection appearances of Jesus in terms of the "subjective vision hypothesis."

Renan's denial and Strauss's explanation are widely echoed in the work of contemporary liberal theologians. John Hick is, perhaps, the most widely read of these at present.[11] Others include Sallie McFague. She argues that "what really happened" in the resurrection was "the awareness of [Christ's] continuing presence. . . . The resurrection is a way of speaking about an awareness that the presence of God in Jesus is a permanent presence in our midst." "Like the awareness of the divine presence in all creation, this new and continuing 'empowerment' brought change only on the side of the disciples, and no change for the dead Jesus Himself."[12]

Hans Kung believes that the empty tomb story represents "legendary elaborations of a message of the resurrection." He states, with a note of surprise, "Even today" a number of influential scholars "hold that the empty tomb is historically probable." But then states,

174 • The Essential Jesus

"Historical criticism has made the empty tomb a dubious fact." Kung manages to imply that all leading scholars take his skeptical view.[13]

In a useful symposium of essays, the work of those espousing the liberal view of the resurrection appears side by side with the work of those both critical of the liberal view and those who espouse the bodily resurrection empty tomb position.[14]

To counter Kung's implication, Gerald O'Collins lists thirty scholars who continue to argue for the bodily resurrection and the empty tomb. He also takes apart the parallel drawn by Hick between the post-resurrection appearances of Jesus and reports of "near-death experiences." Near-death experiences are reported by people who were revived after being clinically dead; no one is saying that Peter, Paul, Mary Magdalene, and the rest had been clinically dead. Further, he points out that near-death experiences are reported by *individuals*, not *groups*.

O'Collins then proceeds to take apart McFague's parallel between the post-resurrection appearances and auto-suggestive experiences reported by those grieving the loss of a loved one. "Unlike the spouse who leaves behind a grieving partner," writes O'Collins, "the pre-Easter Jesus made extraordinary claims to personal authority, which many scholars understand as equivalent to putting his authority on a par with God's. Then he died by crucifixion, a death reckoned to be utterly shameful before God and human beings." In short, the prior claims of Jesus and the specific nature of His death separate His case from "normal" deaths and the bereavement sequences that follow for those who have lost their dear ones. Further, O'Collins asks, how could these so called "waking visions" have been collective? After the resurrection Jesus appeared, not just to individuals, but to groups numbering up to 500 persons.[15]

Closed System Belief

The closed system concept, which is the basis of the rejectionist view, is often attributed to eighteenth-century rationalist philosopher David Hume. Hume argued that we are right to believe only what is normal to human experience. Anything far from the norm—let alone unique—is to be rejected. We live in a closed universe in which there is no supernatural force to crash through the intricate system of natural law. Hume's arguments were the basis of what became known as "the scientific approach"—the idea that we can accept the truth of an event only if it can be proved to have happened repeatedly.

The apostles said, "Jesus rose bodily from the tomb." In response the scientific rationalist says, "Well, let us see what happens when people die." And, of course, it doesn't take much research to demonstrate that when people die they go into the ground, they are buried, and they remain where they are until they decay and merge with the ground around them. In brief, Jesus' resurrection could not have happened because it was not repeatable. To argue that Jesus was a special person cuts no ice with the scientific rationalist. It is the specialness that he cannot accept. That a scientific rationalist should argue in this way is not, of course, surprising. He begins with a premise that all historical events need to be "naturalized" because there is no supernatural. That Christian scholars should argue thus is a little more surprising since if there is no supernatural there is no God.

In their books *Does God Believe in Atheists?* and *Jesus Christ: The Witness of History*, John Blanchard and J. N. D. Anderson, respectively, not only point out the lack of logic in this viewpoint, but present a convincing case against the "closed system universe."[16] Blanchard writes:

> It is not logically valid to use science as an argument against miracles. To believe that miracles cannot happen is as much an act of faith as to believe that they can happen. . . . Miracles are unprecedented events. Whatever the current fashions in philosophy or the revelations of opinion polls may suggest, it is important to affirm that science (based as it is on the observation of precedents) can have nothing to say on the subject.[17]

Having argued the identical viewpoint, Prof. J. W. Montgomery concludes: "The problem of miracles, then, must be solved in the realm of historical investigation, not in the realm of philosophical speculation."[18]

To Montgomery and Blanchard the universe is more like a great thought than a great machine. They argue that we do not have an infallible knowledge of "natural law" so we cannot from the outset exclude every possibility of unique events. The case against miracles is acceptable only if every report of a miracle has been investigated and found to be false. The function of science is to observe, not create. Science can tell us what *has* happened, not what *may* or *may not* happen. Similarly the function of the historian is not to adjudicate upon what history may or may not contain, but merely to investigate the primary sources objectively and write accordingly.

The resurrection cannot be proved scientifically because science collects data from continuous observation of the testing of a hypothesis. Hence the historicity of the resurrection is more likely to be determined by an examination of the testimonies of witnesses and the reliability of the primary sources.

The Evidence

Historians do not force the evidence to fit a preconceived conclusion, but permit it to speak for itself. Here we examine the nature of the sources, the evidence for the death of Jesus, and the evidence for the resurrection of Jesus.

The Sources

F. C. Baur (1792-1860), with many of his contemporaries, assumed that the four Gospels had, in the main, been written in the second century and that the miraculous content represented the embellishment of wishful thinkers. The school of criticism Baur represented did, however, accept Paul's letters to the Corinthians as authentic. In Baur's lifetime, and subsequently, manuscript discoveries were made that enable us to date at least three of the four Gospels to the period prior to the destruction of Jerusalem in A.D. 70 and make it certain to the unprejudiced critic that the fourth Gospel was also written by an eyewitness of the events it records.[19]

John A. T. Robinson, who had belonged to Baur's school of criticism, reached the conclusion, after years of research, that all the Gospels, including the fourth Gospel, were written before A.D. 70. He scolded the earlier critics for their scholarly "sloth," "almost wilful blindness," and their willingness to accept "the tyranny of unexamined assumptions."[20]

R. T. France, after an examination of Robinson's redating of the New Testament books, wrote, "It is, I believe, probable that some, and perhaps all, of the Gospels were written in substantially their present form within thirty years of the events, and that much of the material was already collected and written a decade or two before that. If that is the case . . . we are dealing with four parallel records of quite recent events."[21]

The accounts of the resurrection and appearances of Jesus are to be found in Matthew 28, Mark 16, Luke 24, John 20, and 1 Corinthians 15. These are the sources that contain the testimonies of the witnesses. Is every detail identical in each account? No. There are variations in certain details with regard to the events of the first Easter morning. For example, Luke mentions at least five women at the tomb, Mark mentions three, Matthew two, John one, and Paul none at all.

John Wenham reconciles these apparent discrepancies.[22] The Gospel writers wrote from different perspectives, none of them attempting to tell the whole story. The eleven disciples, the five Marys, Salome, Joanna, and Cleopas were based in three or possibly four different homes on the night prior to the resurrection. Matthew, Mark, and Luke were telling their stories each from the perspective of different groups of witnesses who arrived at the empty tomb at different times. John was writing a personal perspective. Paul, who was marshaling his evidence in a quasi-judicial fashion, excluded all reference to women because he was aware that a woman's testimony was not valid in a law court. By including in his list of resurrection appearances the reference "He [Jesus] appeared to more than five hundred . . . at the same time, most of whom are still living"(1 Cor. 15:6), Paul was, in effect, saying, "You don't have to believe me. Ask them!"

Taking all five sources, it is possible to make a list of ten resurrection appearances in the order in which they occurred.

In or near Jerusalem:

Easter morning—to Mary Magdalene.
Easter morning—to the other women.
Easter afternoon—to Cleopas and his companion.
Easter afternoon—to Peter.
Easter evening—to ten apostles and others.
The following Sunday – to the eleven, including Thomas.

In Galilee, later:
To the seven by the lake of Tiberias.
To more than 500 in the hills about Jerusalem.
To James, the Lord's brother.

Back in Jerusalem:
To the eleven, followed by the ascension from the Mount of Olives.[23]

Lawyers who have examined the resurrection testimonies have been reassured by the variations in detail. These variations accord with standard experience in courts of law. Some who have examined the resurrection sources critically have also been reassured by the variations in the minutiae of the eyewitness testimonies. One authority concludes, "In such cases the surface discrepancies do not mean that nothing happened; rather, they mean that the witnesses have not been in collusion."[24]

Even those who have accepted that it is impossible to harmonize all the details of the recorded appearances of the risen Christ have concluded that "the apparent discrepancies argue rather for the truthfulness of the narrative, for they are evidence that the writers have not tried to obtain artificial agreement on every detail."[25]

Each Gospel account is unequivocally clear that the resurrection of Jesus was a verified and witnessed historical event. Paul told King Agrippa, a shrewd observer of all things Jewish and Christian (Acts 26:3, 26), that the death and resurrection of Jesus were not "done in a corner." As more and more scholarly authorities move towards earlier dates for the four Gospels, it becomes abundantly clear that these testimonies and records were circulated within the lifetime of people who had been "on the spot." Thus they were liable to verification and criticism by the contemporaries of Jesus.

Those who first presented the resurrection message did so in Jerusalem and within a few hundred yards of the empty tomb. Any of those listening could have made the short trip and ascertained whether the tomb was, in fact, empty. Three thousand were converted to the good news of the resurrection in one day (Acts 2:41); five thousand on another day (Acts 4:4); and "a large number of priests" (Acts 6:7). The enemies of those who testified to the resurrection had to acknowledge that something had occurred to transform their early cowardice into courage (Acts 4:13). Speaking about the behavior of the apostles and the wisest course of action to be pursued in the face of it, no one on the Sanhedrin denied the truth of the empty tomb (Acts 5:33-40).

Many had a strong vested interest in disproving the empty tomb and the resurrection. They were extremely hostile to the Christian movement. The apostles were arrested repeatedly. Neither then nor in the years to come did any of the apostles cave in under cross-examination or change their evidence. In the teeth of opposition that could, and did, bring an end to their lives in many gruesome ways, no one recanted. No one budged in the face of the most hostile of cross-examiners. The case for the resurrection stood. Regardless of the likely consequences the witnesses presented it consistently. Those hostile to the Christian movement totally failed to make a valid case.

Sir William Ramsay, a geographer-archaeologist working in the Middle and Near East, made a careful study of the factual accuracy of the writings of Luke, his Gospel, and the book of Acts. After thirty years of study Ramsay concluded, "Luke is a historian of the first rank; not merely are his statements of fact trustworthy . . . this author should be placed among the very greatest historians." "Luke's history is unsurpassed in respect of its trustworthiness."[26]

Evidence for the Death of Jesus

Before the crucifixion verdict was pronounced, the Roman governor had already ordered that Jesus be whipped. Pharisaic rules limited the number of lashes to thirty-nine, but the Romans accepted no such limitation. The *flagrum* used for the whipping had long leather thongs of varying lengths, each with sharp jagged pieces of bone and lead attached to them. In the course of thirty-nine lashes across the shoulders, back, and legs of the prisoner, the blows would cut through the subcutaneous tissue, would render the back an unrecognizable mass of torn, bleeding tissue, and would cause arterial bleeding from blood vessels in the underlying muscles. Many did not survive thirty-nine lashes.[27]

In the recent past Israeli archaeologists have learned much about crucifixion from excavations undertaken on Mount Scopus. A seven-inch spike was driven through both heel bones. A heavy wrought-iron spike would be driven through the front of the wrist causing the incomplete severing of the median nerve. Muscular pain would be excruciating. Air would be drawn into the lungs that could not be exhaled. Carbon dioxide would build up in the lungs and the bloodsteam. Death would come by suffocation.[28]

When Jesus was reported dead at 3:00 p.m. on Good Friday, a spear was thrust into His side. This incident was witnessed by John, who recorded that "a sudden flow of blood and water" was caused by the spear wound. Medical experts have assumed from this that the heart, as well as the pericardium, was pierced.[29]

Romans were grimly efficient with crucifixions. There were no survivors.

Evidence for the Resurrection

Joseph of Arimathea sought permission from the Roman governor to take Jesus down from the cross and bury Him in a tomb he had prepared for himself. Permission was granted. Joseph undertook his work with a fellow member of the Sanhedrin, Nicodemus. Both men had been close supporters of Jesus, and both had great wealth. As they prepared the corpse of the crucified Jesus for burial, they would willingly have relinquished all their wealth and influence for one vital sign that He was alive. The women were witnesses. There were no signs of life. Jesus was buried.

A stone which a modern authority has estimated would have weighed between one-and-a-half and two tons was rolled over the entrance of the tomb. On the Sabbath—the next day—the Jewish authorities, remembering the "after three days" speech of Jesus, went to the Roman governor and asked that the tomb be secured by a guard. A Roman seal was placed on the stone so that it could not be removed without the knowledge of the authorities, and a guard was posted (Luke 23:50-56; John 19:38-42; Matt. 27:57-66).

Some scholars have drawn from Matthew 27:65 the implication that this would have been a detachment of the temple guard; others, because no permission would have had to be sought from the governor to post a temple guard, that it was a Roman guard. The military discipline of the 270 temple police was excellent; they were divided into twenty-seven units of ten. It is the behavior of the guards following the resurrection that has persuaded most authorities that the guard was, in fact, a sixteen-man Roman security detachment. When the resurrection had occurred the soldiers asked the Jewish authorities to intercede on their behalf with the Roman authorities. A temple guard, it has been argued, would hardly have behaved in this way. Roman military historians, including Flavius Fegitius Renatus, were unanimous that discipline in the Roman legions was stricter during the reign of Tiberius than at any subsequent time.

Whether the guard was Jewish or Roman the story that they were bribed to tell—that the body had been stolen by the disciples while they were sleeping—would not have been passed on except by the frightened, the unintelligent, or those who had a strong vested interest. How could the guards have known who stole the body if they were asleep? "Soldiers and priests and Pilate evidently believed that something supernatural had happened. Hence the willingness of the authorities to screen the soldiers."[30] The security precautions taken with the trial, the crucifixion, the burial, the entombment, the sealing and guarding of Christ's tomb make it very difficult for critics to defend their position that Christ did not rise from the dead.

Among the many difficulties is the evidence of the broken Roman seal; those responsible, if apprehended, would have automatically been executed. The idea that a group of disciples would have taken on either the temple guard or a detachment of a Roman legion in order to take the risk of breaking a Roman seal is preposterous. One authority says: "No approach to the origin of faith in Jesus' resurrection will get far unless it realizes what a shattering blow his crucifixion had been for his followers. His execution had been followed by an horrific crisis of faith."[31] "We had hoped that he was the one who was going to redeem Israel"—*had hoped*, past historic tense—was how one disciple expressed it (Luke 24:21). Resurrection morning found the disciples in a state of shock and spiritual disillusionment. Those who believe that the origin of faith in the resurrection came about because the disciples were expecting it, have no foundation for their view. The disciples were not prepared for His resurrection.

It took an objective encounter with the risen Jesus to crystallize the disciples' faith in Him and to cause them to proclaim His resurrection. Visions and subjective experiences would not have done it. Something had to have been seen, something real.

The resurrection witnesses identified the risen Jesus with the earthly Jesus. "After his suffering, he showed himself to these men and gave many convincing proofs that he was alive. He appeared to them over a period of forty days" (Acts 1:3). When Jesus is said to have been *seen* or to have *appeared*, the disciples saw Him with ordinary vision. "Look at my hands and my feet," He said. "I have seen the Lord!" the witnesses announced (Matt. 28:17; Luke 24:34, 39-46; John 20:14,18, 20; 1 Cor. 15:5-8). Jesus is reported to have *spoken* (Matt. 28:9, 18-20), to have *walked* (Luke 24:13-16), to have *distributed food* (Luke 24:30), to have *eaten*(Acts 1:4), to have *performed signs* (John 20:30), to have *given a blessing with His hands* (Luke 24:50), to have *shown His hands and His side* (John 20:20) and to have *been touched* (Matt. 28:9).

The empty tomb was the indispensable Exhibit A of the launch of Christianity on Jerusalem at Pentecost. If Joseph's new tomb had not been empty the very-much-under-pressure temple establishment would have simply aborted the movement by making a brief trip to the sepulcher and parading the body of Jesus around the city. "They did not do this because they knew the tomb was empty. Their official explanation for it—that the disciples had stolen the body—was an admission that the sepulcher was indeed vacant." Both Roman and Jewish sources and traditions acknowledge an empty tomb. The sources range from Josephus Flavius to a compilation of fifth-century Jewish writings called *Toledoth Jeshu.* If a source admits a fact decidedly *not* in its favor then that becomes strong evidence that the fact is genuine.[32]

The high priests and the Sanhedrin had shown their political skill in handling Pilate. It would have required little skill on their part to have handled Christ's followers had they known the location of the body. Instead, the Jewish authorities were reduced to hauling the disciples in from time to time in order to threaten them with death if they did not stop preaching the risen Christ (Acts 5:17- 42). There was little else they could do—with the tomb empty, a strong impression on their part that something supernatural had occurred, and a growing number (including priests) embracing the truth of the resurrection. Those embracing the revolutionary truth were all Jews, either residents or visitors to Jerusalem. These were accepting a revolutionary teaching that could have been discredited by taking a few minutes' walk to a garden just outside the city wall.

Frank Morison entitled his compelling account of the evidence, *Who Moved the Stone?* That question must have baffled those who wanted to believe that the disciples had stolen the body. A stone weighing between one-and-a-half to two tons had been removed. Matthew said that a large stone was "*rolled. . . in front of the entrance to the tomb.*" The Greek verb to roll is *kulio.* In his account of the position of the stone after the resurrection, Mark had to use a preposition with the verb. In Greek, as in English, to change the direction of a verb or to intensify it, a preposition is added. Mark added the preposition *ana,* which means "up" or "upward." Mark's word, *anakulio,* can mean "to roll something up a slope or incline." Luke adds to the picture by using a different preposition, *apo,* which means "a distance from." So the stone was not just moved! It was moved *up a slope, for a distance.*

John (chapter 20) uses a different Greek verb, *airo,* which means "to pick something up and carry it away." Even had the soldiers been sleeping they would have had to have been deaf not to have heard a stone of that size being moved in that way.

> The Jewish authorities must have visited the scene, examined the stone, and recognized its position as making it humanly impossible for their men to have permitted its removal. Here was undeniable evidence which made it impossible for the chief priests to bring any charge against the guard. No twist of human ingenuity could provide an adequate answer or a scapegoat, and so they were forced to bribe the guard and seek to hush things up.[33]

And there is more. John, for one, became a believer in the resurrection *before* he saw the risen Christ. What convinced him was when he entered the tomb and found the grave clothes (John 20:3-8). He remembered Jesus' prediction of His resurrection and recognized His characteristic touch in the way the grave clothes were arranged.[34] For most, of course, belief came when they encountered Jesus. This was even true of Paul (1 Cor. 15:8-11). Christ appeared to Paul last, but Paul may well have been the first to record his account in writing.

The appearances of Jesus were not stereotyped. He appeared in a different manner in a variety of locations. Mary Magdalene at first approached Him as the gardener. To those who walked to

Emmaus He came as a traveling companion. To the apostles in the upper room (twice) He appeared when the doors were closed. On another occasion He prepared breakfast for them on the Galilean shore. Then, also in Galilee, He appeared to five hundred at one time. Reactions varied from fear, being overwhelmed with emotion, to obstinate incredulity. When Christ appeared to Saul at Tarsus, He was appearing to his foremost enemy. Women saw Him first; had the resurrection accounts been concocted women would *never* have been included in the story, let alone as the first witnesses.

Circumstantial Evidence

Any account of the evidence for the resurrection must take into account certain pieces of circumstantial evidence.

The Existence of the Christian Church

The continuous existence of the Christian church can be dated to the preaching of the resurrection of Jesus in Jerusalem on the day of Pentecost. From the first the church expanded in the face of severe opposition. Almost from the first, the blood of the martyrs was the seed of the church. Edward Gibbon notes five major factors in the growth of the early church: her indomitable zeal; the doctrine of the afterlife made certain by Christ's conquest of death; the miraculous powers ascribed to the primitive church; "the pure and austere morals of the Christians;" and her unity and discipline.[35]

How could such a movement be founded on a lie? Why was it Jerusalem that became the center and focus of this fast-growing movement that reached the limits of the Roman world in little more than a generation? Why would men of "pure and austere morals" allow themselves to be beaten, imprisoned, tortured, and executed for a lie? If this were a fraud on the part of such people why, under pressure of death, did not at least some of them break and recant? Knowing what Jesus' followers did and what they taught and what they died for, it is far harder to believe that they were liars or madmen than it is to believe their account of Jesus rising from the dead.

The Communion Service

If there is one thing that gave Christianity a bad name in the intellectual circles of the Roman Empire during the first century of its existence it was the communion service. Gaius Plinius Secundus (A.D.108) and Cornelius Tacitus (A.D. 112) were both determined to view Christianity as a "degraded and extravagant superstition" because it followed the "grotesque" practice of commemorating the horrifying death of its founder by "eating his flesh" and "drinking his blood" in the bread and wine of the sacrament. For Christians, however, even Golgotha was viewed as glorious because of Easter Sunday.

Believer's Baptism

The same preoccupation with the death, burial, and resurrection of Christ was evident in the practice of the baptism of believers, a rite which dates to the earliest years of the primitive church. To become a Christian it was necessary to identify publicly with the death, burial, and resurrection of its founder (see Rom. 6:3-9).

Justification by Faith

A crucial tenet of the developing church was the belief that the sinner was justified (declared righteous) by the grace of God and through faith in the death and resurrection of His Son (Rom.3:22-26; 4:25).

Changed Lives

Gethsemane's cowards became Pentecost's heroes. This is inexplicable without the resurrection. Had prestige, wealth, and increased social status accrued to new believers when they professed Christ and His resurrection, their profession would be logically understandable. In fact, however, their "rewards" were of a different type, eventually involving lions, crucifixion, and every other conceivable method of stopping them from talking. The revolutionary change in the lives of the early apostles has been replicated millions of times in the two millennia of Christian history.

The Inadequacy of the Opposing Arguments

The arguments usually brought against the resurrection of Jesus do not stand up to thoughtful investigation.

That the Authorities Removed the Body of Jesus

If either the Jewish or the Roman authorities had removed and reburied the body of Jesus, all they had to do in the ensuing days and years to quash Christianity was to say, "We gave the orders to remove the body," and then to show where His body had been buried or disposed of. That action was not taken.

That the Disciples Removed the Body

The disciples could neither have taken on the temple guard nor a unit of Roman soldiers. The position and size of the stone was another factor. This story, when it was first put about, was so obviously false that Matthew didn't even bother to refute it. The soldiers' testimony was based on something that they said had happened when they were asleep; they would have been laughed out of any court. Further, we are faced with a psychological and ethical improbability. Stealing the body of Christ would have been something totally foreign to the character of the disciples. Every one of the disciples faced the test of torture, and all except John were martyred for their beliefs and teachings. People will die for what they believe to be true, though it may actually be false. They do not, however, die for what they know is a lie.

That the Women Went to the Wrong Tomb

This theory holds that the women were so distraught that, in the dimness of early morning, they went to the wrong tomb. The seal and the guard, one imagines, would have made the right tomb conspicuous even in the first light of the dawn. Nevertheless, this theory falls because had the women gone to the wrong tomb, the high priests and the other enemies of the faith would rapidly have gone to the right tomb and produced the body. Certainly Joseph of Arimathea, owner of the tomb, could have solved the problem.

That Jesus Swooned and Revived in the Tomb

In short, this theory teaches that despite the flagellation and loss of blood, the spikes in the ankles and the wrists, the hours of exposure on the cross, and the spear in His side—Jesus somehow survived. This theory first appeared in the eighteenth century when, apparently, it was possible to believe that a man could survive burial in a damp tomb without food or water or attention of any kind; that he could survive being wrapped in heavy, spice-laden grave clothes; that he could then summon up the strength to extricate himself from the grave clothes, push away a heavy stone from the mouth of a tomb, overcome the guards—and walk miles on pierced feet to be hailed as Conqueror of Death and Prince of Life. Even David Strauss, a noted nineteenth-century critic who did not believe in the resurrection, rejected this idea as incredible:

> It is impossible that one who had just come forth from the grave half dead, who crept about weak and ill, who stood in need of medical treatment, of bandaging, strengthening, and tender care, and who at last succumbed to suffering, could ever have given the disciples the impression that he was a conqueror over death and the grave. . . . Such a resuscitation could only have weakened the impression which he had made upon them in life and in death; it certainly could by no possibility have changed their sorrow into enthusiasm or elevated their reverence into worship.[36]

That the Risen Jesus Appeared Only to Believers

This is not true. Thomas, at first, was not a believer. It seems likely that James, the brother of Jesus, was not a believer when the risen Christ appeared to him; certainly he had been an unbeliever during Christ's earthly ministry (1 Cor. 15:7; Mark 3:21; 6:3, 4; John 7:5). From the fact that James is listed among the 120 disciples who were together in Jerusalem at the time of the ascension and from the fact that Saul, an opponent of Christ, was converted following an encounter with Him it is clear that some became believers and witnesses *after* seeing the risen Christ.

Richard Swinburne, who recently examined the case for the resurrection from the scientific-rationalist position, reached the conclusion that "the detailed historical evidence" is "so strong" that, "despite the fact that such a resurrection would be a violation of natural laws, the balance of probability is in favor of the resurrection."[37] A dispassionate lawyer or historian would have to consider the case proven.

The Continuing Significance of the Resurrection

Having considered the bleak prospects had there been no resurrection, Paul (1 Cor. 15:20-23) reasserts the resurrection truth and attaches to it another powerful truth. Because Christ rose, we shall rise also; as death came by Adam's sin, so resurrection is guaranteed by Christ's conquest of sin and death. The resurrection of Jesus represents the "firstfruits" of the great harvest of those who will rise to eternal life at His second coming.

The resurrection of Jesus was not just a mighty event on the plane of history. It had altered the direction of that history. It would have eternal consequences. His resurrection was not simply a coming back from the dead. He had awakened Lazarus from what He called the "sleep" of death (John 11:1-44), but Lazarus would die again. When Jesus rose from the dead, He represented the "firstfruits" of a new kind of life. That life was one in which the body was made perfect, freed from restrictions, no longer subject to weakness, aging, or death, but able to live eternally. Jesus had been glorified, and His glorification guaranteed that those who believed would be glorified at His return. The resurrection guaranteed the *parousia*, the return of Jesus, the resurrection of saints to glorification, and the beginning of His everlasting reign (1 Thess. 4:13-18; Phil. 3:20- 4:1).

The Old Testament viewed death as a dreamless sleep (Eccl. 9:5; 12:7; Ps.146:4). It was the prophet Daniel who sounded the trumpet of resurrection to eternal life. "Multitudes who sleep in the dust of the earth will awake: some to everlasting life, others to shame and everlasting contempt" (12:2). By the time of Jesus many Jews, including the Pharisees, looked forward to a *general* resurrection and judgment at the end of history. Only the Sadducees denied the resurrection. The second of eighteen synagogue benedictions current in Christ's day praised the God who kept faith with "them that sleep in the dust" and "who makes the dead live."[38] Thus, having berated Jesus for failing to arrive in time to prevent her brother's death, Martha said, "I know he will rise again in the resurrection at the last day" (John 11:24).

The dualistic—as opposed to wholistic—view of man entered Christian thought from Greek sources. The Greek view of the immortality of the soul—that the body had to become extinct for the soul to escape to another realm—was absorbed by many in the early Christian centuries. This belief in natural immortality, the idea that we don't really die, still exerts a powerful influence on conventional views of death and the life to come. Nevertheless the concept of natural immortality conflicts with the biblical view of death. This is, in the words of Michael Green, "Not survival of the soul as an inherent quality of man: but resurrection of the body as a sheer gift of God . . . anticipated and pledged by the resurrection of Jesus Christ from the tomb."[39] In his great treatise on the resurrection Paul said that death would be the last enemy to be destroyed (1 Cor. 15:26). The body, Paul argued, is "perishable," but when it is raised at the resurrection of the righteous it will be "imperishable" (v. 42). "It is sown in dishonor, it is raised in glory; it is sown in weakness, it is raised in power" (v. 43).

In Paul's reasoning there is no "natural immortality"; it is *conditional*. "Flesh and blood cannot inherit the kingdom of God, nor does the perishable inherit the imperishable" (v.50). Nevertheless, at the time of the *parousia*, some believers would be alive to see the Lord return: "Listen, I tell you a mystery: We will not all sleep, but we will all be changed—in a flash, in the twinkling of an eye, at the last trumpet. For the trumpet will sound, the dead will be raised imperishable, and we will be changed. For the perishable must clothe itself with the imperishable, and the mortal with immortality" (vs.50-53). And all this is made possible by the resurrection of Jesus.

Jesus' resurrection ensures our *regeneration*: "He has given us new birth into a living hope through the resurrection of Jesus Christ from the dead" (1 Pet.1:3). Christ's resurrection ensures our *justification*: "He was delivered over to death for our sins and was raised to life for our justification" (Rom. 4:25). Christ's resurrection is the pledge and power of *our* resurrection: Christ is "the first-fruits of those who have fallen asleep," and we follow after "when he comes" (1 Cor.15:20-23). All who are related to Christ will rise again. Each, however, in his turn: Christ rose first; then when Christ comes back, all His people will become alive again.

The resurrection of Jesus is not only the demonstrably true foundation of Christian faith. It is for us the historical, public, and unbreakable guarantee given by God the Father of our own destiny and future glory.

For Further Reading

P. Beasley-Murray, *The Message of the Resurrection*. Nottingham: InterVarsity Press, 2000.
S. Davis, D. Kendall, and G. O'Collins, eds., *The Resurrection: An Interdisciplinary Symposium on the Resurrection of Jesus*. Oxford: Oxford University Press, 1997.
J. McDowell, *The Resurrection* (Amersham: Scripture Press, 1988.)
J. Wenham, *The Easter Enigma: Are the Resurrection Accounts in Conflict?* Carlisle: Paternoster Press, 1996.
N. T. Wright and M. Borg, *The Meaning of Jesus*. London: SPCK, 1999.

Notes

1. John Hick, *Death and Eternal Life* (London: MacMillan, 1985), pp. 58, 71, 172; William Barclay, *The Letters to the Corinthians* (Edinburgh: St. Andrews Press, 1954), pp. 156,157.
2. 1 Cor. 15; Paul Beasley-Murray, *The Message of the Resurrection* (Downers Grove, IL: InterVarsity Press, 2000), pp. 120, 121.
3. N. T. Wright and M. Borg, *The Meaning of Jesus* (London: SPCK, 1999), p. 116.
4. 1 Cor. 15:19, *The Message: The New Testament in Contemporary Language* (Colorado Springs, CO: Navpress, 1993).
5. C. S. Lewis, *Surprised by Joy* (London: HarperCollins, 1955), pp. 178, 179.
6. *Ibid*; D. Marshall, *Joy in Jesus* (Grantham: Autumn House, 1998), p. 87.
7. J. McDowell, *The Resurrection Factor* (1st. edit., Alpha (1993); 2000 edit.), p. 17. See also J. McDowell, *The Resurrection* (Amersham: Scripture Press, 1988).
8. M. Green, *The Empty Cross of Jesus* (London: Hodder and Stoughton, 1984), pp.102, 103.
9. Ross Clifford, *Leading Lawyers Look at the Resurrection* (Sutherland, NSW: Albatross,1991), pp. 41-55; P. Beasley-Murray, *The Message of the Resurrection*, p. 23.
10. Clifford, p. 126; V. Grieve, *Your Verdict on the Empty Tomb of Jesus* (Downers Grove, IL: InterVarsity Press, 1988), p. 17.
11. J. Hick, *The Metaphor of God Incarnate* (London: SCM, 1993).
12. S. McFague, *Models of God: Theology for an Ecological, Nuclear Age* (London: SCM, 1987), p. 192, n. 37.
13. H. Kung, *On Being a Christian* (London: Collins, 1977), pp. 364-366.
14. S. Davis, D. Kendall, G. O'Collins (eds), *The Resurrection: An Interdisciplinary Symposium on the Resurrection of Jesus* (Oxford: Oxford University Press, 1997).
15. *Ibid.*, pp. 6-16.
16. J. Blanchard, *Does God Believe in Atheists?* (Evangelical Press, 2000); J. N. D. Anderson, *Jesus Christ: The Witness of History* (Leicester: IVP, 1985), p.

80. See also J. W. Montgomery, *Where is History Going?* (Grand Rapids, MI: Zondervan, 1969).

17. Blanchard, p. 564.

18. Montgomery, p. 71.

19. F. F. Bruce, *The New Testament Documents: Are They Reliable?* (Fifth edition, London: InterVarsity Press, 1960); F. F. Bruce, *The Books and the Parchments* (Paternoster, 1984); D. Marshall, *The Power of the Word* (Grantham: Autumn House, 1999).

20. A. T. Hanson, *The Prophetic Gospel* (Edinburgh: T.and T. Clark,1991),p. 7; McDowell, *The Resurrection Factor*, pp. 39, 40.

21. R. T. France, *The Evidence for Jesus* (London: Hodder and Stoughton, 1986), p. 121.

22. J. Wenham, *The Easter Enigma: Are the Resurrection Accounts in Conflict?* (Exeter: Paternoster, 1996). See also E. G. White, *The Desire of Ages* (Mountain View, CA: Pacific Press, 1898), pp. 788-801.

23. Wenham, Appendix 4.

24. N. T. Wright and M. Borg, *The Meaning of Jesus* (London: SPCK, 1999), pp. 121 ff.

25. J. O. Sanders, *The Incomparable Christ* (London: SPCK, 1982), p. 225.

26. Cited in McDowell, p. 49.

27. C. T. Davis, "The Crucifixion of Jesus," *Arizona Medicine*, March 1965, p. 185.

28. *Ibid.*, p. 186; McDowell, pp. 61-65.

29. John 19:33-35; medical experts cited by McDowell, pp. 65-67.

30. Wenham, pp. 78-80.

31. G. O'Collins, *Contemporary Christian Insights: Interpreting Jesus* (London: Mowbray, 1983), p. 115; Green, p.102.

32. Blanchard, pp. 579-581; P. L. Maier, "The Empty Tomb as History," *Christianity Today*, vol. XIX, 28 March, 1975, p. 5.

33. W. L. White, *A Thing Incredible* (Yanetz, 1976), pp. 42, 43; D. N. Marshall, *Risen Indeed* (Grantham: Autumn House, 1992).

34. E. G. White, p. 789. See also McDowell, pp. 89, 90.

35. Edward Gibbon, *The History of the Decline and Fall of the Roman Empire* (London: Folio Society, 1984), vol.2, p. 94.

36. D. Strauss, *The Life of Jesus* (second edition, 1879), 1: p. 412.

37. R. Swinburne, "Evidence for the Resurrection," *The Resurrection: An Interdisciplinary Symposium on the Resurrection of Jesus,* (eds.) S. Davis, D. Kendall, G. O'Collins (Oxford: Oxford University Press, 1997), p. 202.

38. Cited in C. K. Barrett, *The New Testament Background: Selected Documents* (London: SPCK, 1961), p. 162.

39. Green, p. 111.

Jesus—the Man for Others
Roy Adams

Deep down in the soul of each of us is the need for acceptance. We seek those who receive us, regardless. Those who are always there for us. Those who would not turn their back on us when we're "dirty" or when we blow it.

In Jesus we have that person. He is truly the man for others.

One reason for my interest in this dimension of the Jesus story is that it's the area in which I personally feel most unlike Him. I sense a profound selfishness at the very core of my personality, a feeling that grows deeper every passing day. Bombarded by reports of global calamities and disasters, I find myself becoming callous, numb, insensitive. I've learned to eat supper in front of the evening news, with its graphic scenes of terrorist carnage, earthquake destruction, famine and starvation, bloody conflicts, political assassinations, the massacre and torture of innocent people, and a myriad other incidences of human tragedy.

Is this some kind of built-in psychological defense mechanism designed by "nature" to protect my sanity? Is it a consequence of the sheer volume of stuff thrown at us by the media, leaving us no time to process it all—no time, so to speak, to grieve? Or is its cause the flippant, show-biz nature of what passes today as news— the report of a massacre, for instance, followed immediately by a couple dancing in excitement over the wonders of <u>Viagra</u>? Whatever the cause, I feel myself becoming more indifferent, less caring. And I have the feeling I'm not alone.

What follows is an attempt to take another look at the life of

Jesus in the context of His caring concern for others. I want to be softened by the experience. And I want all who read this chapter to experience again that softening as though for the first time.

We focus first on *Jesus' concern for others*. Next, on what He taught and lived in regard to *ethics and values that matter*. Finally we address the issue of whether a person of the stature and complexity of Jesus was able to form *meaningful and fulfilling relationships* with those He met.

Caring Concern for Others

"Jesus went throughout Galilee, teaching in their synagogues, preaching the good news of the kingdom, and healing every disease and sickness among the people. News about him spread all over Syria, and people brought to him all who were ill with various diseases, those suffering severe pain, the demon-possessed, the epileptics and the paralytics, and he healed them. Large crowds from Galilee, the Decapolis, Jerusalem, Judea and the region across the Jordan followed him" (Matt. 4:23-25).

The topic of the radio program I was listening to a few years ago was televangelism, a phenomenon just then coming into its own. The focus of the discussion was an article just off the press. The source of the piece, unfortunately, turned out to be one of those off-color magazines not appropriate for footnoting here. But here's the substance of what it told.

The investigators wanted to learn, among other things, the true source of the uncanny insight into people's private ailments that had become a core ingredient of these evangelistic shysters. How did they come to know, for example, that the man in the blue shirt near the middle aisle was suffering from gallstones? Or that the lady sitting in the tenth row on the left side in the red blouse had back trouble? The investigators discovered that the source of their incredible intelligence lay in discrete pre-meeting interviews of selected attendees by personnel from the faith-healing team. By the time the healing portion of the service commenced those well-trained helpers, monitoring closed circuit television of the audience, were ready to feed the information they'd gleaned directly into the tiny electronic ear piece worn by the evangelist.

And there was another troubling finding. Another major tactic of these televangelists was the vigorous encouragement of viewers to send in their prayer requests. The investigators watched staff pick up the mail sent in by listeners, open letters on the spot, fish out the enclosed checks, then dump the prayer requests right there in the post office waste bins.

I was stunned. How profoundly different this attitude was from that of the Master whom they claimed to follow! In the key passage cited above we read of Jesus traversing the entire area of Galilee, with large crowds following Him—from Decapolis, Jerusalem, Judea, and points across the Jordan. It is an extensive area, as one looks at a map of the region. And when Matthew returns to this same theme in chapter 9, he adds a crucial element that forever distinguishes Jesus from modern faith-healing charlatans. He says: "Jesus went through all the towns and villages, teaching in their synagogues, preaching the good news of the kingdom and healing every disease and sickness. When he saw the crowds, he had compassion on them, because they were harassed and helpless, like sheep without a shepherd" (9:35, 36).

The word "compassion" here comes from the Greek word *splagchnon,* meaning originally "the inward parts," the "entrails," and referring to "the seat of feelings" or "emotions."[1] In this sense, compassion goes beyond sympathy, which can be wholly cerebral and intellectual. Compassion comes from the depth of a person's soul, from the very seat of the emotions and feelings.

That's what Jesus had. For Him, playing Sherlock Holmes with people's personal ailments would have been unthinkable; and dumping people's heartfelt prayer requests in post office garbage bins, totally unacceptable. Again and again in the Gospels the quality of compassion identifies His attitude toward the people. A leper begs Him: "If you are willing, you can make me clean." Jesus, filled with compassion, reaches out to him: "I am willing. . . . Be clean!" (Mark 1:40, 41). Two blind men are sitting by the roadside just outside Jericho and—much to the annoyance of the crowd accompanying Jesus—shout their request to him. "Son of David, have mercy on us!" "What do you want me to do for you?" Jesus asked them. "We want our sight," they respond. Then He "had compassion on them and touched their eyes" (Matt. 20:29-34; cf. Mark 10:46-52).

Even under intense pressure the same trait emerges. Following the beheading of John the Baptist and the return of His disciples from a missionary tour, Jesus felt the need for rest and quiet. "Come with me by yourselves to a quiet place and get some rest," He said to the twelve (Mark 6:31). The multitude, however, learning of the plan, preceded them to the place designated. Under those circumstances, how easy and natural it would have been to feel used! *Can't a person ever get away without being trailed?* Most of us might have reacted in that way.

But Matthew reports an entirely different attitude in Jesus. When He landed and saw the crowd, Matthew says "he had compassion on them. . . . So he began teaching them" (Mark 6:30-34). Not only did He teach them, He healed them (Matt.14:13,14). And when, as evening approached, the disciples tried to dismiss the hungry crowds, Jesus had a different plan: He fed them (Matt.14:15-21). Unlike some who claim His name today, Jesus was in the *feeding*, not in the *fleecing*, business.

If you can imagine someone doing all this with never a thought of personal gain or aggrandizement, with no desire whatsoever that the events in question be picked up by the press, or that they at least leave the kind of impression that could come in handy in some future promotion, then you're thinking about Jesus. The sole motivation was genuine love coming from deep inside—love from the belly. The Gospels call it "compassion." And it always put people first. It's something more Christians talk about than actually do.

Speaking of his time in the city slums, Indian theologian Samuel Rayan confessed, "It is the stench I cannot stand, and the filth. I am middle class, bourgeois, clerical."[2] There was probably little in Jesus' time that could be equated with the slums of India today, but everything we read about Jesus in the Gospels tends to suggest that He would feel at home with the outcasts, physical or psychological, who inhabit the wretched places of this planet.

Lepers were outcasts in Jesus' time; but the Gospels mention numerous instances where He touched and healed them. Simon, at whose place Jesus once had dinner, had been a leper (Matt. 26:6).

Prostitutes were outcasts in Jesus' time, but He mingled with them; Mary of Bethany, the sister of Martha and Lazarus, had been a prostitute. Samaritans were outcasts in Jesus' time, but Jesus went out of His way to make contact with them (see John 4), and in His parable of the Good Samaritan He immortalized the positive about them. Gentiles were an outcast group for Jews in Jesus' time, but in His sensitive dealing with the Syrophoenician woman (Matt. 15:21-28; cf. Mark 7:24-30), He sought to correct the prejudice in the minds of His own disciples and break down the artificial barriers that religious jingoists had erected. No one was outside the circle of His concern.

In Jesus we see a person whose entire life is framed by a burning love for others. For Him, there was no inconvenient time when it came to service. Once following the Sabbath, Mark says, the people brought all the sick and demon-possessed to Him. Indeed, "the whole town gathered at the door" where He was. And He ministered to them (Mark 1:32-34). Look how He spent His Saturday nights! I would hazard a guess that most Christians in the industrialized world typically spend theirs around the TV or with family or friends, or at a concert, or engaged in some other form of entertainment. But surrounded by the sick and needy? How extraordinarily dull!

We conclude this section with the twin stories of a sick woman and a dead girl. By themselves, they encapsulate everything we have been saying about Jesus' caring concern. Mark's narrative carries the deepest pathos.

According to Mark 5, the bleeding woman had suffered for twelve years. He does not describe the exact nature of the problem but one can imagine that in that society it was accompanied by considerable pain and embarrassment, almost impossible for us today to comprehend. She'd "suffered a great deal," Mark says, "under the care of many doctors and had spent all she had, yet instead of getting better she grew worse" (v. 26). Her doctors, however, never stopped taking her money. And now she's poor, bankrupt, lonely, bleeding, dying.

But she learns that Jesus is in town. Summoning what little strength she had remaining, she finds the place, comes up behind

Him in the crowd, and touches His cloak (v. 27). Instantly, her ailment vanishes. Imagine the thrill of that exciting moment! Imagine the emotion, the joy! Healed! After twelve years of misery! She's walking on air, strutting on cloud nine, ready almost to burst with sheer exuberance. But she must not make a scene. Better to slip away quietly, she thinks.

Then, just as quickly, her newfound peace is shattered. Still close enough, she hears the Master's question: "Who touched my clothes?" (v.30). Suddenly she's shaking all over. What does this question mean? Would she be asked to pay up? The physicians who had prescribed those worthless remedies had emptied her bank account. What would she be expected to pay now in return for the fantastic healing she'd just experienced? Trembling, she falls down before the Saviour and tells Him everything.

Jesus' gracious response is recorded in verse 34: "Daughter, your faith has healed you. Go in peace and be freed from your suffering." Here Jesus uses the Aramaic equivalent of the Hebrew *shalom* (peace) to refer to the "wholeness," the "completeness" into which He had brought her by His power, and into which He desires to bring all who are wounded, bleeding and less than whole.

Something very similar happened with the influential Jairus, whose twelve-year-old daughter had contracted a disease from which she was dying. Large crowds impeded Jairus' journey to Jesus to get help. By the time he got there it was too late. Messengers brought the devastating news that his daughter was dead (Mark 5:35). But the keen ears of Jesus—ever sensitive to the cry of those around him—picked up the terrible message. "Don't be afraid," He told the trembling father, "just believe" (v. 36). An hour later Jairus is embracing his little daughter, who was bubbling with radiant health.

Such was the tender touch felt by those who came into Jesus' presence. Truly, He was the Man for others, the Man for people, all people. The statement made in mockery at the cross was true, after all: "He saved others . . . , but he can't save himself" (Mark 15:31). For He could not save Himself and others too. So He made the critical choice—for others. It was the hallmark of His ministry, of His whole life.

Ethics and Values That Matter

Ethics and values are big issues today. They were high on Jesus' agenda, too, if we read the Gospels aright. Yet it is quite amazing how warped our thinking can become in regard to the values Jesus taught and lived. "I guarantee you Christ would be the toughest guy who ever played the game," proclaimed an American football writer in his book *On God's Squad*. "He would be a star in this league."[3] Poor Jesus! What will His friends do with Him next! Said the South African theologian Albert Nolan: "The supreme irony is that some of the things . . . [Jesus] opposed most strongly in the world of his time [in this case supremacy and mastery over others] were resurrected, preached, and spread more widely throughout the world—in his name."[4]

So, is it possible to get from the Gospels a sense of what Jesus really was about? Can we discover the fundamental ethical principles and values that guided Him, and which He still holds out to us today? We turn now to this important question. We will deal first, and together since they are so interrelated, with the core values of *unselfishness, self-denial,* and *humility.* Then we will examine briefly Jesus' involvement in *social action* and *the political order.*

Unselfishness, Self-denial and Humility

"You know that the rulers of the Gentiles lord it over them, and their high officials exercise authority over them. Not so with you. Instead, whoever wants to become great among you must be your servant . . . just as the Son of Man did not come to be served, but to serve, and to give his life as a ransom for many" (Matt. 20:25-28).

What does it mean to be utterly unselfish? Where can we find it modeled? Can we even imagine it? And how about those qualities that run so completely against the contemporary grain—self-denial, for example, sacrifice, or humility? A few soundings into the life and teaching of Jesus will help us in this quest.

A passage in Luke is probably a good place to start. At this point in Jesus' ministry, He was teaching each day in the temple. In the evening He would go out "to spend the night on the . . . Mount of Olives." Then, "early in the morning," it is recorded, "all the people [would come] . . . to hear him at the temple" (Luke 21:37, 38).

From this account we may draw the conclusion that during these days of the passion week in His nation's capital, Jesus had no roof over His head. How rough it must have been for Him! Where, for example, did He actually sleep? Did He have access to any of the common nighttime comforts so many of us take for granted—bedding, for example, or a pillow? How about His toilet needs? What did He do for baths and showers? What about personal grooming—His hair, His teeth? And what about breakfast, clean clothes, and laundry?

It would be inappropriate to conclude that these stressful days of Jesus' ministry are to be a model for ours today. But its Spartan quality certainly points up the obscenity of our natural and inordinate reach for the most comfortable and prestigious roles in the kingdom—the point, surely, of Jesus' statement reflected in the words above. By both teaching and demeanor, Jesus meant to convey the impression that reality as we know it radically changes at the door of His kingdom. In that kingdom, He said, there is no room for superstars or celebrities. Indeed, it was the jockeying among His disciples for supremacy that elicited one of His strongest statements on self-denial and humility: "I tell you the truth, unless you change and become like little children, you will never enter the kingdom of heaven" (Matt. 18:3).

This is not a text for the unchurched at an evangelistic meeting, where we expect people, in the language of the King James Version, to be "converted, and become as little children," so they can be baptized or join the church. No, this is admonishment for seasoned Christians, for ecclesiastical politicians, for church members who have been around the block a time or two.

Notice, Jesus was deadly serious here. In the original language, the statement is preceded by the word *amen*, the same word we use today at the end of our prayers, or when we strongly agree with something. Whenever it precedes a saying of Jesus, we can expect a very important or solemn pronouncement to follow. "Amen," Jesus said, "Verily I tell you the truth, unless you change and become like little children, you will never enter the kingdom of heaven." He didn't say, "You're not likely to enter the kingdom of heaven." He didn't say, "You'll find it difficult to enter the kingdom of heaven." He didn't say, "Chances are, you might not enter the kingdom of heaven." No, He said, "You will NEVER enter the kingdom of heaven"—unless you become like little children.

The particular characteristic of little children He had in focus was humility. "Therefore," He went on to say, "whoever humbles himself like this child is the greatest in the kingdom of heaven" (v. 4). Moreover, considering the question that elicited the statement, "Who is the greatest in the kingdom of heaven?"(v.1), it would seem that He was talking about humility in the context of position and power among His followers. Realist that He was, Jesus knew that the struggle for influence and power would always be a hallmark of the "Gentiles" (Matt. 20:25). But "not so with you," He said (v. 26).

The extent to which Jesus' words have been ignored or forgotten over the centuries is astonishing. The struggle to become big fishes in the ecclesiastical pond has thrown us all too frequently into a state of mass amnesia.

One of those who heard Jesus' startling statement was Peter. His admonition to church leaders, toward the end of his life, shows how deeply he had internalized what he'd heard that day: "The elders who are among you I exhort, I who am a fellow elder and a witness of the sufferings of Christ, . . . Shepherd the flock of God which is among you, serving as overseers, not by constraint but willingly, not for dishonest gain but eagerly; nor as being lords over those entrusted to you, but being examples to the flock; and when the Chief Shepherd appears, you will receive the crown of glory that does not fade away" (1 Pet. 5:1-4, NKJV).

Humility and self-denial are basic Christian attitudes, required by the gospel in all who follow Jesus, not only in leaders of the church. True humility led Jesus to deny Himself and relinquish the position He held in heaven (Phil. 2:5-11), not merely for His own sake, but as a model for others: "Let this mind be in you, which was also in Christ Jesus" (KJV). Humility and self-denial are related, but as William Lillie so perceptively remarks, true self-denial in the gospel is more than humility, more even than self-forgetfulness:

Our Lord's challenge to a would-be follower is to "deny himself and *take up his cross* and follow me"(Mk. 8.34), or to *"bear his own cross and come after me"*(Lk. 14.27). The carrying of a cross seems to be an integral part of self-denial and an indispensable condition of disciple-ship.[5]

Lillie sees this cross-bearing, this self-denial, as dying with Christ, being crucified with Him, "making room for Christ in us."[6] It is the opposite of self-seeking, wherever it may be found, in the pulpit or in the pew, and it is always accompanied by humility. Thus it was in Jesus.

Social Action and the Political Order

Social action and the political order are issues over which Christianity as a whole has often been divided. Yet regardless of our philosophical differences, whether as churches or as individuals, none of us is really neutral. By either action or inaction we make an impact.

So what should be our position in the face of incredible moral and social evil in the world? What is our Christian duty? Should we be involved in changing the social order in the interest of the poor, the oppressed, the marginalized? And what about the difficult and contentious issues of abortion, euthanasia, homosexuality, cloning, civic and religious freedom, immigration and refugee policies, the sordid traffic in human beings, especially women and children, and a host of other pressing humanitarian, economic, and sociopolitical issues today? We certainly cannot address these issues in full here. But what general guidance can we find in the life and teachings of Jesus?

At the beginning of His ministry, during His maiden appearance at His hometown synagogue in Nazareth, Jesus chose a pivotal passage from the book of Isaiah as the paradigm for His mission: "The Spirit of the Lord is on me, because he has anointed me to preach good news to the poor. He has sent me to proclaim freedom for the prisoners and recovery of sight for the blind, to release the oppressed, to proclaim the year of the Lord's favor" (Luke 4:18, 19).

It is possible to give a completely spiritual application to this text and be entirely credible. After all, the explicit motivating influence described in it is the Holy Spirit, with the preaching of the gospel listed first on the agenda. A good case could be made that everything else in the passage—freedom for prisoners, sight for the blind, release for the oppressed, proclaiming the year of the Lord's favor—flow from and are a consequence of the preaching of the gospel. Evidence is abundant in the Gospels themselves, and throughout the Scriptures, that all are prisoners whom Jesus came to free. We have all been blind and deaf and dumb. When Jesus healed the bent woman, did He not refer to her as "a daughter of Abraham, whom Satan has kept bound for eighteen long years"? (Luke 13:16).

The spiritual application of the passage is altogether appropriate. In fact, I would argue that that is its fundamental meaning. If it were not, then Jesus' ministry was, ultimately, a failure. For He left His nation in as great a condition of political bondage as He found it.

All that said, however, can we deny that there is also a sociopolitical (a literal, or nonspiritual) dimension to the Isaianic passage Jesus cited? All one has to do to see the point is go back again to the bent woman in the synagogue. Presumably, many a spiritual leader before Jesus had ministered to her. And the fact that she was perhaps present in church each Sabbath probably meant she'd received the *spiritual* release that God had promised. But on that critical Sabbath when Jesus came, she found release on a different level—and how sweet it was! Forever afterward, no sermon on the spiritual meaning of the Isaiah text would be complete without covering the part where Jesus straightened her back and delivered her from eighteen years of physical bondage.

Across the centuries, people who have had it all together, who have known nothing of hardship and hunger and exploitation and oppression, are very quick to gravitate toward the spiritual application of the Nazareth passage. But those whose backs are breaking under a load of misery and care welcome that added dimension. To borrow words from J. H. Yoder, it's not hard for them to understand the messianic expectation "in the most expressly social terms."[7]

We proceed with caution here. For Jesus does not lend credence to every argument. Not every revolutionary can claim Him on his side. He had His own agenda. And that agenda was unabashedly spiritual. His mission was to build the kingdom of God, which certainly did not envision a realm of tanks and explosives. It was a different kingdom. But—and this is the point—it was a kingdom that recognized and sought to meet the physical and social needs of the unfortunate, the poor and the marginalized.

Picture the scene, for example, when a confused John the Baptist sent messengers to verify Jesus' identity. "Are you the one who was to come," John wanted to know, "or should we expect someone else?" (Matt. 11:3). Jesus' response to the Baptist's emissaries, based on actual happenings before their very eyes, reads like a paraphrase of the scripture he had read in the Nazareth synagogue: "Go back and report to John what you hear and see: The blind receive sight, the lame walk, those who have leprosy are cured, the deaf hear, the dead are raised, and the good news is preached to the poor" (vs. 4, 5).

It wouldn't be very perceptive for a person who has read the Gospels to ask whether Jesus was involved in politics. It is clear, as we have indicated, that He understood His mission as fundamentally spiritual, with no political subtext. The question, rather, is whether Jesus, operating purely from His own spiritual agenda, did not nevertheless rattle the political order of His day? And the answer is Yes. Indeed, that is the guiding principle we should take from His example. While party politics, and politics as such, are entirely foreign to Christian mission, involvement with people is at its heart.

Since our mission is to people, it must address their needs in toto—the physical and the social, as well as the spiritual, and often in that order. As the perceptive religious writer E. G. White put it: "Christ's method alone will give true success in reaching the people. The Saviour mingled with men [and women] as one who desired their good. He showed His sympathy for them, ministered to their needs, and won their confidence. Then He bade them, 'Follow Me.' "[8]

We make a fundamental mistake if we suppose that Jesus was killed simply because He "broke" the Sabbath or because He claimed to have power on earth to forgive sins or for any number of other strictly "religious" infractions. The trilingual sign on His cross read: "Jesus of Nazareth, the King of the Jews." That was not a religious title. And Yoder, arguing against the "spiritualistic-apologetic exegesis," which insists that Jesus "never really meant to bother the established order," makes the following penetrating observation. We must ask the question, he says, "why a Jesus whose main concern . . . [was] to be apolitical would be misunderstood in just this way instead of some other way." "The events in the temple court," he notes, "and the language Jesus used were *not* calculated to avoid any impression of insurrectionary vision. Both Jewish and Roman authorities were defending themselves against a real threat."[9]

It is in the light of similar concerns that one New Testament scholar puts the following penetrating questions: "What did the historical Jesus do and say in the late 20s of that first common-era century that made some people say, 'He is criminal; we must execute him,' and others say, 'He is divine; we must follow him'? How could people look at the same Jesus and judge so divergently?"[10]

The answer, simply, is that He was consumed with the needs of people. And anyone today who could mount an operation approximating the magnitude of what Jesus did would inevitably confront similar political consequences. In today's economy, for example, it would instantly bring the vast medical and pharmaceutical establishment to its knees, and he would quickly become *persona non grata* in those circles of contemporary society where people earn their living from the misfortune of others. It would upset the entire political order—in any country.

That thought was suggested recently in a report from the *Ecumenical Courier*.[11] It called attention to the Dalits (formerly "the untouchables") of India, describing them as being "born into a caste" that relegates them to the most menial tasks imaginable. They're "manual scavengers," it said, which among other things, "means cleaning up human excrement by hand . . . [and] dealing with dead bodies, including human carcasses." Does being a follower of Jesus mean turning a blind eye to such revolting humiliation of our fellow human beings? Frankly, I can't see how. Placing Jesus in the middle of that situation and His love for people, completely apart from questions of common politics, would rattle that horrible status quo.

The totally apolitical approach arouses very little attention, since the focus is on what we may call individualism or gradualism. That is, as long as we are content to deal with one individual or one family at a time, and project decades, if not centuries, for the world's social plight to change. This is not in any way to downplay the need for concern at the individual level. But if our mission ever began to approach the magnitude of Jesus,' then political implications are bound to arise, as they did for Him.

Meaningful and Fulfilling Relationships

What kind of individual was Jesus? How did He relate to other people? Were those relationships warm and meaningful? Or were they remote and stilted?

We cannot, of course, paint a detailed picture of the personality of the Saviour. But we know enough to get a fairly accurate view of the way He connected with people in the various strata of first-century Palestinian society—ordinary people, wealthy people, family and friends. We will briefly discuss each of these dimensions of Christ's relationships, and then conclude with the way in which Jesus, mysteriously, has continued to relate to people *personally* across the centuries.

Relating to Ordinary People

Our generation does not take kindly to snobs, elitists, and conceited eggheads. Jesus was not any of these. Here comes this itinerant preacher with no financial resources, no academic credentials from the learned institutions of the day, and no support from the ruling religious establishment. He spreads His sawdust under the open canopy of the skies, and the crowds flock to Him. And beyond the miracles and the healing, we know—thanks to Mark—how they responded to His message. "The large crowd listened to him with delight," (Mark 12:37).

The statement indicates not only how the people heard the Master, but also contains, I think, undertones of the way He spoke, even the way He related. The mood is captured better by the more emotive translation of the King James Version: "And the common people heard Him gladly." As one commentary observes, this is a reference to "the great mass of the people, or the crowd at large."[12] Mark's comment points beyond the immediate audience that elicited it to a broader acceptance of Jesus and His message among the common folk—the *amhaarez,* the people of the land, or "sinners," as they were known in Hebrew society. "Much of the appeal of Jesus . . . [lay] in his ability to touch wounded hearts. People down on themselves, feeling they were no good or had no future, could hear in his preaching a gentle counsel never to lose heart."[13]

The way Jesus related to children is an example of the way He related to the common people as a whole. In Mark 10:13-16 "people" (parents, probably) bring children to Jesus, "to have him touch them." What a powerful vote of confidence—and trust! But a ghastly thing happens. The disciples, like a posse of modern political handlers, "rebuked them." Jesus should not be distracted by these insignificant little people. Don't these parents know that the Master needs to concentrate on more important things?

Jesus was mortified. "Indignant" is the word the Bible uses; "much displeased" (KJV). It comes from the Greek *aganakteo,* meaning to be aroused, indignant, angry. The behavior of His well-meaning disciples actually angered Him. "Let the little children come to me," He commanded, "and do not hinder them."

Just think of it. He was concerned about the children. Children who could not give Him anything in return. Children who were regarded by the disciples as insignificant, unimportant—not worth Jesus' time. One of the tests of our true concern is the way we relate to the powerless in society. Children, as such, have no power. Retirees, too, are no longer at the controls. The feeble and infirm who not only have no power, but actually are dependent on others for their well-being or survival. The poor. Those on the margins. The way we treat these, how we relate to them, determines the genuineness of our concern. Jesus saw these helpless little ones for who they are: children of His Father, authentic citizens of His kingdom. "Do not hinder them," He said, "for the kingdom of God belongs to such as these."

Aboriginal activist Boori (Monty) Pryor goes around Australia telling stories of his life, his pain, and hopes. With humor, compassion, and sensitivity, he relates chapters in the dark history of his people. And in his book *Maybe Tomorrow,* he tells the moving story of a little girl in one of his meetings. It is an incident that highlights the tenderness of children and the reason for Jesus' anger that day over the treatment they'd received at the hands of His own men.

> I was at this beautiful school in Sydney near the Royal National Park. . . . After the performance the children were all coming up and wanting to talk. This little one said, "Thank you, Monty." She was about seven, I suppose. All the other kids were around. I looked at her and gave her a big hug. She looked up at me with her beautiful eyes and said, "Can you make me an Aborigine?"[14]

Like Monty, Jesus was at home with the little folk. And I believe that each one, as they left Him, longed to be like Him. "The common people [yes, even the little people] heard him gladly."

Relating to Wealthy "Undesirables"

"Zacchaeus, come down immediately. I must stay at your house today" (Luke 19:5). In ancient Oriental culture—as it still is today—much of intimate social life in community centered around the meal. Breaking bread together was an expression of solidarity and acceptance. In these dinner encounters, then, as the Pharisees knew all too well, Jesus was entering into one of the most intimate and meaningful relationships with undesirables.

I'm not aware of a contemporary equivalent to the ancient tax collector—at least not in the West. No single person in Western society today wields the kind of power and generates the level of repugnance that a tax collector did in first-century Palestine. Accordingly, it was no small matter for Jesus to sit down with such loathsome specimens of humanity. Perhaps we come close to understanding the tension if we consider how Blacks in the 1950's American South, say, would have felt if Jesus had come into their community and had been found hobnobbing with wizards of the Ku Klux Klan. Or, to turn it around, if a group of Klansmen had found him sitting down to dinner with Black Southern sharecroppers.

The people were scandalized. The shame of it! The outrage! The perfidy! He had abandoned elevated society for the scum of the earth. Yet, if we can imagine it, Jesus' action was not for show. Nor was it political correctness in advance of its time. His was, instead, a genuine desire to come close to these individuals who, though well-placed and affluent, were yet so spiritually needy. He wanted to bless them, to encourage them, to bring hope.

As a tax-collector, the wealthy Zacchaeus was vermin in his community—a traitor who had sold out his own soul, betrayed his own people. Perhaps one of the loneliest persons in town, he'd heard of Jesus, about His miraculous work, about how He received sinners. A deep yearning, mixed with a good dose of curiosity, flooded his soul. He was determined to see this person.

It was a desperate man who climbed the sycamore tree that day, hoping his unseemly perch would pass unnoticed. The intention, notwithstanding his deep need, was perhaps simply to satisfy his curiosity, then slump back into his own solitary world. But to his acute embarrassment, mixed perhaps with a touch of joy, Jesus noticed him, even knew his name. And to his shock, Jesus invited Himself to his house as a guest! We might wish we had an audiovisual record of the event—to be able to see Jesus' face at that moment, hear His voice, review the cadence, the pathos in it, the note of true concern. Zacchaeus saw and heard all that, and it was enough. "Look, Lord!" he said, "here and now I give half of my possessions to the poor, and if I have cheated anybody out of anything, I will pay back four times the amount"(Luke 19:8).

Some of us are used to "sinners" surrendering publicly at a meeting, in response to repeated calls and organ music. But who ever heard of a sinner "coming to the altar" from a call to come down a tree, and from the preacher inviting himself to dinner! It had something to do with the mystique of Jesus; something to do with His uncanny ability to establish, almost instantly, the most enduring and fulfilling relationships.

Stunned by this amazing development, the people gave voice to the prevailing prejudice of the day. "He has gone to be the guest of a sinner," they declared. But Jesus had a different view. "Today," He said to the flabbergasted Zacchaeus, "salvation has come to this house" (Luke 19:9).

Relating to Family

The Gospels do not provide a great deal of information about the home situation of Jesus, on how He related to His immediate family. But here and there we find hints. On one occasion, for example, His detractors asked: "Isn't this the carpenter's son? Isn't his mother's name Mary, and aren't his brothers James, Joseph, Simon and Judas? Aren't all his sisters with us?" (Matt.13:55, 56).

We owe a great deal to these detractors. For through them we learn that notwithstanding the unusual circumstances of His birth, Jesus grew up as a regular member of Joseph's household, so much so that He was regarded as one of the carpenter's sons. We learn that in Jesus' upbringing there were siblings to relate to: four "brothers"(whose names are given) and at least two "sisters." One searches almost in vain for information on how these siblings interacted, or how Jesus related to His parents. But in several significant instances, we have something. Here are two examples.

When He Was "Lost" in the Temple

This is the well-known story of Jesus being left behind in Jerusalem while His parents headed home. When they found Him, He was in the midst of the legal experts of the temple (Luke 2:46). It was His mother who spoke, scolding Him mildly, and in her words we get an insight into the internal dynamics of the family. "Son," she says, "why have you treated us like this? Your father and I have been anxiously searching for you" (Luke 2:48).

It is an encounter at once tense and tender. Tense, obviously, because of the anxiety and apprehension that had led the parents back to Jerusalem in search of Him. Tender because of the solicitude manifested on the part of both parents for the lad. Incredibly, the eminent New Testament scholar Joseph Fitzmyer uses Mary's language at this tender moment to deny the virgin birth of Jesus. According to him, Mary uses the expression "your father and I" with "no qualifications such as 'foster father' or 'putative father.' " And, he goes on, "Matthew 13:55 records the query, 'Is not this the carpenter's son?' "[15]

But the very language Fitzmyer points to as evidence of a tradition that did not accept the virgin birth stands, rather, as testimony to Jesus' complete integration into His earthly family. It suggests that as a child He had been accepted by Joseph as a son, and Mary's language ("Your father and I") is eminently natural, precisely the kind of sentiments any contemporary mother in that situation would use. And the fact that Jesus is called the carpenter's son (and

later Himself "the carpenter"—Mark 6:3) suggests the depth of His
identification with His immediate family.

When They Came to Take Charge of Him

What He had said to Mary and Joseph in the temple when they
found Him ("I must be about my Father's business," Luke 2:49,
KJV) had now come into full operation. As Mark tells it, Jesus and
His disciples had been under such heavy pressure of ministry that
they "were not even able to eat" (Mark 3:20). When that report
reached His family they decided to take action, saying "He is out of
his mind" (v. 21).

Jesus, holed up in the house of some needy person, has just finished defending Himself against the Jerusalem legal heavyweights
who had charged Him with demon possession, when a message
reaches Him. His "mother and brothers are outside looking for
[him]" (Mark 3:22-32). "Who are my mother and my brothers?" He
asked the messenger. "Then he looked at those seated in a circle
around him and said, 'Here are my mother and my brothers! Whoever
does God's will is my brother and sister and mother' " (vs.33-35).

With this, the Gospels leave us hanging in midair. Did Jesus ever
go out to His folks? And if He did, what did He say to them? That
would have been an intriguing exchange to hear. But we have nothing. What the incident makes clear, however, is that Jesus has left
home. His mission is in full swing. And His family (especially
when, however well-meaning, they launch an effort to impede that
mission) must come second.

We know, however, that Mary later followed Him. And we know
that at least one of His brothers also took his stand and played a
prominent role in the early church. When Paul, three years following
his conversion, went up to Jerusalem for a briefing visit, he saw just
two of the church's leaders: Peter, with whom he stayed fifteen days
and "James, the Lord's brother" (Gal. 1:18, 19). Many scholars
believe this was the James who served as moderator of the Jerusalem
council (Acts 15) and who later authored the Epistle of James.

We see final evidence of Jesus' concern for His family in His treatment of His mother at the cross. His dying agony notwithstanding,
one important detail needed caring for—the future of His aging

mother. "When Jesus saw his mother there, and the disciple whom he loved standing nearby, he said to his mother, 'Dear woman, here is your son,' and to the disciple, 'Here is your mother.' From that time on, this disciple took her into his home" (John 19:26, 27).

Here, in the midst of gloom and tragedy, stands this tender moment—a dying man caring for His beloved mother. It is a powerful testimony.

People Across the Centuries

We can, perhaps, readily understand how Peter and Mary and Martha and Lazarus (warm, personal friends of Jesus, whose story we have not had space to tell) could enjoy such meaningful relationships with Him. But how has it come about that people all over the world—and across the centuries—also have been able to claim Him as a bosom friend? How is it possible that they could enjoy this experience almost as if they had been in real, physical contact with Him? As I feel it in my own soul, this thing is real. In the words of the Samaritans after the woman of the village had introduced Jesus to them: "We no longer believe just because of what you said; now we have heard for ourselves, and we know that this man really is the Saviour of the world" (John 4:42).

Millions in the past and millions today can bear a similar testimony. How is that possible? I don't know that anyone can explain it adequately. But I suspect it has nothing to do with His appearance, real or imagined. It comes from who and what He was. "It is the man Jesus—his kindness, holiness, ability to heal life, ability to express how people ought to relate to one another—that solicits most people's faith. It is the way Jesus depicts God and makes life hopeful."[16]

He not only taught people how they should relate to one another. He modeled it. He *lived* the essence of perhaps His most remembered and widely-quoted words: "Do to others as you would have them do to you" (Luke 6:31). There has never been, in all human history, an individual who has lived so completely and utterly for others.

Jesus is still able to enter into meaningful and enduring relationships with individual human beings, and does so. It is a great mystery, and a great reality. Millions can testify to this personal connection with someone none of us alive today has seen, someone we have met only, or to begin with, in a book. Ultimately, and at its very core, that is the essence of Christianity: an intimate and life-changing relationship with a person. Indeed, *the* Person. Jesus Christ, the Man for others.

For Further Reading

D. Armstrong, ed., *The Truth About Jesus*. Grand Rapids, MI: Eerdmans, 1998.
F. F. Bruce, *The Hard Sayings of Jesus*. Downers Grove, IL: InterVarsity Press, 1983.
D. L. and J. T. Carmody, *Jesus: An Introduction*. Belmont, CA: Wadsworth Publishing Co., 1987.
M. Littleton, *Jesus: Everything You Need to Know to Figure Him Out*. Louisville, KY: Westminster Press, 2001.
J. H. Yoder, *The Politics of Jesus*. Grand Rapids, MI: Eerdmans, 1972.

Notes

1. G. Friedrich (ed.), trans. G. W. Bromiley, *Theological Dictionary of the New Testament*, (Grand Rapids, MI: Eerdmans, 1971), VII, pp. 548-54.
2. Quoted in D. L. and J. T. Carmody, *Jesus: An Introduction* (New York: Wadsworth Publishing Co., 1987), pp. 85, 86.
3. Cited in M. Littleton, *Jesus: Everything You Need to Know to Figure Him Out* (Louisville, KY: Westminster John Knox Press, 2001), p. 176.
4. Cited in Carmody and Carmody, p. 81.
5. W. Lillie, *Studies in New Testament Ethics* (Philadelphia, PA: Westminster, 1963), p. 158.
6. *Ibid.*, p. 159.
7. J. H. Yoder, *The Politics of Jesus* (Grand Rapids, MI: Eerdmans, 1972), pp. 34, 35.
8. E. G. White, *The Ministry of Healing* (Mountain View, CA: Pacific Press, 1942), p. 143.
9. Yoder, pp. 58, 59.
10. J. D. Crossan, in M. J. Borg, ed., *Jesus at 2000* (Boulder, CO: Westview Press, 1997), p. 22.
11. Sonia P. Omulepu, *Ecumenical Courier*, Summer 2001, vol. 61, no. 2, pp. 8, 9.
12. *Seventh-day Adventist Bible Commentary*, vol. 5, p. 648.
13. Carmody and Carmody, p. 150.
14. B.(Monty) Pryor, *Maybe Tomorrow* (Ringwood, Victoria, Australia: Penguin, 1998), p. 34.
15. Cited in Carmody and Carmody, p. 94.
16. *Ibid.*, p. 149.

Jesus and Ourselves
Andrea T. Luxton

In Trafalgar Square, London, there are four <u>plinth</u>s. On three are figures of great historic importance to England. The fourth <u>plinth</u> has become the home of a variety of sculptures, each left there for a short term only. Surprisingly, perhaps, for the late twentieth century in secularized England, Je<u>sus Christ was selected as the subject for the first</u> temporary statue. On first thought, it might have appeared that skepticism and secularization had played their role in this portrayal of Jesus, for beside the other statues, this figure looked overpowered, marked by ordinariness rather than heroism. He was short, every man's neighbor, with only the barbed wire crown of thorns to give Him any identity. But then that "only" is perhaps the whole point: this was the Messiah, the One who according to Isaiah had no grace or comeliness, but who was marked instead by His commitment to suffering and sacrifice. Quite fittingly, the sculpture is named *Ecce Homo*, "<u>Behold the</u> Man," Pilate's words to the crowd just before the beaten Jesus is handed over to be crucified: the Messiah who is to be treated as a criminal.[1]

Questions About Jesus

Arguably the two most important questions Jesus asked His disciples are found in Luke 9, "<u>W</u>ho do the people say I am" (v. 18, NEB) and then, "<u>W</u>ho do *you* say I am?" (v. 20, emphasis supplied). One only has to pick up a book such as Jaroslav Pelikan's *Jesus Through the Centuries* to realize the impossibility of a simple answer to the first question. Was Jesus the rabbi, the revolutionary, the universal man, the monk, the liberator, or all of these? [2] *Ecce Homo* was just one more depiction of a Christ whom art has tried to capture, film has tried to portray, literature has tried to evoke, and theology has tried to understand. All have their value and to some degree speak of the answers others have found to Christ's second question.

It is that second question, "Who do you say I am?" that is finally the question that confronts each individual who seeks to understand and know this Man who has so dominated history. It is not a question Jesus asked the disciples after a lecture that weighed up all the evidence. Although Peter's answer may be in one sense a factual one, "The Christ of God," there is no doubt that his response was intended as more than that and that Christ sought for more also. This was not a question about Jesus' place in history; it was a question about Jesus' place in the hearts and minds of His disciples. They had been given time to weigh up Jesus, both man and lord. What was their verdict? Had they discovered the essence of who and what Jesus was: His lordship and servanthood, His saving and sacrificial commitment, His divinity and humanity? It was Jesus asking His closest friends: "Do you know Me well enough to know what it means to have your life intersect with Mine? Do you know what you are to Me, and where you will go if you remain with Me?"

Jesus' claims do not allow Him to remain simply a man in history. One way or another we who are confronted by the questions of Jesus' authenticity and historicity, must finally face the question of Jesus and ourselves. Who is Jesus, the person who reaches out to humanity, and what personal claims does Jesus make in relation to us? What does it mean to have Jesus' life intersect with ours and to make a confession of His lordship—to accept His gifts, to face the difficult reality of truth and to believe, sometimes even in the midst of silence? Do such experiences authenticate the claims and promises of the gospel? And what responsibilities does such personal faith place on one who comes to believe?

Exploring His Claims

It is not surprising that Jesus attracted both crowds and enemies. His claims were audacious—and yet supported by the way He lived

His life and related to His followers. His claims were usually unambiguous. From the perspective of a nonbeliever they were also arrogant. To a leader in the Jewish community they were blasphemous. To His followers, they defined His mission and His intent of a relationship with both them and His Father.

The Gospel of John records Jesus pronouncing a series of direct statements regarding His identity. "I am the bread of life," Jesus claims (6:35) and "whoever drinks the water I give him will never thirst" (4:14). He further adds: "Before Abraham was born, I am" (8:58). "I am the good shepherd" (10:11); "I am the resurrection and the life" (11:25); "I am the Way and the Truth and the Life" (14:6) and "I am the true vine" (15:1). The words to the Samaritan woman, "Whoever drinks the water I give him will never thirst," perhaps most directly exemplify the nature of all these claims. Jesus is trying to lead the woman to realize the difference between the physical and the spiritual, to point her to the more satisfying way of living He knows she longs to find and which by believing in Him she can discover. In all the claims of Jesus recorded throughout the Gospels, He similarly identifies Himself as the One who can bring deep, personal satisfaction and that confidence of faith which transforms lives.

In many of these assertions Jesus also points more directly to His impending sacrifice and the unselfish nature of the relationship He sought. The bread of life will be given "for the life of the world" (John 6:51). The good shepherd will give His life for His sheep (10:15). Just as Jesus resurrects Lazarus from the dead, He too will soon die so that life can be given to many others who believe.

Jesus' claims also relate to the close link between Himself, His Father, and His followers. Jesus may be the vine, but the Father is the gardener and the disciples and His followers are the branches. All are inextricably linked together. He is the way, the truth, and the life, but the way that He speaks of and shows is the way to the Father. And His unity with the Father throughout timeless ages is no better expressed than in His claim, "before Abraham was born, I am" (John 8:58). Jesus' incarnation made sense only if He truly was God and one with His Father, and if His purpose was to offer His followers a better life in the present and hope for the future through

His sacrifice. This was the essence of His claims.

The expectations arising from Jesus' claims, however, become a little more complex when His differing assertions reflect the intrinsic contradiction of a relationship that offers uncertainty as well as security, a cross as well as restoration. So, while Jesus can promise His disciples that if they come to Him they will find rest (Matt.11: 28, 29), He also warns that He did not come to bring peace, but a sword (10:34). He promises that if His disciples ask, seek, and knock, they will receive, find, and the door will be opened to them (7:7, 8). But if that seemed like the offer of a life in which all problems were to be resolved on request, Jesus also promises that any follower of His would need to deny himself, take up his cross, and follow Him (16:24). This does not indicate a life of easy answers or of rapidly won power or glory. So Jesus offers hope on one hand and challenge on the other. His challenge to the status quo is not just focused on the Jewish establishment or on the Roman occupiers, but also on the individual.

Jesus' claims and promises throughout the Gospels never change their central focus. Rather like a multifaceted diamond, His varied assertions may highlight different perspectives, but the basic reality remains the same. Jesus' life and death are essentially about Jesus and the disciples, about Jesus and us. His life and death are a revelation aimed at each individual so that humanity can discover truth, recognize God's astonishing gifts, and come to faith. They are about a visible and concrete representation of a God who is compassionate, who wishes His followers to develop ever stronger faith, and who will give everything to bring hope and salvation to those He deeply loves. They are not about a remote God who manages the processes of the world from a distance. Rather, they are evidence of a personal God to whom ultimately relationship is everything, for that was the fundamental purpose of the incarnation.

So here is a Man who not only shows that He can perform physical miracles, but who more importantly claims something greater—the right to forgive sins (Luke 7:48). Here is a Man who not only talks of His own death and resurrection (9:22), but who also promises the resurrection of other believers (John 5:28, 29).

Here is a Man who not only promises to return to the Father from whom He came (14:28), but who also promises to come again to take His followers back with Him (v. 3). It is all about the restoration of lost relationships.

The claims of Jesus, however, did not remain as words. The Gospel accounts are far more about story and reality—stories Jesus tells in order that His message may be understood and events in which He interacts with His followers, touches their hearts, opens their minds, and helps them explore the unimaginable depths of what His claims and promises mean. It is largely by reflecting on these means of interaction between Jesus and His followers that we are still able to explore the inner realities of Jesus' presence in human lives.

Accepting Grace

If one of the most often-repeated promises of Christ in the Gospels is that He, representing the Father, provides His followers with good gifts, perhaps one of the greatest difficulties His followers have is to recognize those gifts and accept them. Yet in that interaction of Jesus' giving and our acceptance lies one of the most important keys to understanding who Jesus truly is. And here, it is important to understand the nature of the gifts of Jesus. While the scribes and Pharisees sought for the removal of Roman oppression, and the disciples fought among themselves for a greater place of prominence in God's kingdom, Jesus offered very different gifts. He sought to provide gifts that could bring peace, fulfillment, hope, and a personal home. Yet these gifts were neither then or now always comprehended or embraced.

Perhaps the parable of the great banquet in Luke 14:15-24 defines the problem. Here is a man who has clearly gone to great effort to provide a banquet for many guests. The indication is that all has been well prepared. The guests have not said they cannot come, and the host has every justification to believe that when he sends his servant to bring the guests to the feast they will come. However, not only do the guests not come, but their excuses are insulting. "I have just bought a field, and I must go and see it." Can he not see it the next day? "I have just bought five yoke of oxen, and I'm on my way to try them out." Is that a reasonable choice of priority? "I just got married, so I can't come." Perhaps a better excuse, but did the guest care so little about the host that he is only telling him now? And would not the new wife have been just as welcome? And so, turned down by those he had invited to the banquet, the host now sends out for more appreciative guests: the crippled, the blind, the lame, the homeless, itinerant travelers—those who recognize their need of his proffered hospitality.

What is most astonishing about the behavior of the guests is their apparent total lack of awareness of the host's efforts to prepare the best possible banquet for them. Caught up in their own world, where they buy their own way, they miss out on the free gift that was being offered, just waiting for them to accept. This parable had immediate significance. Jesus told it to the Jewish leaders who had been waiting so long for the gift that in reality He Himself was, but who didn't recognize Him when He was there among them. However, in the context of the gospel message as a whole, this parable takes on wider significance.

Still using the central image of a banquet Jesus tells another parable, recorded just one chapter later: the parable of the lost son. As is often found in the Gospels, the main thought of this parable lies at its center—the father's unequivocal acceptance of his returned son. He is to receive the best robe, a ring, sandals and there will be a banquet. Why? "For this son of mine was dead and is alive again; he was lost and is found" (Luke 15:24). The wandering son at last recognized the true nature of his father's intentions and resources, and came home. There is no better expression of the gospel and of the way Christ wishes to interact with all human beings: free and unconditional acceptance, forgiveness and grace from Him and a willing and open acceptance of those gifts by each individual.

The younger son had struggled with this concept when he decided to return home. He had planned his return a little differently: not as a son, but as a servant. Surely what he had done was too much for total forgiveness. Maybe, however, he would be acceptable as a servant, and in a way this would be an easier return. For to be a son means accepting much more and taking responsibility for much more than a servant. Speaking of the experience of the younger son and relating it to his own spiritual journey, Henri Nouwen writes:

> Sometimes it even seems as though I want to prove to God that my darkness is too great to be overcome. While God wants to restore to me the full dignity of sonship, I keep insisting that I will settle for a hired servant. Do I truly want to be restored to the full responsibility of the son? Do I truly want to be so totally forgiven that a completely new way of living becomes possible?[3]

Christ's invitation to the banquet includes acceptance of all the gifts and responsibilities that come with being a son or daughter. Nothing is earned. All can be accepted. That is what kept the older brother away from the celebration when the younger brother returned. He was still "earning" the right to be a son—how could he be anything but jealous of one who had done nothing to earn his gift of grace?

Jesus' interactions with those He contacted consistently mirrored His wish to give freedom and full acceptance. The woman caught in adultery could leave, uncondemned, from Jesus' sight. The man lowered through the roof on his bed of sickness could take up his bed and walk, healed but also forgiven. Peter, who had spent so much time confident of his loyalty, could be raised to be leader of the early church after his public denial of his Lord. The Gospels never once record Christ turning away any prodigal who seeks a better way or a better life. He always restores, forgives, and offers hope.

Jesus' focus on grace and forgiveness—two of the good gifts He offers—and this difficult offer of full acceptance reaches right to the center of the interaction He wants between human beings and Himself. Christ's gospel asks that we dare stop focusing on the field or the oxen we have just bought, and instead be willing to accept something we have not had to work for, with complete openness and vulnerability.

This need for us to come from our far country and allow ourselves to be embraced by the father becomes of heightened importance when we face the reality of the cross of Christ. It is difficult in a society that has grown up aware of the story of the crucifixion for the cross to have personal meaning beyond tradition. It is difficult also in an increasingly individualistic society for people to accept gifts without wanting to offer something equally valuable in return. But the reality of the cross is just that. Jesus is only in a position to offer the gifts He does because of the high cost He first paid on the cross. And there is nothing we can do of equal value in return. In fact, we miss the whole point of the gift if we believe we can either earn it or reciprocate. Jesus is the one who gave up everything, suffering beyond our understanding, in order to give to us, without cost, the gifts of forgiveness, freedom, and life—in other words, salvation. And yet those barriers of self-doubt and the determination to earn what we receive still keep us at a distance.

Telling the Truth

Perhaps the greatest problem in dismantling the barriers we erect to prevent us receiving the fullness of God's gifts is that we do not always recognize the nature, or even the existence, of those barriers. Time and again Jesus, in the Gospel accounts, helps individuals to identify the obstacles to deeper relationship and faith. The challenge often is whether the individual can accept the possible pain of facing personal truth and what that might mean. Or will a relationship with Jesus come at too high a cost?

Perhaps the most important sentence in the telling of the story of the rich young ruler is found in Mark 10:21: "Jesus looked at him and loved him." This young man is not one of the ruling class trying to catch Jesus out. He had not become so hardened that he could not hear truth when it was spoken to him. Here is a young man who had seriously tried to do what he says: to live in obedience to the law of God as fully as he could. He has clearly been taught the intricacies of the law, and he has earnestly driven himself to fulfill every part of it, so the story suggests. Now, he wants to know, is there anything else he needs to do to receive eternal life? He is earnest but confident, and Jesus, who recognized his worth, is not prepared to let him go without the truth. As Jesus looks into the heart of this young man He knows that money is the barrier to his acceptance of God's true gifts. Jesus loves him and so tells him the truth. And the young man knows it is the truth. There is no defensiveness, no parrying with the reality of what Jesus has said. Yet the truth is too difficult and sadly the young man turns away (v. 22).

Nicodemus is another who cannot face all the truth—at least not immediately. His journey to Jesus is made in the safety of the night, and his initial approach is impersonal and as a representative of the Sanhedrin: "We know you are a teacher who has come from God" (John 3:2). However, Jesus penetrates to the heart of the matter very quickly. This is not a time for intellectual discussion or prevarication, and He immediately shifts the ground of the discussion to the personal, "I tell you the truth, no one can see the kingdom of God unless he is born again" (v. 3). The two parry for a while, Nicodemus finding it difficult to move past his intellectual barrier of what makes reasonable sense, and Jesus speaking of that which is humanly unreasonable: the new birth, the variableness and unpredictableness of the Spirit, and the nature of the kingdom of heaven. This was nothing like the security of religious laws and hierarchy: the truth Jesus presents is often uncomfortable, and this was no exception.

Robert Badinas speaks of the nature of the truth that Jesus presents to Nicodemus:

> Nicodemus knows so much. Religion is his area of expertise. He moves in a world of theological debate and argument. He stands out as a learned scholar. But somehow he has missed the most elementary of lessons. He has not learned that the spiritual life depends not upon his own theological knowledge about God but upon his relationship with him.[4]

As the conversation continues, Nicodemus becomes silent. Jesus' focus is on relationship, belief, accepting the "light" that has come into the world openly. However, Nicodemus, who came seeking Jesus by night, does not yet seem ready to leave in the light. He has heard the truth spoken, however, and as Badinas says, "Nicodemus returned to his own world. But beyond the shadows, in the distant horizon of his own life, an inescapable sunrise had begun to dawn."[5] Later Nicodemus came out of the shadows: first when the Jewish leaders threatened Jesus' life (John 7:40-52) and then after the crucifixion (19:38-42).

Perhaps one of the most outstanding examples of someone who responded to the truth with which Jesus confronted her was the woman of Samaria. With cultural, religious, and gender barriers between them, it would not have been surprising if this encounter had remained at best superficial, and at worst had soured. However, ignoring the natural barriers to communication, Jesus seeks to reach beyond the superficial and beyond the harshness of her life to share with this woman a glimpse of great truth. The point of vulnerability seems to be her relationships: five husbands and now one that is not her husband. The Bible doesn't tell us what lies behind the life the woman has led—the hurt, the failures—because Jesus sees no need to comment or condemn. He merely states the facts.[6] Yet this appears to begin to open the woman's heart, for immediately she responds, "I can see that you are a prophet" (John 4:19). And it is His understanding and knowledge of her that she will later use in her witness to those in the village.

In this interaction, Jesus also makes another important point. As they speak, the woman distinguishes between the worship of her "fathers" and that of "you Jews," in the circumstances another barrier to communication. Jesus' response, though, is unequivocal—true worship is not to do with traditions, but is an attitude of the heart—it is worship "in spirit and truth." And that is possible for all. Forget the form of worship or whether the worship takes place in a temple or on a mountain. What is most necessary is the honest, personal search for truth and understanding. This woman is open to hearing the truth, aware of her own vulnerability and needs. She leaves her water jar unfilled and rushes to the village to tell of the truth she has heard.

The Gospels suggest there is no one pattern which Jesus used to confront people with truth. It is only by being open and honest, by hearing and being willing to accept the truth, that we become open to change and growth. For any individual—and for us—that means taking the risk of being vulnerable, of being willing to know ourselves in a way that may leave us uncomfortable. Jesus' invitation to each individual to look with Him at truth wherever it may be found is an inevitable part of an enriching relationship between Him and ourselves.

Embracing Belief

Jesus invites human beings through the ages to accept His gifts and to risk facing the truth. Neither of these experiences, however, is likely to be a reality without an individual daring to commit himself or herself to believe. The need to believe remains central to all Gospel accounts of Jesus interacting positively and successfully with any human being.

It is this question of belief that is the focus of John's Gospel. At the very beginning of his explanation of who Jesus is are two responses to Christ's person and the purpose of His incarnation: those who do not recognize Him or receive Him (John 1:10-11), and those who do receive Him and believe in Him (v. 12). For the remainder of his Gospel John invites his readers to experience for themselves the fulfillment of belief that was reflected in his own life. The challenge to believe is no more clearly explored than in the final miracle recorded in the Gospel of John—the miracle that stands right in the center of his Gospel and which lies at its heart and which introduces the last events leading to Christ's death.

On one level, the record of the raising of Lazarus from the dead prefigures the death and resurrection of Christ that is to follow. If Lazarus can be raised from the dead so can Christ. That in itself is a reason for belief. This story, though, can be seen as less about reasons for belief than about the human struggle to find belief amidst the unknown, frightening, and sometimes threatening environment to faith. This again reaches right to the heart of the complexity of the interaction between Jesus and ourselves. Belief involves the intellect, but more than that, it touches our fears and demands our vulnerability. It invites us to remove our safety barriers and not seek limitations to our understanding of God or our relationship with Him.

Mary and Martha are key characters in this story and those we would most expect to exemplify belief. They are some of Jesus' closest friends. They know Him; they love Him. He has changed their lives dramatically, and nobody was more likely to believe in His promises than these two sisters and their brother, Lazarus. And yet they are suddenly faced with a doubly unknown and frightening situation. Jesus, who as their friend they might well have expected to come immediately to their help as soon as He heard Lazarus was sick, did not come. So their brother died. It is not surprising that when Jesus eventually arrived both sisters separately expressed their disappointment at his delay: "If you had been here my brother would not have died" (John 11:21, 32).

However, it is Martha's response that is perhaps most interesting, for she continues, "But I know that even now God will give you whatever you ask" (v. 22). No doubt Martha means exactly what she says, but Jesus immediately challenges her, "Your brother will rise again." Yes, "at the last day," Martha responds, putting limits on her belief and evoking from Christ a response that contains one of His most far-reaching claims, "I am the resurrection and the life. . . . Do you believe this?" "Yes, you are the Son of God," Martha affirms. She believes. Yet, standing by her brother's tomb a few moments later Jesus asks for the gravestone to be taken away, and her very natural, human response belies her earlier statement of faith. "But there will be a bad smell," she says—he has been dead four days. And Jesus gently says, "Did I not tell you that if you believed, you would see the glory of God?" (v. 40). And the unbelievable, that which is even beyond Martha's faith in her friend and Saviour, happens.

The disciples also struggle with belief in this incident. They want to understand, but Christ's actions belie their limited comprehension. First of all Jesus does not go immediately to His friend when the message of his sickness arrives, and then when He does go it is through a region where His own life has recently been threatened and after He knows that Lazarus is dead. Jesus' explanation does little to convince the disciples. Although they go with Him it is not because they believe that they will be safe or even because they are convinced that He knows what He is doing, but as Thomas says, "Let us also go, that we may die with him" (John 11:16)—a wonderful expression of friendship, if not of belief. Here is another group of individuals who know Christ well, yet who also find that belief is threatening and difficult to grasp or put into practice.

There is a third group of individuals who are also important in this story: the mourners by Lazarus' tomb. From the time John first describes them to us he separates them into two camps—those who are willing to see the best in Christ ("see how he loved him !") and those who take the critical approach ("could not he . . . have kept this man from dying?") (vs. 36, 37). The two groups continue to respond differently to what they see happen, for after the resurrection of Lazarus one group will believe in Christ's messiahship and the other will see the miracle as a reason for deciding that He must be destroyed. We do not know exactly who those who believed were; we do know that the sparse support Jesus received at the time of His death would unfortunately suggest that their amazement at this act did not change their long-term natural human instinct for self-preservation and propensity for doubt.

Jesus' claims, when accepted as true, demand a level of belief difficult for humans to comprehend, and more difficult still to live out in practice. In this short story we see several human dilemmas. There is a call to believe that the laws of nature we have learned to take for granted do not limit this man. There is a call to accept that belief in Christ may mean moving outside the limits of our own logic to accept apparently unreasonable conclusions. There is a call to believe in miracles, and also to believe that if miracles do not happen Jesus is no less the Christ. And there is a call to believe at all costs, despite the threat that that belief might pose to our sense of security.

Frederick Buechner writes tellingly of the gospel as tragedy, comedy, and fairy story. He does not suggest by this that the gospel is not true, but that belief in what the gospel tells us takes us to the depths of the darkness of our own souls (tragedy), astonishes us with ultimate happy endings (comedy), and presents us with the humanly unbelievable (fairy story).[7] And that is why the gospel call to belief is so difficult. It will shows us the depths of sin, even in ourselves. It will ask us to believe that in the midst of those depths, Jesus' voice can call us to new life. It will constantly ask us to move beyond our safely-constructed boxes into the unknown, amidst our fear, and with limited understanding.

One of the greatest encouragements in the Lazarus story, however, is the evidence that when Jesus calls us to believe it is not without understanding how difficult that call is. How gently Jesus treats the disciples and the two sisters with their deep desire to believe and their love of their friend and Saviour, and yet still possessing a limited faith. Jesus raises Lazarus despite Martha's limits of faith, and He continued with His disciples toward Jerusalem despite their remaining fears. And in the account Jesus makes it clear that much of what happens is, in fact, not primarily for this group of followers and believers, but for those who are standing by, watching, and finding it hard to believe at all.

The difficulty of belief is present for all who are confronted with the daily call of Christ. Like the disciples and Martha some will discover that their response, which seems great in faith, instead only denies the full extent of the love and power of the Saviour. Some will doubt their ability to believe in the first place and will not even find the limited confidence shown by these friends of Jesus. However, the reality of the gospel message is that even the seeming impossibility of belief is made possible with Christ. The one who personally called forth Lazarus, by name, from the dead and performed the impossible miracle, also personally calls all individuals by name to belief. In the strength He supplies the impossible can happen.

Living With Silence

Human experience in all ages testifies that the impossible can and does happen. The joy at the grave of Lazarus is repeated throughout the Gospels and throughout history when faith is validated by what Jesus does both in our lives and in the lives of others. Yet joy is not always the immediate outcome and sometimes a deepening relationship with Jesus also includes the difficult experience of living with silence.

For a while silence is the experience of Mary and Martha. Where is Jesus? Yet the dilemma goes further. Philip Yancey describes his childhood conviction that miracles were "absolute proofs of Jesus' claims" and "guarantees of personal safety." But then his adult eyes also saw the times when miracles did not happen, for while Lazarus was raised from the dead and his grieving sisters were comforted, not all who died that day saw resurrection, and not all mourners found joy. For Yancey the conclusion is that miracles are signs, God's way of stating His intent to right the wrongs of the world, "the early glimpses of restoration."[8]

In Luke 18:1-8, Jesus tells His disciples a parable about continuing to pray and not giving up. It is told in the context of a Jewish nation waiting for the freedom anticipated in a coming Messiah. It was recorded by Luke in the context of a young Christian church suffering persecution and longing already for the second coming of Christ. Why did God delay? Here the widow, pleading with an unjust judge, continues to badger him until he finally gives in because, as he expresses it, "Even though I don't fear God or care about men, yet because this widow keeps bothering me, I will see that she gets justice, so that she won't eventually wear me out with her coming!"(vs. 4,5). And so, Jesus points out, those who continue to cry to God can similarly rely on His justice. However, that promise does not deny that miracles do not always happen when they are requested. John the Baptist was beheaded even while those who believed in Christ and followed Him at a more respectable distance were healed. The silence of God continues to beleaguer many who have like Peter confidently declared the messiahship of Christ.

There is a final twist at the end of this parable of the persistent widow, for Jesus asks, "When the Son of Man comes, will he find faith on the earth?" What Jesus wanted from the disciples was not a relationship based on miracles, but on who He was and how He could transform lives despite the darkness and in the presence of silence. His claims in the gospel are not those of a magician but of one who will bring light, truth, wholeness, and a sense of direction—even though His call may be to sacrifice and the cross.

Kathleen Norris, in The Cloister Walk, describes the Easter when she was confronted with the harshness of the death of Christ. As a young child she was watching the Easter story on television. She was watching because it was about Jesus, and she liked the story because she had heard about Jesus in Sunday School. But then the story goes where she has not known it go before. She sees the cross and watches Jesus die. Horrified, she runs for comfort to her grandmother, but her grandmother's words do not help her to understand. So the young Kathleen flees into her room, into her wardrobe, and shuts the door. She recalls her feelings: "I am going to stay here a long time. I am not going to come out, ever. The grown-ups have gone crazy or they've lied to me; they've kept it hidden, what a terrible world this is, where Jesus dies."[9]

In the silence of the cross, the despair of the disciples, the grief of Mary, the Gospels recount the difficulties of the darkness, the silence, the unanswered questions. It is in this silence that all individuals must finally face themselves. In the words of Ajith Fernando, at the cross our "personal" and "theological arrogance" are both "shattered."[10] Here is injustice, extreme pain, suffering beyond our imagination, and its dark reality exists only because of that intersection between our lives and that of Christ, because of His wish to restore the broken relationship between Himself and His Father and ourselves. In that environment of love, the cross is more than just a place of uncertainty, of fear, of the unknown. It is perhaps a place where truth itself lies—or where a question lies, waiting until we are ready to face the truth. Speaking of Pilate's unanswered question to Jesus, "What is truth?" Buechner posits: "Before it is a word, the Gospel that is truth is silence, a pregnant silence in its ninth month, and in answer to Pilate's question Jesus keeps silent, (and) even with his hands tied behind him manages somehow to hold silence out like a terrible gift."[11]

Certainly the silence of the cross held out truth about the nature of Jesus' messiahship to the disciples, a truth they had long not wanted to accept. It continues to hold out the truth of who we are and who we can be, as well as truth about Jesus Himself.

And then the resurrection becomes more poignant because of what has gone before. The resurrection puts all in order and gives a reality to hope and a reason for belief. Yet the call to believe is to accept and experience the cross, the resurrection, and the silence that may lie between the two. All three are part of the gospel, in the experience of Jesus Himself, and in all subsequent human experience.

Jesus never promised that a relationship with Him was one which would provide all the answers or no questions; all the joy without some sadness; total victory without any loss; all the fulfillment, without vulnerability, challenge and fear. Nevertheless, answers, joy, victory, and fulfillment *are* also a very real part of this relationship, indeed are its ultimate objective.

Writing the "Fifth" Gospel

Jesus' important questions to His disciples in Luke 9 about who He is do not stand alone. Even while Peter is still confessing Jesus as the Messiah, Jesus is framing the words that give shape to His personal mission. They point to the cross, recognize the silence, and promise the resurrection: "The Son of Man must suffer many things and be rejected by the elders, chief priests and teachers of the law, and he must be killed and on the third day be raised to life" (Luke 9:22).

This in itself offers a challenge to belief, but it is only half of what Christ wants the disciples to understand. The rest follows: "If anyone would come after me, he must deny himself and take up his cross daily and follow me" (v. 23). The point is not just who Christ is, but who are the disciples, and who are we, in relationship with Christ. It is not just about acceptance of God's gifts, about facing the truth we are shown, about belief and faith in the salvation He offers. There is a more visible consequence of opening ourselves to the realities of Jesus of Nazareth. It is the inevitable consequence of Jesus moving off the pages of history and into the minds and hearts of individuals. Their lives, their service, are to mirror His life, His service. They too learn to experience the cross and the silence. Their hope then is also of resurrection.

The apparent harshness of the three short dialogues Luke records at the end of chapter 9 carry the same message. It is perhaps exemplified in the second conversation. "Follow me," Jesus says. "First let me go and bury my father," is the response. And Jesus replies, "Let the dead bury their own dead, but you go and proclaim the kingdom of God" (vs. 59, 60). The issue is one of priority. Don't refuse to experience the gracious gift of God's banquet because of the immediate material needs or requirements confronting you. Don't focus too intently on the realities ahead, even those in the future (many commentators suggest that the man's father was probably not actually dead yet). To follow Christ, recognizing the reality of His kingdom, present and future, demands the same wholehearted commitment that Jesus' Himself showed in both life and death. This means finding the grace to forgive like the father in the parable of the prodigal son, because we have ourselves known forgiveness. It means representing the gospel through humility, not power. It means being confident in witness because of who Christ is and not because we trust in our own loyalty or ability.

Peter was one who was confident of his commitment and loyalty. After all, he knew who the Messiah was. Jesus was not just a historical figure and a miracle worker. He would never deny Him. How devastating for Peter to find out, when he did exactly what he said he would never do, that he did not know himself and that his confidence in himself had left him blind to his own weaknesses. However, when we move briefly out of the Gospels into Acts 2, we find an interesting portrayal of this same man. It is the day of Pentecost. Peter is preaching. He still has confidence, but the source of the confidence is now different. He does not trust in himself, but in the assurance of the Christ who has died and been resurrected. He is totally clear: "Therefore let all Israel be assured of this: God has made this Jesus, whom you crucified, both Lord and Christ" (v.36). Peter's whole sermon reverberates with certainty, belief, and hope. It was an honest and effective witness, born of experience.

Jesus does not merely ask His followers to witness, He expects that witness will flow from their relationship with Him, inseparable from the call to follow Him. It is to be witness to the Jesus whose humanity touched our humanity, whose deep passion would not remain silent amidst wrongs, whose grace and compassion draws all to Him and gives self-worth, whose own life was totally in harmony with His teachings. Elizabeth Johnson sees this responsibility as writing the "fifth gospel," "telling the story" (our story) and "living the story" (our story) of Jesus.[12] To the individual who knows belief and to the church that shares belief this is not a choice. It is the natural and inevitable result of belief that is vibrant, if not always easy.

"Who Do *You* Say I Am?"

Jesus' claims in the Gospels cannot be left on the pages of a text or as mere historic evidence. By their very nature they reached into the lives of those among whom Jesus dwelt. They were lived out through His personal interactions, they were explored through His teaching and parables. Yet these claims, by their very nature, reach out past the barriers of time and ask each generation to allow them to be proved true once again. And these claims can only be fully understood and authenticated through the relationship He taught was necessary—and possible.

No service is done to Christian faith when this relationship is oversimplified, when Jesus is seen merely as a miracle worker or the divine Father Christmas. Like any valued relationship, interaction with Jesus demands considerable investment of self. More than any other relationship it will challenge our arrogance, self-sufficiency, or lack of self-esteem. It will ask us to face ourselves with almost brutal honesty, and it will push us to the bounds of belief time and again. It remains the most important encounter any of us can ever experience, although it may not always leave us feeling comfortable. And it will demand that we speak our story, our gospel encounter, with amazement, with excitement, with conviction, to others.

The statue of Jesus that rested briefly in Trafalgar Square is no longer there. Perhaps after all that was not where it belonged—the very human Christ, among the heroic, the military, the famous, the nationally-honored leaders. Nevertheless, it did belong. It belonged in that Christ has greatly influenced human history, English history included. It belonged in that Christ's claims, gifts, and challenges are for all people in all lands in all ages. It belonged in that it raised uncomfortable questions regarding the nature of Christ and the purpose of His life, a life that constantly challenged, and challenges, the status quo of individuals and the establishment alike. Yet there is yet no permanent place in Trafalgar Square for this contemporary portrayal of Jesus Christ. Perhaps it is a fitting symbol of the difficulty we have of giving the biblical Jesus a place, not just in history, but also in our own hearts and minds. "Who do *you* say I am?" It is a question that, like Jesus Himself, will not go away and that cannot, with honesty, be avoided.

For Further Reading

R. Badinas, *Meet Jesus*. Grantham: Autumn House, 1995.
A. Fernando, *I Believe in the Supremacy of Christ*. London: Hodder and Stoughton, 1997.
H. Nouwen, *The Return of the Prodigal Son*. New York: Doubleday, 1994.
J. Pelikan, *Jesus Through the Centuries*. New Haven, CN: Yale University Press, 1999.
P. Yancey, *The Jesus I Never Knew*. London: Marshall Pickering, 1995.

Notes

1. The sculptor was Mark Wallinger. Further information on this sculpture and the contrasting sculptures on the fourth plinth can be found on the project web site www.fourthplinth.com.
2. Jaroslav Pelikan, *Jesus Through the Centuries* (New Haven, CN: Yale University Press, 1999), *passim.*
3. Henri Nouwen, *The Return of the Prodigal Son* (New York: Doubleday, 1994), p. 53.
4. Robert Badinas, *Meet Jesus* (Grantham: Autumn House, 1995), p. 24.
5. Badinas, p. 27.
6. Badinas discusses this story and the woman's situation with insight and sensitivity, pp. 29-33.
7. Frederick Buechner, *Telling the Truth: The Gospel as Tragedy, Comedy, and Fairy Tale* (New York: Harper and Row, 1977), *passim.*
8. Philip Yancey, *The Jesus I Never Knew* (London: Marshall Pickering, 1995), pp. 178-180.
9. Kathleen Norris, *The Cloister Walk* (New York: Riverside Books, 1997), p. 168.
10. Ajith Fernando, *I Believe in the Supremacy of Christ* (London: Hodder and Stoughton, 1997), pp.153, 154.
11. Buechner, p.16.
12. Elizabeth Johnson, *Consider Jesus: Waves of Renewal in Christology* (London: Geoffrey Chapman, 1990), pp. 61, 62.

Jesus: Priest and Coming King

Ivan T. Blazen

In the developing story of the New Testament, Jesus, following His resurrection, functions first as intercessor and priest for His people and then as One who returns in royal power to receive them. However, in this chapter Jesus' high priestly ministry is set forth after consideration of His second advent so that it may become the more apparent that His work as priest is what provides assurance and makes readiness for His coming possible.

The Second Advent Hope in the New Testament

At the core of the New Testament is the message that Jesus in His life, death, and resurrection is the embodiment and unique expression of God's salvation process in the world. Indeed, He is set forth as Saviour and Lord. In consequence of, and as the climax to, the outworking of redemption initiated and revealed in His first coming, "he will appear a second time" (Heb.9:28) to bring this process to completion. Earth has never had better news!

The joyous note that Jesus is coming again is struck, in one form or another, explicitly or implicitly, throughout the pages of the New Testament. It is found, for example, in those reports which the Gospels of Matthew and/or Luke share in common with Mark, which good evidence indicates to be the earliest of the Gospels and which Matthew and Luke probably had before them as they wrote. Utilizing Mark's version, we find Jesus saying in a climactic statement at the end of chapter 8, that the way people have reacted to Him will be the basis for how the Son of Man reacts to them "when he comes in his

Father's glory with the holy angels" (8:38). This pithy but pictorial statement is expanded in Mark 13, with parallel chapters in Matthew 24 and Luke 21. In these three salient chapters the destruction of the temple is linked with a large-scale description of the coming of the Son of Man in power and glory and the events leading up to it.

The return of Christ is also found in those passages that only Matthew and Luke have in common. Here again the references to Jesus' coming are striking. We may note a few passages from Luke. Jesus compares the coming of the Son of Man with the coming of a thief, the point being that we should be ready at all times, "because the Son of Man will come at an hour when you do not expect him" (Luke 12:40). The inhabitants of Jerusalem, soon to be desolated, will not again see the Jesus they have rejected until belatedly, but without avail, they say at the consummation of all things: " 'Blessed is he who comes in the name of the Lord' " (13:35). Furthermore, when Jesus comes it will be like a lightning flash to all those who will be, as in Noah's day, engrossed with the ordinary pursuits of life, oblivious to what is ahead (17:20-37).

In material unique to either Matthew or Luke we learn such themes as the nearness of the Son of Man's coming (Matt.10:23) and the judgment that will take place when the angels gather out of His kingdom "everything that causes sin and all who do evil"(13:41). If we add to the testimonies of the first three Gospels that of John 14:1-3, where Jesus promises to return to take His people to dwelling places He has prepared for them in His Father's "house,"[1] we can say that the frequency and force of the second advent passages in every stratum of the Gospels is impressive indeed.

Other portions of the New Testament state that people will see Jesus come in the same manner in which the disciples saw Him ascend (Acts 1:11), that the day of His return is fast approaching, and that light rather than night should characterize God's people (Rom. 14:11-13). Two entire chapters of the five in 1 Thessalonians are devoted to eschatological themes relating to Christ's coming, the resurrection of God's people, and the spiritual/ethical walk of the "children of light" in faith, hope, and love in view of Jesus' reappearance (1 Thess.4,5). 2 Thessalonians contrasts two comings: one of Antichrist and the other of Jesus who will destroy Antichrist (2:1-10).

The New Testament further provides information on the transformation that Christ will effect in His people and in their bodies when He comes (Phil.3:21; 1 Cor.15:35-54). When He appears His people will be like Him (1 John 3:2) and will appear with Him in glory (Col.3:4). There will also be a change in the created world itself (Rom.8:20, 21; 2 Pet. 3:10, 12, 13). Furthermore, the disparate and disharmonious elements in heaven and earth will be brought into unity in Christ (Eph.1:10).

As that day draws nearer believers are exhorted to come closer together through frequent assembly and mutual encouragement (Heb.10:25). James admonishes his readers to be patient until the coming of the Lord (5:7, 8), and 2 Peter warns believers against letting the passage of time become a reason for accepting the argumentation of scoffers who, on the basis of the uniformitarian principle that "everything goes on as it has since the beginning of creation," deny the reality of Christ's coming. Such encourage lustful indulgence rather than lives of holiness that are necessary in view of the impending divine dissolution and restitution of all things (3:3-13).

The biblical text provides a variety of words and expressions to designate the fact of Jesus' return. In addition to the frequently used word "come," *erchomai* (Matt. 25:31; Mark 13:26; Luke 18:8; John 14:3; Acts 1:11; Rev. 1:7), there are a number of other terms. One of these is *parousia,* which has become an English word meaning presence or arrival. It may have a secular sense, as with the presence of Paul with his converts (Phil.2:12), but in the New Testament a religious sense with reference to the second coming predominates, as in Matthew 24:1, 3, 27, 37, 39 and 1 Thessalonians 5:23. The word *apocalypsis*, meaning unveiling or revelation, occurs seven out of eighteen times in the New Testament for the dynamic revealing of Christ at the end of history. Examples are 1 Corinthians 1:7; 2 Thessalonians 1:7; and 1 Peter 4:13. The verb *phaneroo* means to manifest or appear and is found, for example, in Colossians 3:4; 1 Peter 5:4; and 1 John 3:2. *Epiphania*, from which the word epiphany, the revelation of the divine, is derived is utilized of the second coming in such texts as 2 Thessalonians 2:8 and Titus 2:13.[2]

All this is sufficient to demonstrate the ubiquity of the concept of Christ's second coming in the New Testament. It is also sufficient to

236 ● The Essential Jesus

show, as Paul affirms, that we are saved in hope (Rom. 8:24). And for the New Testament that hope, regardless of the language used to refer to or describe it, is that Jesus, as Saviour and Lord, will come again to consummate His salvific work and openly reveal His Lordship over all things. This is a major element in the pulse beat, the fiber, of New Testament faith. To eliminate it, either by outright rejection or existentialist reinterpretation, which makes the future entirely present, would be to lose the hope of the gospel and the goal of salvation history.

Imminence and the Second Advent

We have shown that in the New Testament the teaching that Jesus will return is pervasive and prominent. It must also be said, however, that in a certain sense it appears problematical.

The problem is related to the time of the second advent. Frequently the New Testament presents Christ's coming again not only as certain, but as near. For example, the idea of the last days, expressed in a variety of ways, is used of the period following the resurrection of Jesus and the coming of the Spirit. As Peter makes his speech on the day of Pentecost to explain the bestowal of the Spirit on the disciples, he claims that what took place was a fulfillment of the prophecy of Joel 2:28, 29. What makes his quotation from this passage especially noteworthy is the way Peter introduces it. The Hebrew text of Joel says "afterward" God's Spirit will be poured out, which the Septuagint (the Greek translation of the Hebrew Old Testament) renders "after these things." Peter, however, says, "In the last days, God says" (Acts 2:17). Thus, the last days are present in the events of Pentecost.

Similar expressions are found in a number of texts. According to 1 Corinthians 10:11, Old Testament references to judgment had been written down for use by Paul's readers, upon whom the end of the ages had come. 1 Timothy 4:1 and 2 Timothy 3:1 both refer to heretical teachings and practices already occurring in the first century as indicators of the latter or last times. Hebrews 1:2 and 9:26 equate God's revelation in Jesus and His sacrifice with the last days or the end of the age. 1 Peter 1:20 declares that Christ had been chosen before the creation of the world, but "revealed in these last times for your sake." In this text the beginning and the end of time are clearly contrasted. According to Jude 17-20 "in the last times" there would be "scoffers" who would "follow their own ungodly desires." It is clear that this refers to Jude's own time, for he says in verse 19 that these scoffers create (present tense) divisions, and they and their work are contrasted with the believers to whom Jude offers pastoral advice in verse 20. Jude's warning is parallel to 2 Peter 3:2-7 which similarly emphasizes the presence of scoffers in the last days who follow their own evil desires and deny the second coming of Christ (vs. 3, 4). Finally, 1 John declares that the presence in his own day of antichrist figures indicates that it is the "last hour" (2:18).

In addition to various statements speaking expressly about the last days, there are many others declaring in one way or another that the end is near. In Romans Paul asserts that salvation and "the day" are near, nearer than when his readers first believed (13:11, 12). He further states that God will shortly crush Satan under their feet (16:20). 1 Corinthians speaks of the shortness of time and the present dissolution of this world (7: 29, 31). Philippians explains that the Lord is near (4:5), James that the Lord is at hand, the Judge at the doors (5:8, 9), 1 Peter that the end of all things is at hand (4:7), and Revelation that the time is near, and Christ is coming soon (1:3; 3:11; 22:20).

It is easy to contemporize such statements and read them principally as relating to the twenty-first century. However, while the waiting may indeed be applied to us and to our time, the immediate contextual reference is to first-century Christians. They waited in hope of Christ's coming in their time. "Adventists" existed in the first century!

How can these many indications of early Christian belief that the last days were present and that Christ's coming was near be explained? In answering this question, two errors must be avoided: The first is that the early Christians were simply wrong and that their belief must be jettisoned, and second, that since they could not possibly have made any miscalculation, their statements must refer to times just ahead for twenty-first century believers. The following considerations suggest what may be a better approach.

First, with reference to the last days, what else could the early

Christians have believed in view of Christ's resurrection from the dead? Apocalyptic Judaism, which much affected early Christian thought, had come to believe that instead of there being one age of human history in which God would ultimately transform all things and effectively be present, there were two totally distinct, successive ages (2 Esdras 4:26, 27; 6:7, 8, 20; 7:28-32). Jesus Himself represented this position (Matt. 12:32; Luke 18:30). The first age was the present evil age, in which God's will did not prevail, but in which evil grew worse and worse, and the second, the age to come, which would inaugurate the new creation.

The resurrection of the dead was one of the outstanding markers indicating the transition from the present evil age to the age to come. Inasmuch as the early Christians believed that Christ, the representative man, had risen from the dead, He was the firstfruits of them that sleep (1 Cor.15:22). Thus in the midst of the old age, rather than at its end, the new age had begun, and its reality, already inaugurated, would be consummated at the return of Christ. What else could Christians call this period of time but the last days? It made good theological sense. If we are also in the last days, then in some meaningful sense Christ and the end are near for us as they were indeed for the early believers. There may be more to imminence than chronology (the horizontal dimension), for every day we live in the presence and by the Spirit of the Christ who will come (the vertical dimension). We feel the impingement of the coming Christ on our lives. If this is not the case, then all ages prior to the actual end of history, lacking close proximity to the chronological consummation of all things, would be unable to have any sense of imminence and any conviction of belief in the Parousia. For them "soon" would lose all meaning.

In response to the lengthening of time before the Parousia one can either revert to new chronological schemes or turn from chronology to Christology, the contemplation of Christ and His work. The latter is the only path to follow, for up to now every speculation about the time of Christ's coming has proven wrong. However, the truth about who Christ is and what God has done through Him is the basis for strong and continuing faith and hope.

Romans 5 is very helpful in this regard. In the first verses Paul teaches that justification by faith brings peace, continual access to

God's grace, and the hope of one day sharing the glory of God (vs. 1, 2). The certainty of this hope of future glorification and the grounds for it are expressed in verse 5, one of the most significant texts of Scripture: "And hope does not disappoint us, because God has poured out his love into our hearts by the Holy Spirit, whom he has given us." In other words, we may be certain of the fulfillment of our future hope by reason of what God has already done for us. God's love in our hearts through the Spirit is our guarantee of future inheritance. What is the content of that love which makes the future secure? Paul answers: It is the death of Christ for the weak and ungodly (v. 6), sinners (v. 8), and those hostile to God (v. 10). In this act God shows His love to us (v. 8). The conclusion is inevitable: If God was willing to give His Son to die even for enemies, how much more will He finally and fully save those who have become His friends (the reconciled) through that sacrifice (vs. 9, 10)? No matter how much time has passed or will pass before Jesus comes again, those who trust in Christ know that they will live with Him.

Furthermore, in the interim, believers have something to do that is vitally related to Christ's second coming. We are explicitly told that despite the sense of nearness deriving from the unfolding events of history (Mark 13:29, 30), it is not for us to know the times and seasons which the Father has under His own authority (Acts 1:11), and that no one knows the day or the hour (Mark 13:32). However, we are called to be His witnesses to the ends of the earth (Acts 1:8), taking the gospel to the whole world as a testimony to all nations. The completion of this mission will bring the end (Matt. 24:14). And as the gospel is proclaimed, in the outworking of God's time clock, which is different from ours "for him a thousand years are like a day" (2 Pet. 3:8), God is giving everyone time to come to repentance, for He wants no one to be lost. This, not that the Lord is being slow about His promise, is the truth that should be emphasized (v. 9).

Major New Testament Passages

We may now turn our attention to a few major New Testament passages that give special emphasis to the doctrine of Jesus' second coming.

1 Thessalonians 4:13-18

1 Thessalonians 4:13-18 is one such passage. This epistle is of particular significance since it is probably the earliest of the New
Testament writings, composed about A.D. 49 or 50. It is of great
interest to see what this first known Christian writing is concerned
with. After discussing personal matters in the first three chapters, the
focus of the letter shifts entirely to the return of Jesus. At the end of
chapter 3 a prayer introduces the subject matter in chapter 4. Paul
prays that the Thessalonians' love will increase and that they will be
found unblameable in holiness at the coming of Jesus (3:13).
Eschatology and ethics, the second advent and the character of
Christians in view of it, is what concerns the apostle here.

It is the same with Paul's prayer at the conclusion of the letter.
"May God himself, the God of peace, sanctify you through and
through. May your whole spirit, soul and body be kept blameless at
the coming of our Lord Jesus Christ" (5:23). Again eschatology and
ethics are prominent in Paul's supplication. He calls his converts to
holiness in readiness for the Lord's coming and rests that possibility
squarely on the fact that the God who called them is faithful and "will
do it" (v. 24).

It is within this prayerful context that Paul discusses the coming of
the Lord (4:13-18). His purpose is entirely practical—not to present
a detailed panorama of eschatological events, but to overcome
Thessalonian grief with the comfort of Christian hope. Paul's message is clear and simple. In essence he says: "Do not grieve (v. 13),
rather comfort one another (v. 18), because those of your fellowbelievers who have fallen asleep in Jesus (v. 14), and who hence
remain even in death in Christ (v. 16), will most certainly rise from
the dead at the Parousia and together with the living be forever with
the Lord (vs. 15-17)."

The Thessalonian believers had been grieving over those who had
died, apparently believing that unless one lived until Christ came he
or she would have no part with Christ.[3] It may well be that since they
believed the advent was near they worried that not to live until that
time meant that one was under God's wrath for some wrong. That
would then be the reason why Paul highlights deliverance from wrath

when he says of the newly converted Thessalonians that they were waiting for God's Son from heaven, "Jesus, who rescues us from the coming wrath" (1 Thess.1:10). This in turn harmonizes with what Paul says in chapter 5 in a passage which is parallel to 4:13-18: "For God did not appoint us to suffer wrath but to receive salvation through our Lord Jesus Christ. He died for us so that, whether we are awake or asleep, we may live together with him" (vs. 9-11).

Verse 14 is of fundamental importance as a summary of Paul's main point, namely, that all who believe will be with Christ after the resurrection. It shows that the fundamental realities of Christian faith, Jesus' death and resurrection, have a future orientation. What happened to Jesus is basic to and finds its fruition in the resurrection of believers at the coming of Christ. There is a material and insepa-rable connection between what happened to Christ long ago and what will happen to believers at the end of time. Jesus' resurrection, itself an eschatological event, demands the Parousia and the resurrection it brings. Christ's resurrection gives assurance that history will close with Christ and further resurrection, notwithstanding the time between the two events.

In verses15-17 Paul declares that what he will say comes not by human speculation but by divine revelation. He teaches that Christ's coming will be a personal event for "the Lord himself will come down from heaven" and a public event involving a shout of com-mand, an archangel's call, and a trumpet blast. Death will be chal-lenged by a command that cannot be resisted. The archangel's voice and the trumpet sound, associated in part with the idea of gathering,[4] speak here to the summoning of God's people. Christ will first call those whose death has brought great grief, and they, together with the living, will ascend to meet with the Lord in the air. The word employed for meeting the Lord (*apantesis*) is colorful. It was used in ancient times for meeting a dignitary en route to a town. As he drew near, the town gates would be opened and the citizens would stream forth to meet the arriving nobleman and in procession escort him to the town.[5] Thus, when Jesus comes again, the gates of this world and of death itself will open wide, and ascending believers will meet their descending Lord and be forever with Him.

Paul urges his readers to "encourage each other with these words"

(v. 18). This comfort is unlike that offered by those without Christian faith. From a second century A.D. letter we read:

> Irene to Taonnophris and Philo good comfort. I am as sorry and weep over the departed one as I wept for Didymas. And all things, whatsoever were fitting, I have done, and all mine. . . .But nevertheless against such things one can do nothing. Therefore comfort ye one another.[6]

Irene was right, we can do nothing about death, but Christ can, and that is what Paul's words are about. He offers believers a sure hope that transcends death, rather than a sense of resignation in the face of death. That is the message of 1 Thessalonians 4:13-18.

Mark 13, Matthew 24, Luke 21

With deep concern for His disciples in the tumultuous times that would follow His death Jesus discourses on the future. The tone of His discourse is apocalyptic in nature. Apocalyptic utterances and writings arose in connection with present or projected periods of severe suffering and trial. They were tracts for bad times, designed to give encouragement and inspire hope in view of God's coming great victory. Their central message is quite simple: Signs in earth and heaven show that God's deliverance of His persecuted people is near. The words of Jesus in Luke's account convey the idea exactly: "When these things begin to take place, stand up and lift up your heads, because your redemption is drawing near" (Luke 21:28).

Jesus' prophetic outline begins with a prediction of the complete destruction of the temple and culminates with the dissolution of the cosmic order and the coming of the Son of Man. The end of the temple and the end of the world are linked in each account, though most explicitly in Matthew. In Mark and Luke, in response to Jesus' temple prophecy, the disciples asked when it would happen and what sign would indicate that it was about to take place. In Matthew however, the question about "when" refers to the temple's destruction, but the sign concerns Jesus' coming and the end of the age. What is implicit in Mark and Luke is explicit in Matthew. For any Jew of the time the demise of the temple, the holiest place on earth because of God's presence there, could not but suggest the end of all things.

Consequently, in Jesus' address two periods are envisioned, the period prior to the overthrow of the temple and the period following it until the Son of Man comes. Utilizing details from all three Gospels, the precursors to the temple's overthrow include the appearance of false Christs and prophets, the threat of war, earthquakes, and famines, plagues on earth and portents in heaven, trials before high officials, persecution, apostasy, betrayal, and then, more significantly, the universal proclamation of the gospel (cf. Col.1:6, 23). A specific sign of the temple's end is sacrilege in the holy place or, as Luke describes the matter, the surrounding of Jerusalem by armies.

With the imminence of the destruction of Jerusalem and its temple, the signal to flee from Judea is given. This inaugurates a period of unparalleled tribulation which, according to Luke, includes the captivity of Israel and the trampling of Jerusalem by Gentiles. The tribulation is accompanied by the reappearance of false Christs and prophets who attempt to deceive the elect. Immediately succeeding the tribulation are disruptions in the heavens—sun and moon are darkened, the stars fall and the powers of heaven are shaken—and distress on earth over what is coming upon the world. On the heels of celestial and terrestrial chaos the Son of Man appears as a flash of lightning across the heavens. The tribes of earth mourn as they behold His power and glory, and the elect are gathered from every corner of earth.

What distinguishes Jesus' apocalyptic discourse from Jewish apocalypses of His era is the practical underpinning to all that He says. He is not merely forecasting the future, but is offering instruction and exhortation on what His followers should look out for, and how they should conduct themselves until He returns in glory. In Mark 13 there are no less than twenty imperatives telling them what to do or not to do. In four of these Jesus solemnly urges His disciples to take heed or beware. They are to beware of being deceived (v. 5), of being surprised at harsh treatment by authorities (v. 9), of forgetting Jesus' warnings of what was to come (v. 23), and of being lulled to sleep because of their uncertainty as to when the Lord would appear (vs. 33-36).

Accompanying the manifold need to take heed the disciples are to keep awake (v. 33) and, in the climactic word of the chapter, to watch. The sentence that contains the call to watch is especially significant due to its universal scope: "What I say to you [the disciples], I say to everyone: 'Watch!' "(v. 37). This summons to watch harmonizes with the fact that Jesus has made it crystal clear that no one knows the time of the advent (Mark 13:31-36; Matt. 24:36, 42; 25:13). Furthermore, according to Jesus, the advent will come unexpectedly (Mark 13:36; Matt. 24:37-39), and that is why readiness is needed (Matt. 24:44).

In Mark 13 Jesus also cautions His followers about being alarmed by wars and rumors of wars as if they proved the immediacy of the end when actually they are only the beginning of sufferings (vs. 7, 8). In addition, the disciples are not to believe those who announce the location to which Christ has come (v. 21)—He will not be found in any private place, reports Matthew; His coming will be as public as a lightning flash across the sky (24:26, 27). And, in view of family breakdown and betrayal, as well as hatred by all, the disciples are called to endure until the end (Mark 13:12, 13).

The parables of Matthew 25 that follow and give point to the discourse in chapter 24 further underline Jesus' practical concerns. Here Jesus' disciples, with their eyes on the advent, are called to be faithful to the Lord (vs. 45-51), ready for the Lord (25:1-13), and give compassionate service to the Lord by ministering to the needy, a criterion for acceptability in the final judgment by the Son of Man when He comes (vs. 31-46).

It is clear that the nature of discipleship in view of the end rather than isolated and esoteric knowledge of the end itself is what Jesus is concerned about. And while the signs should create a strong sense of nearness (Mark 13:29, 30), the equally strong awareness that no one knows the time (Mark 13:32; Matt.24:36, 42; 25:13) should lead to the conclusion that Jesus is concerned more with vigilance and readiness than speculation and calculation.[7]

John 14:1-3

While 1 Thessalonians 4:13-18 is probably the earliest New Testament statement about the return of Jesus, John 14:1-3 is one of the latest. In the former Paul, at the midpoint of the first century, speaks to a grieving church for its comfort. In the latter, John, near century's end, reports Jesus speaking to His troubled disciples for their comfort, a message directed to these disquieted disciples of

Jesus in John's own community and also to all who read his Gospel.

This important passage in John brings New Testament reflection on Jesus' coming to an advanced point. In non-apocalyptic terms, in contrast to Mark 13, Matthew 24, and Luke 21, John, whose basic emphasis is on Jesus as the bringer of eternal life in the present, focuses our attention upon the future coming of Christ. That the passage refers to Jesus' coming at the consummation of history, rather than a spiritual coming in the present, has been much debated, but it will be argued here, on the basis of evidence from the Gospel itself, that the eschatological future is indeed in view.

Jesus begins His farewell address with the words, "Do not let your hearts be troubled" (John 14:1). This exhortation to put away anxiety and fear is related to His announcement that same evening of His imminent departure: "My children, I will be with you only a little longer. . . .Where I am going, you cannot come" (13:33). To speak of Jesus going or going away is equivalent to speaking of His death and subsequent ascent to His Father in heaven. As recounted in John the disciples did not know what this going away meant. Peter asks, "Lord, where are you going?" (v. 36). The prospect of Jesus' impending departure filled them with fear. Thus He exhorts them to not be troubled. Later He expands this in the memorable words: "Peace I leave with you; my peace I give you. I do not give to you as the world gives. Do not let your hearts be troubled and do not be afraid" (14:27).

At the end of His discourse and in view of the persecution that would come upon them after His departure, Jesus says: "I have told you these things, so that in me you may have peace. In this world you will have trouble. But take heart! I have overcome the world" (16:33). Jesus has not yet gone to the cross, and yet He speaks as if from the other side of His resurrection! It is the victorious Jesus who speaks in the Gospel of John. That is why He can give encouragement.

The admonition to be without anxiety is followed by a challenge to believe in God *and* also in Jesus (14:1). Faith in Jesus as well as in the Father is crucial and is the answer to the disciples' distress. In John's thought faith in Jesus is not a mere addendum to faith in God, but is integral to such faith. According to John, understanding of God before Jesus came was inadequate. Jesus is the full and indispensable

246 • The Essential Jesus

revelation of God. Thus Jesus' words may be paraphrased to say: "Have faith in God by having faith in me." This means that Christology (understanding Christ) is the key to theology (understanding God). Jesus' call to faith comes down to this: Faith is the answer to fear. As He says in Mark 5:36: "Don't be afraid; just believe."

We now know *who* we are to believe, but *what* should we believe? The answer is simple. Just as surely as Jesus is going to the Father, believing disciples may know that ultimately they also will dwell with the Father: "In my Father's house are many rooms" (John 14:2). As Son, Jesus' place with the Father is permanent (8:35); so also for those who belong to the Son. There is not only one dwelling place in the Father's house (for the Son) but many places (room enough for all).

Furthermore, the Son is going away to make ready these places, and will return to take His disciples to them "that you also may be where I am" (14:3). This statement represents the high point in what Jesus has said thus far. To His troubled disciples He promises that though it is necessary for Him to depart, He will come again and welcome them into an everlasting union with Himself in the Father's "house." In this connection one is reminded of a saying in the book of 1 Enoch (much beloved by Jews of the intertestamental period): "With him [the Son of Man] shall be their dwelling places and with him their heritage, and they shall not be separated from him for ever and ever and ever" (71:16).[8]

Jesus had said, "In my Father's house are many rooms." Where is the house and what are the rooms? The house can be nothing other than heaven, the dwelling place of God (Ps. 2:4; 33:13, 14; Isa. 63:15; Eccl.5:1, 2) for, as several texts in John point out, Jesus is returning to the Father (7:33; 13:1,3; 14:28; 16:5, 10, 28; 17:11, 13) from whom He had come (8:42). As for the rooms, these should not be thought of as "mansions" (KJV) in the modern sense. The picture of heaven is that of one "house" with many abiding places. This can be seen in John 14:23 where the same word occurs as in 14:2. Jesus says, "If anyone loves me, he will obey my teaching. My Father will love him, and we will come to him and make our *home* with him." The word mansion would not fit here; it is clear that the sense of a dwelling place is intended. The wonderful promise is that if we love

Christ, He and the Father will take residence in us here and now. And as surely as it is true that God dwells in us in this world, we can be confident that we will have a dwelling place with God in His heavenly world.

A crucial problem that arises, however, has to do with the specific reference in Jesus' statement, "I will come again." Does this refer to the final Parousia of early Christian expectation? There is a divergence of views here. Some say, "Yes," others speak ambivalently, some talk of a reinterpretation of the early Parousia hope, and still others deny the Parousia reference altogether. In my judgment, the text *does* point to the future Parousia, and this is not nullified by reinterpreting the text according to the meaning that the "coming" of Jesus carries elsewhere in the following Johannine passages (14:18-23, 28; 16:16-22). C. H. Dodd was one of those who read John 14:2, 3 in the light of these other passages. For example, having spoken of 14:3 and then 14:19, 20 he says:

> By now it is surely clear that the "return" of Christ is to be understood in a sense different from that of popular Christian eschatology. It means that after the death of Jesus, and because of it, His followers will enter into union with Him as their living Lord, and through Him with the Father, and so enter into eternal life. That is what He meant when He said, "I will come again and receive you to myself, that where I am you too may be" (cf. also 17:24). This is the true epiphany, and it is essentially an epiphany of the love of God, as the evangelist has set forth clearly and emphatically in 14:21-24.[9]

Now, it must be admitted that the discussions concerning Jesus' coming in John 14:18-23, 28 and 16:16-22 refer primarily to His resurrection appearances that inaugurate the era of the Spirit and the spiritual communion of the believer with the Son and the Father. The final Parousia does not seem to be in view. That this is so is suggested by a number of considerations:

1. Each of the passages referring to the coming of Jesus is preceded by a passage dealing with the coming of the Paraclete or Holy Spirit:

Coming of the Spirit	Coming of Jesus
14:14-17	14:18-24
14:25, 26	14:27, 28
15:26; 16:7-15	16:16-22

It is hardly accidental that the coming of the Spirit and the coming of Jesus are so often placed in juxtaposition. There must be a fundamental relationship. This is particularly clear in John 14:16ff. After the promise that the Paraclete is to be with the disciples forever (v. 16), dwelling with and in them (v. 17), Jesus declares: "I will not leave you as orphans; I will come to you" (v. 18).

2. The coming of Jesus in 14:18ff. has the marks of an inward rather than an outward event. Commandment-keeping love on the part of the disciple is the condition for relationship with the Son and the Father. Where this love is shown, the Son and the Father reciprocate with love. This leads to the manifestation of the Son to the believer and the coming of the Father and the Son to make their dwelling with the believer (14:21, 23).

3. The world does not see this manifestation of Christ, only believers (14:19, 22).

4. In 16:16ff. Jesus says that in a little while His disciples would no longer see Him, but in a little while they would see Him again, an event which would turn their grief into joy. It is difficult to resist the conclusion that this passage is speaking primarily of the resurrection appearances of Jesus that followed His death.[10]

It seems clear that the "coming" passages of 14:18-23 and 16:16-22 refer to that first Easter and the subsequent coming of the Father, Son, and Spirit to abide with the believer. But does this mean that the same significance is to be attached to the promise of the coming contained in 14:2, 3? I think not. Christ's reception of His disciples in 14:3 goes beyond the "you will see me" and "I will see you" of 16:16, 22 and brings this seeing to an end. The promise of a heavenly dwelling and being with Christ is different from the promise of that joy in seeing Christ that will overcome the grief of the disciples in being separated from him (16:20, 22). The opening verses of John 14 are more easily understood as the promise of a once-for-all future return of Christ to take the disciples to Himself and the heavenly home He has made ready for them. The language of this section is different from 14:18ff and 16:16ff. For example, in 14:2, 3 the Father and Son make their dwelling place on earth with the believer, whereas in 14:2, 3 the believer enters his dwelling place in heaven with Christ.

More significantly, there is a real affinity in thought between John 14:2, 3 and 1 Thessalonians 4:13-18. Even allowing for the differences involved in the fact that the Johannine passage does not use the apocalyptic symbolism Paul employs, and that it does not speak of the resurrection as Paul does in 1 Thessalonians 4 (though John does teach the future resurrection in 5:28, 29), the following similarities between the passages are present: (1) Jesus' coming inaugurates the period of blessedness; (2) the believers are taken to the Lord; (3) the essence of the future life is being with Christ. These similarities certainly do not suggest any dependence of John on Paul, but they do show that John also could proclaim the early Christian message of the Parousia, and that he, notwithstanding all his difference of emphasis, stands in continuity with the recent theological past of the developing church.

If it is granted that the "I will come back" of John 14:3 does refer to the final Parousia, a further problem arises: How can John in the very same discourses speak of the coming of Christ in two different ways? How can he emphasize so strongly that a coming is realized in the appearances of the risen Lord, in the giving of the Spirit, and in the fellowship of the believer with the Son and the Father, and yet in John 14:1-3 refer to the coming at the end-time? Can the coming be both present and future?

Such a question has to do not only with the passage under consideration but also with other texts in John. For it is clear that while John's great emphasis falls on the present, he can still place in the future those very elements that he has so vividly described as present (or past). Examples are as follows: The one who does not believe is judged already (3:18, 19) and the wrath of God abides upon him (v. 36); nevertheless, he will come forth in a resurrection of judgment (5:29) and Christ's words will be his judge on the last day (12:48). Again, Christ is the resurrection and the life (11:25), the believer has passed from death to life (5:24), and "a time is coming and *has now come* when the dead will hear the voice of the Son of God and those who hear will live"(v. 25). Indeed, with regard to life and resurrection, Jesus declares: "Whoever eats my flesh and drinks my blood *has* eternal life, and I *will* raise him up at the last day" (6:54). Here the paradox of present and future is expressed in the very same sentence! In John 21:22, 23, which many take to be a Johannine addition to the Gospel of John, the future coming seems plainly intended. In view of the evidence, the conclusion seems inevitable: While John has a very strong "already," he still retains a genuine and significant "not yet."

If we accept this, and the varying materials in John point in this direction, we may also take encouragement from the fact that other parts of the Johannine literature similarly point to the future, and, in so doing, lend support to its presence in the Gospel of John. In relation to the final Parousia it may be noted that 1 John reflects a number of those elements that in the Gospel are bound up with the present coming of Christ to the believer, for example fellowship with the Father and His Son Jesus Christ (1:3); the mutual indwelling of believers with the Father and the Son (2:24, 27); that commandment-keeping love and the presence of the Spirit which make this union possible (3:24; 4:16,13). Yet this epistle also points forward to the time of Christ's Parousia (2:28; 3:2). He can also speak of the coming day of judgment (4:17) and of his time as "the last hour" (2:18).

In conclusion, the promise of the future Parousia is a key element in a reoriented picture of eschatological hope that John draws. John's reinterpretation is that the Parousia which the Church looked for only at the end is something that has three tenses: past, present, and future. John speaks not merely of the Christ who will come at the end but of the Christ who comes from now on, beginning with the resurrection and the coming of the Spirit, and consummating in His final return for His own. In all this, however, John's main focus is on the period that lies between the time when Christ came unto His own and His own received Him not and the time when He comes to His own and receives them into the heavenly kingdom. This middle time is also eschatological time, and it is filled with the presence of the coming Christ. It is the time in which we live as we await the final coming of the Saviour.

Jesus: Mediator, Intercessor and High Priest

It is one thing to accept the New Testament message that Jesus is coming again. It is quite another to know that we will be accepted by Him when He returns. Jesus Himself asked the relevant question:

"When the Son of Man comes, will he find faith on the earth?" (Luke 18:8). This question was not about faith in general, but is quite specific. The context in which the question is asked is the parable in Luke 18:1-8 in which Jesus admonishes His disciples that they should pray continually without giving up (v. 1). The parable depicts a widow before whose persistent cries for justice a judge finally says, "I will see that she gets justice" (v. 5). Jesus counsels the disciples to take note of the statement of the unjust judge.

The point of the parable is that if an unjust judge will finally yield to a widow's persistent pleas and deliver her from her adversary, will not God, who stands in contrast to such a judge, provide deliverance for His chosen ones who cry out to Him continually? Jesus asserts that God will ensure that His people are quickly delivered. Then comes Jesus' question as to whether the Son of Man will find faith on the earth when He comes. The issue is clear: At the second coming will God's people have faith that, in response to their prayers, they will be delivered by the Son of Man? Or will they doubt? Human weakness makes people wonder if they will be saved at the end of time. And when one considers that Jesus is not only Saviour but Judge (e.g. Matt. 25:31-36), the question might well be: Who will be able to stand on the day of his wrath? (Rev. 6:17). The issue thus becomes: How can one have the assurance of salvation now and at the second advent? It is here that the New Testament vision of Christ as mediator, intercessor, and priest is of inestimable value.

This concept of Christ as mediator is of fundamental significance in 1 Timothy 2:3-6. In this passage God is pictured as a Saviour who desires everyone to be saved. Such salvation is made possible by the fact that between God and humankind there is one mediator, Christ Jesus, who gave Himself as a ransom for all. This assertion was probably intended to counter three prevalent Gnostic beliefs: that there were many powers standing between God and the world; the docetic[11] view that Christ was not truly human; and the idea that salvation comes through esoteric knowledge possessed by only a few. Christ's mediatorial role, however, is grounded in the fact that He gave Himself as a ransom for all people. The concepts of mediator and sacrifice are connected. 1 Timothy does not say more, but the connection is fully established in the book of Hebrews.[12]

That Christ is mediator and intercessor is also hinted at in Romans 5 and made explicit in Romans 8. According to Romans 5:2, it is through Jesus Christ that we have gained access to grace, and this is the basis for the joyful hope of future glorification. The word "access" in this text makes one think of Christ's mediatorial ministry in heaven and the realities spelled out in the related text, Hebrews 4:16: "Let us then approach the throne of grace with confidence, so that we may receive mercy and find grace to help us in our time of need."

Also in Romans 5 there are parallel thoughts that now that we have been justified or reconciled by Christ's death, we can be sure that we will be saved from the day of wrath (v. 9) by Christ's life (v. 10). The life that is spoken of here is not the earthly life of Christ, as if Paul argued backwards from the cross to Christ's life. This will not do, for Paul is the theologian of the cross and resurrection. He is moving forward in verse 10 from the cross to Christ's risen life.

This movement is spelled out in Romans 8:31-34. Paul opens this passage with the question, "If God is for us, who can be against us?" He continues by delineating the content of the "for us" and that of the "against us." In the course of his exposition he asks who there is to condemn us (v. 34) and answers with a series of statements, each of which is qualified by "for us" at the end of the verse: Christ died for us; He rose for us; He is at the right hand of God for us; He is interceding for us. Here is how we are saved by Christ's risen life. He is at God's right hand and is making intercession on our behalf. In the light of His cross and resurrection He represents us before God. There can be no doubt about the outcome; it is the same as found in chapter 8:1: "There is now no condemnation for those who are in Christ Jesus."

The epistle to the Hebrews presents the most complete New Testament picture of the priestly work of Christ. It is designed to promote the efficacy of Christ's atoning sacrifice and the necessity of holding on to it, for through Christ's sacrificial offering alone can complete assurance of salvation be found. That Christ is a high priest is explicitly stated nine times (2:17; 3:1; 4:14, 15; 5: 5, 10; 6:20; 7:26; 8:1; 9:11); is implicit two times (7:28; 8:13); and for the six times He is called a priest (5:6; 7:16, 17, 21) contextual associations show clearly that the term refers to His high priestly ministry. Obviously, every high priest is a priest, but not every priest is a high priest. In Hebrews Jesus is presented exclusively as a high priest, and that means that His heavenly ministry is related to the Day of Atonement and its significance.

The high priestly ministry of Jesus has been in focus since the opening verses of the epistle. After affirming that the Son is the ultimate revelation of God, the Creator of all things, and the exact representation of God's being (1:1-3), Hebrews goes on to say that when the Son "had provided purification for sins, he sat down at the right hand of the Majesty in heaven" (v. 3). Clearly, Christ is thought of here as high priest (in analogy with the high priests in Old Testament times who made purification for sins (Lev. 16:19, 30) and as possessing the kingly authority of God. When the text says that He made purification for sins and sat down, this finds a parallel in Hebrews 10:12 where Jesus, in contrast to the earthly priests and their repetitive sacrifices, offered one sacrifice for sins for all time (cf 9:25), and then sat down at the right hand of God.

There are other parallels as well. According to Hebrews 9:25, 26 Christ as high priest did away with sin by the sacrifice of Himself. This in turn finds its counterpart in 9:28 where it is written that "Christ was sacrificed once to take away the sins of many people." Indeed, the efficacy of Christ's offering of His own blood was so great that it obtained not a temporary remission of sins but "eternal redemption" (9:12; cf 5:9 which speaks of "eternal salvation").

The message comes through clearly and emphatically that no believer need fear, but can have utmost confidence due to the work of Christ, his high priest, who has "entered heaven itself, now to appear for us in God's presence" (9:24). It is to that very presence that Christ's sacrifice takes us. Jesus is at the right hand of the throne of God (12:2), and it is there that we are bidden to come with boldness and receive the grace we need (4:16). It is there that we may place our hope "as an anchor for the soul, firm and secure" (6:19). Because Christ lives forever, He has a permanent priesthood" (7:24) and thus "is able to save completely those who come to God through him, because he always lives to intercede for them" (v. 25).

Moreover, we may have complete assurance not only because

Christ is our heavenly high priest but also because what qualified Him to be priest was that He shared in our humanity. He who is not ashamed to call us brothers (2:12) had to be made like His siblings in every way and be temptable in every way as they are "though he did not sin" so that He might become a merciful and faithful high priest, able to help those who are tempted and to sympathize with their weaknesses (2:17, 18; 4:15). Being thus fully qualified to be our high priest, He became the source of eternal salvation to all who obey Him (5:7-9). It is for this reason that we are exhorted to approach God's throne of grace with assurance and find all the help we need in times of difficulty (v. 16). It was such assurance that led Charles Wesley to write one of his most confident hymns:

> Arise, my soul, arise, shake off thy guilty fears,
> The holy sacrifice in my behalf appears;
> Before the throne my Saviour stands,
> My name is written on His hands.

The completion of Christ's high priestly ministry brings us back again to the promise and the hope of His second coming and the eternal salvation that event will bring to full and final fruition. Hebrews states it thus: "Christ was sacrificed once to take away the sins of many people; and he will appear a second time, not to bear sin, but to bring salvation to those who are waiting for him" (9:28). Christ has been ministering as high priest; now He returns as King. And so we who still wait for Him can say confidently, as did first-century Christians, "Amen. Come, Lord Jesus" (Rev. 22:20).

For Further Reading

J. T. Carroll, *The Return of Jesus in Early Christianity*. Peabody, MA: Hendricksen, 2000.

C. Holman, *Till Jesus Comes: Origins of Apocalyptic Expectation*. Peabody, MA: Hendricksen, 1996.

W. G. Johnsson, *In Absolute Confidence: The Book of Hebrews Speaks to Our Day*. Nashville, TN: Southern Publishing Association, 1979.

A. L. Moore, *The Parousia in the New Testament*. Leiden: E. J. Brill, 1966.

V. N. Olsen, ed., *The Advent Hope in Scripture and History*. Washington, D.C.: Review and Herald Publishing Association, 1987.

S. H. Travis, *I Believe in the Second Coming of Jesus*. London, Hodder and Stoughton, 1982.

Notes

1. In the course of this chapter, I will argue that on the basis of textual evidence in the Gospel of John that 14:1-3 refers to the coming of Christ at the end of time.
2. The word "day" occurs frequently in relation to the second coming, deriving from the concept of the day of the Lord in the Old Testament. Hence, the day of the Lord (1 Thess. 5:2), the day of our Lord Jesus Christ (1 Cor. 1:8), the day of Christ (Phil. 2:16), the Son of Man in His day (Luke 17:24), the day of God (2 Pet. 3:12), the day of redemption (Eph. 4:30), the last day (John 6:39), the great day (Jude 6), that day (2 Thess. 1:10), the day (Rom. 13:12).
3. Cf. Ellen G. White, *The Acts of the Apostles* (Mountain View, CA: Pacific Press Publishing Assn., 1911), p. 258.
4. See Matt. 24:31 and 1 Cor. 15:52.
5. See E. Peterson, "Die Einholung des Kyrios (1 Th IV, 17)," *Zeitschrift fur systematische Theologie 7* (1929-30), pp. 682-702; F. F. Bruce, *1 and 2 Thessalonians, Word Biblical Commentary* 45 (Waco, TX: Word Books, 1982), pp. 102, 103.
6. Adolf Deissmann, *Light from the Ancient East,* trans. Lionel R. M. Strachan (Grand Rapids,MI: Baker, 1965), p. 176.
7. Re. the practical significance of the discourse in Mark 13 for the life of the church, see William L. Lane, *Commentary on the Gospel of Mark, The New International Commentary on the New Testament,* ed. F. F. Bruce (Grand Rapids, MI: Eerdmans,1974), pp. 446-448.
8. Translation by R. H. Charles in *The Apocrypha and Pseudepigrapha of the Old Testament,* II (Oxford: Oxford University Press, 1913), p. 237.
9. C. H. Dodd, *The Interpretation of the Fourth Gospel* (Cambridge: Cambridge University Press, 1960), p. 405.
10. A number of themes in these passages stand out: the troubled and fearful hearts of the disciples (John14:27); the coming (vs. 18ff., 28); seeing the Lord (16:16ff.); peace (14:27); joy (16:22); the coming of the Spirit (14:14-17, 25, 26; 15:26; 16:7-15). These same themes reappear in John 20 in relation to the first resurrection appearance of Christ: "On the evening of that first day of the week, when the disciples were together, with the doors locked for *fear* of the Jews, Jesus *came* and stood among them and said, *Peace* be with you! After he said this, he showed them his hands and side. The disciples were *overjoyed* when they *saw* the Lord. Again Jesus said, '*Peace* be with you! As the Father has sent me, I am sending you.' And with that he breathed on them and said, '*Receive the Holy Spirit*'" (John 20:19-22, emphases supplied).
11. Docetism, one of the heresies of the early centuries, regarded the humanity and suffering of Jesus as apparent rather than real.
12. Christ's mediatorial ministry in Hebrews is implicit in His priestly activity. However, three times in Hebrews He is explicitly called mediator (8:6; 9:15; 12:24). In each of these cases He is called the mediator of a better or new covenant, which in 13:20 is called the eternal covenant.

The Victorious Jesus
Jan Paulsen

One of the most important and recurring themes of the biblical revelation is the conflict between good and evil. Beginning in the very early chapters of Genesis with the warning that enmity would persist between the serpent and the seed of the woman (Gen.3:15), it culminates in the closing chapters of Revelation with the eventual triumph of good and the destruction of evil. This conflict portrays opposing forces and envisages repeated confrontations at many different levels. It anticipates deception, discouragement, even defeat at points along the way—but ultimately victory and a victor. In biblical teaching and Christian belief, Jesus is that Victor. Speaking specifically of the "crushing defeat" inflicted on the enemy at Calvary, Michael Green asserts "Christ is the conqueror over all the power of the Enemy."[1] And to draw on the triumphant title of Gustav Aulen's important book, *Christus Victor,* it is Christ who emerges as conqueror and who carries the ages. He will be, indeed already is, victorious over the amassed forces of evil, and those who are Christ's are victorious with Him.

In this chapter we examine briefly a few of the more important aspects of Christ's triumph, many already accomplished, some yet to be seen.

Prophetic Projections of the Coming Victor

The concept of a returning, victorious leader is one that evokes great longing in a people held in captivity. The anticipation of a coming Messiah in the prophetic books of the Old Testament gave much meaning and purpose to those who suffered, whose daily lives were filled with pain and injustice, sorrow and disappointment. That one day this present time of oppression and tragedy would be transformed by the arrival of the Victor gave hope and reassurance through successive generations. They found comfort in the promise that God had not forgotten His people and that they would have a future: "For I know the plans I have for you," declares the Lord, "plans to prosper you and not to harm you, plans to give you hope and a future" (Jer. 29:11).

This assured promise of the divine guarantor is not only linked to a temporal salvation and rescue of the oppressed. The conquering Victor also returns to re-establish the rule of right, to restore truth and to remedy the wrongs of the former era:

> "See, I will send my messenger, who will prepare the way before me. Then suddenly the Lord you are seeking will come to his temple; the messenger of the covenant, whom you desire, will come," says the Lord Almighty. . . . "So, I will come near to you for judgment. I will be quick to testify against sorcerers, adulterers and perjurers, against those who defraud laborers of their wages, who oppress the widows and the fatherless, and deprive aliens of justice, but do not fear me," says the LORD Almighty (Mal. 3:1,5).

This is the response to a continued cry for truth and right, for God to usher in a kingdom that is not based on the present world's evil ways.

Habakuk best exemplifies this desperate appeal for God, the anticipated Victor, to speed the implementation of His kingdom and restore justice and righteousness:

> How long, O Lord, must I call for help, but you do not listen? Or cry out to you, "Violence!" but you do not save? Why do you make me look at injustice? Why do you tolerate wrong? Destruction and violence are before me; there is strife, and conflict abounds. Therefore the law is paralyzed, and justice never prevails. The wicked hem in the righteous, so that justice is perverted (Hab. 1:2-4).

The arrival of Messiah as the victorious One will remedy this intolerable situation. These assurances of God address both present realities and future longings, providing confidence and trust in the omnipotence of God and His assured intervention. In the words of the eighth-century B. C. prophet Isaiah, "In that day the deaf will hear the words of the scroll, and out of gloom and darkness the eyes of the blind will see" (Isa. 29:18; see also 35:3-10). We can already detect in these prophetic projections of the coming Victor, hopes that go beyond the boundaries of Israel and the constraints of the time.

These principles of Old Testament anticipation can be projected even into the present age. That God Himself is also distraught over the condition of the world is a truth we need to reaffirm. All the unfairness, injustice, and evil then existent, or current in our present world, are not part of God's eternal purpose. The world needs to know that He intervenes to reestablish His rule of truth and right. The words of a prophetic message, familiar to many, project that hope right into our own time: "In the time of those kings, the God of heaven will set up a kingdom that will never be destroyed, nor will it be left to another people. It will crush all those kingdoms and bring them to an end, but it will itself endure forever" (Dan. 2:44).

The grand theme here is *intervention*. God is not sitting idly by, He is not unmoved by the present pain, suffering, and distress. He purposes to destroy the works of evil. He is there to hold men, women, and children close to Himself and ultimately to set them free and share with them His victory over every evil force. Daniel again points to the future:

> In my vision at night I looked, and there before me was one like a son of man, coming with the clouds of heaven. He approached the Ancient of Days and was led into his presence. He was given authority, glory and sovereign power; all peoples, nations and men of every language worshiped him. His dominion is an everlasting dominion that will not pass away, and his kingdom is one that will never be destroyed (Dan. 7:13, 14; see also Mic. 5:4; Hag. 2:7; Zech. 3:8; 6:12, 13; 9:8, 9).

One noted Old Testament scholar concludes from his survey of Daniel's prophetic message, "In the latter days the God of heaven will erect a kingdom that will never be destroyed." Although there will be hardship, oppression, even persecution, for God's people "the Messiah will come, and the eternal kingdom will be established."[2] It is this reassuring message of ultimate victory that is as appropriate for today's generation as it was for those who first heard the words of the prophets in the pre-Christian centuries of Old Testament oppression.

Jesus' Perception of His Own Role as Victor

The arrival of Jesus is the arrival of the Victor. This is true regardless of the passing of many centuries. In Christ the victory is already accomplished—it is irrefutably and irrevocably won.

His Own Statements

In announcing His mission at the beginning of His ministry Jesus states precisely:

> "The Spirit of the Lord is on me, because he has anointed me to preach good news to the poor. He has sent me to proclaim freedom for the prisoners and recovery of sight for the blind, to release the oppressed, to proclaim the year of the Lord's favor." Then he rolled up the scroll, gave it back to the attendant and sat down. The eyes of everyone in the synagogue were fastened on him, and he said to them, "Today this scripture is fulfilled in your hearing" (Luke 4:18-21).

With considered deliberation Jesus applied the words of the prophet to Himself. "I am He," Jesus is saying. "I am the Victor, I am the One you have waited for, the One of whom the prophets have spoken. Through My work the chains of darkness will be broken, the blinded eyes will see once more, and through Me you will receive both physical and spiritual healing." But there is more. Jesus knew very well that all could not be accomplished immediately or in the manner many of His hearers expected. So He also says, in effect, "I care about the *now*, but I also care about the *future*."

Mark's record of Jesus' proclaiming the arrival of God's kingdom has long been understood as a recognition by Jesus of His kingdom role. One writer clearly brings together this connection between the present and the future in the work of Jesus:

> According to Mark Jesus announced the nearness of God's reign to be the "gospel of God.". . . . Mark understood this to be a prediction. God is about to reveal a glorious reign of justice and mercy that has been hidden until now in suffering. Luke understood this to be a declaration. God has begun to reign in the ministry of Jesus, and the future will look like the dominion of this Lord and Messiah.[3]

Whether now or in the future, victory is inherent in Jesus. It may or may not be immediate, but it *will* be.

The "I am" statements of Jesus in the Gospel of John reinforce this self-identification. "I am the bread of life." "I am the light of the world." "I am from above." "Before Abraham was born, I am." "I am the gate for the sheep." "I am the good shepherd." "I am the resurrection and the life." "I am the way, the truth and the life." "I am in the Father." "I am the true vine."[4] These amazing assertions come from the lips of the consummate Victor, the One who also says, "Anyone who has seen me has seen the Father" (14:9). Not only do we see in the face of Jesus the victorious One, we see God as He truly is. Moreover, Jesus' victory is the victory of God Himself.

Commenting on one of these profound "I am" claims of Jesus, the New Testament Greek scholar, R. C. H. Lenski, captures the sense of self-awareness and shared victory inherent in them all. Pointing out that Jesus' claim to be the way to the Father summarizes all His teaching and work, Lenski declares:

> Only this ONE Way takes us to the Father. The astounding thing is that this way is a person, this one person. This is not a dead road that one travels with his own strength, but a way such as never existed on earth, that picks us up in its arms and carries us to the destination. . . . This way, we may venture to say, is like a vast stream which takes our little boat and with its flood-power bears it to the ocean.[5]

The victory inherent in Christ is not, in the end, primarily of a national or political nature. It comes to bear principally on the realm of the human spirit, each individual human spirit. All Christ's "I am" claims are ultimately for others—for us.

That the contemporaries of Jesus had come to misunderstand the role of the Messiah as that of a nationalistic hero, a Maccabean-style leader who would throw off the yoke of Roman oppression, should not blind us to the wider and conclusive role played by Christus Victor. The prophetic expectation of Messiah was indeed to set right what had been wronged, to restore true spiritual values, to set prisoners free, to open the eyes of the blind. From the time of Jesus' declaration in the synagogue at Nazareth we see exactly that—a tearing down of the evil works of the prince of this world and the establishment of the kingdom where righteousness dwells.

The message Jesus sent to convince John the Baptist of His authenticity focused on the results already achieved by Christ as Victor. Tell John, He said, that "the blind receive sight, the lame walk, those who have leprosy are cured, the deaf hear, the dead are raised, and the good news is preached to the poor" (Matt. 11:5). But Christ conquers more than the evil forces of His own day. As Aulen says, "Christ—Christus Victor—fights against and triumphs over the evil powers of the world, the 'tyrants' under which mankind is in bondage and suffering, and in him God reconciles the world to himself."[6] Christ's conquest began in His own day with victory over human suffering and has continued ever since with countless victories in countless human lives. It was thus that He understood his mission.

Demonstrations of Fulfillment

Such a perspective sums up the way in which Christ defined His ministry—helping those around to recognize the divine impact. In the Gospels, Jesus sought to demonstrate to the dull and slow-to-believe disciples something of the true nature of this person among them: the vanquisher of evil, the One who had come to undo the structures of evil, the One before whom evil and its architect stand judged and doomed. The originator of evil may for a few fleeting moments be perceived as the "prince of this world," but he is only a supplanter who has usurped the rulership of this world. Over against Jesus Christ he has nothing to offer. Jesus said of him: "The prince of this world is coming. He has no hold on me" (John 14:30). In His monumental battle with the devil—the temptations in the wilderness—Jesus again and again refutes the devil's claims to supremacy and lordship.

Maybe the most dramatic presentation of this truth is seen in the passion of Christ, especially in the cosmic war waged in the garden of Gethsemane. In the death struggle of Jesus we recognize the climactic conflict, the hosts of evil arraigned against the suffering servant. Yet despite the consolidated attacks of the evil one, the righteous servant is victorious, and though He dies, His triumphant resurrection assures final and cataclysmic success when "death is swallowed up in victory" (1 Cor. 15:4). Christ's primary work is the conquest of evil through a complete demonstration of God as He truly is. In contrast to the lies of the devil, whose accusations lie at the heart of the great controversy, Jesus lives the truth of God in His fullness. He is not as the devil has painted Him, and through this supreme victory of Gethsemane and the cross, He demonstrates not simply the might and power of God, but His own true spirit and commitment to redeem and save.

With regard to the divine victory we must not miss the significance of the Gethsemane experience:

> Amid the awful darkness, apparently forsaken of God, Christ had drained the last dregs in the cup of human woe. In those dreadful hours He had relied upon the evidence of His Father's acceptance heretofore given Him. He was acquainted with the character of His Father; He understood His justice, His mercy, and His great love. . . . By faith, Christ was victor.[7]

There is thus great meaning in the pre-passion words of Jesus. He says, "*Now* is the time for judgment on this world; *now* the prince of this world will be driven out" (John 12:31, emphasis supplied). "The prince of this world *now* stands condemned" (16:11, emphasis supplied). Lenski declares, "The devil receives his doom in the death and the resurrection of Jesus." It is not, he says, "a gradual pressing back of his control that runs its course through the centuries," but "a sudden dethronement in the hour that is now at hand."[8]

It is *now!* The defeat is so sure, so complete, and so final that the victory is absolutely certain. And it is this victorious Christ that we follow, supremely confident in Him. Jesus is now seated at the right hand of the Father. All has been entrusted to Him. Jesus has already overcome; He has destroyed the foundation of evil. It's history! So He says again, "I have told you these things, so that in me you may have peace. In this world you will have trouble. But take heart! I have overcome the world" (John 16:33).

It is more than of passing interest that Jesus said in His prayer to the Father before He went to the cross, "I have finished the work" (John 17:4, KJV). He was very positive even though He had not yet been crucified. And on the cross He said again, "It is finished" (19:30). Jesus' thinking was objectively victorious. He knew that the outcome of the conflict was now settled. By His suffering, death, and resurrection Jesus is the assured Victor. Already the enemy and his whole philosophy are defeated. So, speaking proleptically, Jesus views the end-time conclusion as vividly real in the present, for He has totally vanquished the rebellion of sin and vindicated God before the universe. Therefore, He says to His followers "Take heart! I have overcome the world" (16:33).

The Apostolic and Early Church View of Christ as Victor

The reality of the cosmic powers of evil is something of which the New Testament is very conscious. Paul speaks of the Christian battle against "the powers of this dark world" and "spiritual forces of evil in the heavenly realms" (Eph.6:12).[9] In the words of Robert Webber, "their debilitating effect on human life and on political, economic, social, institutional, and family structures" is all too evident.[10] Over against these forces of evil the apostles and the early church clearly saw Christ as the Victorious One. As such He becomes the centerpiece of human history—the only solution to human trauma, suffering, and defeat. It was clear to these early believers that the reason for Christ's coming was "to destroy the devil's work" (1 John 3:8). They believed that He did it, that He does it still, and that He will complete it.

The unanimous voice of the early church declares that the devil's work in rebelling against God, in perverting His creation, in charging God with tyranny and as possessing a hostile and arbitrary character—with all its consequences for this fallen planet—is destroyed by Christus Victor. The victorious Christ answers the devil's charges, denies the devil's claims to authority, and breaks the power of the devil over his enslaved followers. Based on Christ's claim to have bound the devil (Matt. 12:22-29), the early believers were quite clear that Jesus had power over evil because He had entered the domain of evil, confronted and arrested its source. Hence, "having disarmed the powers and authorities, he [Christ] made a public spectacle of them, triumphing over them by the cross" (Col. 2:15).

The cross is the center of this victory theme. The assertions of the apostles and the early church are those of transformation—for the object of persecution becomes the means of salvation. In the ultimate irony, the crucified One is the Victor, for the cross, the symbol of shame and oppression, is made the defining emblem of victory and redemption. Instead of being the weapon of defeat, the cross is transformed into the most meaningful sign of God's sovereign power and victory:

> And being found in appearance as a man, he humbled himself and became obedient to death—even death on a cross! Therefore God exalted him to the highest place and gave him the name that is above every name (Phil. 2:8, 9).

> Let us fix our eyes on Jesus, the author and perfector of our faith, who for the joy set before him endured the cross, scorning its shame, and sat down at the right hand of the throne of God (Heb. 12:2).

> For the message of the cross is foolishness to those who are perishing, but to us who are being saved it is the power of God (1 Cor. 1:18).

While emphasizing the centrality of the cross in the conquest of evil at a cosmic level, such references also show that the apostles, especially Paul, are clear and emphatic in stating that the victory of Christ is effective at the individual, personal level. Especially in his "gospel" of Romans, Paul highlights the battle at this level, declaring that Christ's all-encompassing victory brings us atonement, restoring harmony and ending lostness. As a consequence, Paul argues, humanity is "set free from the law of sin and death" (Rom. 8:2), is "freed from sin" (6:7), and the "result is eternal life" (6:22).

The outcome of Christ's action is that "he condemned sin in sinful man" (8:3). This is not simply a statement of condemnation against sin. By what He did, Jesus pronounced the doom of sin. Sin itself, wherever it reigns, has been conquered. This is the victory. This is the triumph won by Christus Victor. Thus in the apocalyptic vision of the end times the utter and total destruction of all satanic forces closes the chapter on cosmic disharmony and human suffering (Rev. 20:10). "Christ was victor over Satan; and, as the result of his triumph, millions were to be victors with him in his glorified kingdom."[11] Those triumph at last with Christ in whom Christ's victory has already become established, those in whom sin has already been condemned and conquered.

In his book *The Cross of Christ*, John Stott refers to Gustav Aulen's *Christus Victor*, cited at the beginning of this chapter. Stott explains that Aulen was concerned to reestablish in Christian thinking a "neglected truth," namely the significance of the cross as a victory over the powers of evil in counterbalance to other views of the atonement that in isolation can easily lead to an unbalanced position.[12] Stott says that Aulen was "right to draw the church's attention to the cross as victory, and to show that by his death Jesus saved us not only from sin and guilt, but from death and the devil . . . as well."[13]

Stott and Aulen both point to the "note of triumph" that "sounds like a trumpet-call through the teaching of the early church." It is triumph in the victory achieved in the cross. It did sound through the early church as it does throughout the New Testament. And it *was* a triumph, a victory, both cosmic and personal.

Proleptic and Anticipated Fulfillment

While the cross remains central to the work of Christ and His victory over evil, there are other dimensions of that work. For now—after His life, death, and resurrection—Jesus sits at the right hand of God. *Already, now.* The universe acknowledges that Christ has gained the victory, that the decisive conclusion has been fully accomplished. There is no doubt. That is why the New Testament is replete with references to the glorified Christ, now seated at the right hand of God's throne, in a position of power and authority. While the final events remain future, the outcome is sure, for the victory is already achieved.

Even during His earthly ministry, prior to Gethsemane and the cross, Jesus pointed to this vision of exaltation. In response to the high priest's question, "Are you the Christ, the Son of the Blessed One?" Jesus replies, "I am, . . . and you will see the Son of Man sitting at the right hand of the Mighty One and coming on the clouds of heaven" (Mark 14:62). Similarly in Luke's account, Jesus responds to the council's question as to who He is, "From now on, the Son of Man will be seated at the right hand of the mighty God" (Luke 22:69).

Jesus is speaking in both instances with proleptic assurance of His victory and His return to the position in heaven He had relinquished in coming to earth as Saviour. For that is His destination and His destiny. Mark records that at the ascension Jesus "was taken up into heaven and he sat at the right hand of God" (Mark 16:19). Thus, after the resurrection, at the martyrdom of Stephen, heaven is opened and Christus Victor is seen is just this position. Stephen's announcement of the exaltation of Jesus precipitates his own death. "But Stephen, full of the Holy Spirit, looked up to heaven and saw the glory of God, and Jesus standing at the right hand of God. 'Look,' he said, 'I see heaven open and the Son of Man standing at the right hand of God'" (Acts 7:55, 56).

The truth of the exalted Christ finds fullest expression in the New Testament in the epistle to the Hebrews (Heb. 1:3; 8:1; 10:12; 12:2). But it is important to note that Christ is here depicted as more than priest, vital though that doctrine is in itself. He is priest after the order of Melchizedek, the king-priest. His priesthood has a regal dimension. It is associated in the text with "majesty" (1:3; 8:1) and therefore with power, regency, and conquest.

William Johnsson, speaking of this kingly priesthood of Christ, says that "while he has not attained full rule yet, he is now *seated*. That seating carries with it deep significance for the now time." Then he adds, "It enables Christians to anticipate the heavenly goal as they await its realization."[14] We may also add that they can do so in full confidence, for they are assisted by the heavenly priest-king, who has already conquered the forces of evil and who now sits enthroned above.

This is the ongoing conviction of the early church—that the exalted Jesus continued to work for them from His position of power and authority: "Christ Jesus, who died—more than that, who was raised to life—is at the right hand of God and is also interceding for us" (Rom. 8:34). The stress on the righteous power of God, working through Christ, is consistent and emphatic throughout the New Testament. Paul writes again to the Ephesians of the power which God "exerted in Christ when He raised Him from the dead and seated Him at His right hand in the heavenly realms, far above all rule and authority, power and dominion." This enthronement and authority relates not only to "the present age" but also to "the one to come." Thus God has "placed all things under His feet and appointed Him to be head over everything for the church" (Eph. 1:19-22). Christ, once the suffering servant, is now the exalted priest-king; once the despised One, He now reigns and intercedes.

The consequence for the believer and the church is that such a position infuses immense confidence. It also directs attention to the primary focus, ensuring that the spiritual perspective is paramount both in the life of individuals and in the corporate life of the church. True spirituality draws its life from the power of the victorious One. "Since, then, you have been raised with Christ, set your hearts on things above, where Christ is seated at the right hand of God" (Col. 3:1). "Let us fix our eyes on Jesus, the author and perfecter of our faith" (Heb. 12:2), "Jesus Christ, who has gone into heaven and is at God's right hand—with angels, authorities and powers in submission to Him" (1 Pet. 3:21, 22).

In a chapter entitled "The Conquest of Evil," John Stott points to "the objective, decisive victory of the Lamb over all the powers of darkness," reminding us that the victory of Christians "consists of entering into the victory of Christ and of enjoying its benefits."[15] It is made possible through the continuing intercession of Jesus, the victorious priest-king, now seated at the right hand of the Father.

Reality of Christus Victor in the Lives of Individual Believers

As the foregoing paragraphs suggest, the conviction that Christ is truly the victorious One affects radically the lives of individual believers. It is a theme to which Paul returns continuously. We are "in Christ," he says. We are "clothed" with Christ; we are empowered by His Spirit; He lives in us. Webber comments, "Just as Christ is Victor over the powers [of evil], so this victory extends to us. Spirituality is a union with Christ and His victory over the powers of evil."[16] While true spirituality is not a matter of works—it is a life in Christ constantly refreshed by Him—yet true spirituality is constantly at work. It expresses itself in what we do with our lives. It is a force for good. It is active, rather than passive. It is, as Webber says, a union with the victorious, conquering Christ. So, the role of Christians in the world is to be a transforming and redemptive influence that both nurtures good and condemns evil.

Christ's own words are similarly indicative. "You are the salt of the earth . . . You are the light of the world" (Matt. 5:13, 14). Using the metaphors of salt and light Jesus clearly identified the role that individuals are to play in the world. They are beacons of truth and light; they are the salt that protects and purifies, giving true taste and meaning to life itself. For that to happen the believer must have a strong, creative role to play in society. He or she must not withdraw from the life of the communities of which they are a part. Ellen White wrote of this interaction with those in the community:

> Jesus says, "Ye are the light of the world. . . . Let your light so shine before men, that they may see your good works, and glorify your Father which is in heaven" (Matt. 5:14, 16). There are some who will observe the example and feel the influence of a consistent Christian life. Jesus does not bid the Christian to strive to shine, but just to let his light shine in clear and distinct rays to the world. Do not blanket your light. Do not sinfully withhold your light. Do not let the mist and fog and malaria of the world put out your light. Do not hide it under a bed or under a bushel, but set it on a candlestick, that it may give light to all that are in the house. Neither take pains to exalt yourself to shine nor go into the cave as did Elijah in his discouragement, but come out, stand with God and shine. God bids you shine, penetrating the moral darkness of the world. Be the salt, the savor of men.[17]

Just as the victorious Christ is Himself the light of the world, so believers also are to be the light of the world (John 1:9; Matt. 5:14). When that is believed with true conviction, the believer becomes a bearer of the light that conquers darkness. The believer cannot stand idly by in a needy society. He or she must be fully or completely engaged, making faith real and relevant to all around. Involvement is essential. Christians cannot be inactive, uninvolved in society with all its cares and needs. As colight-bearers with Christ we are called to a redemptive ministry in all possible areas, to change and transmute the lives of others by our very presence.

Moreover, the role of the Christian is to be a sanctifying presence in an unsanctified world. Through influence and example it is to transform the experience of our fellow human beings, to raise them from despair to hope, from sadness to joy, from defeat to victory. Without compromising the final outcome of Christ's victory, it is to make the world a better place inhabited by better people.

For this reason Paul says, and we catch again the note of conquest in his words, "But thanks be to God, who always leads us in triumphal procession in Christ and through us spreads everywhere the fragrance of the knowledge of Him. For we are to God the aroma of Christ among those who are being saved and those who are perishing" (2 Cor. 2:14, 15). We are the fragrance, the aroma of Christ. We make Christ smell good. We make Him look good and sound good. Just like the woman who anointed Jesus with precious perfume, such actions cannot be hidden. By its very nature perfume wafts through the air and spreads all around. So it is to be for the Christian—to spread throughout the world the glorious good news of the graciousness of God. We share His victory and our victory with others so that they too might conquer. This is the ethical imperative. As James puts it, this is true religion (Jas. 1:27).

Christ's victory thus has a twofold impact on the believer, on his or her own living and lifestyle. We are called to be different. Because we are truly different—our *raison d'etre* is different. Our world view is different. Our values are different. Our philosophy of life is different. Our hope is different. Most of all, our very lives are different, because the victory that Christ has accomplished is complete and assured. So the believer meets the ups and downs of life with a strong sense of inner assurance.

And then Christ's victory is the destruction of sin and the achievement of betterment and salvation for mankind as a whole. The Christus Victor motif draws our attention not only to the theoretical provisions for dealing with sin, but also to the practical conquering and annihilation of sin itself. In other words, it highlights the shattering impact of the death and resurrection of Jesus on all the works of the devil that are thereby to be destroyed, now, as well as at the end. It is this good news, this assurance of Christ's ultimate victory and its implications, that we are called to share with our neighbors and friends.

So, in sum: the Christus Victor theme helps us find meaning here and now, before He returns to fulfill the final aspects of His promise. It provides a strong mandate for an active and proactive role in society. Most of all we smell and taste the elements of the victory feast already while here, thereby deriving courage for the present and investing our involvement with others with deeper meaning. The victory of Christ, attained through the cross and the resurrection, makes it possible for us to enter into that state of victory here in the present. It provides a sense of assurance that becomes a stabilizing and motivating factor in the life of every authentic believer.

The "Victor" Reality in the Life of the Church

The "Victor" reality is also central to the life and mission of the church. If Christ truly is the conqueror of death and evil, of sadness and despair, then the church is called to live and communicate the truth of the victorious Christ. The church is continuously to recall what happened at the cross, witnessing to it and proclaiming the vision of ultimate triumph and the destruction of evil, which Christ's second coming brings about. So, whether the church looks back in time, or at the present society of which the believing community is a part, or at the future apocalyptic consummation, the church's mission is to testify consistently to the victorious One.

In the end—meaning both termination and goal—death is destroyed, evil is wiped out of existence, and the reign of eternal righteousness is inaugurated. The church thus has both a wonderful opportunity and an inescapable obligation to participate in this ultimate and glorious event, for the victory is ours as well as His. Paul anticipates it in these familiar and reassuring words:

> When the perishable has been clothed with the imperishable, and the mortal with immortality, then the saying that is written will come true: "Death has been swallowed up in victory." "Where, O death, is your victory? Where, O death, is your sting?" The sting of death is sin, and the power of sin is the law. But thanks be to God! He gives us the victory through our Lord Jesus Christ (1 Cor.15:54–57).

The ultimate victory is the final conquest of death. It is made possible through Christ and lies at the heart of the church's proclamation.

For some, the repeated emphasis on victory may sound vainglorious, overly triumphant—the voice of a church militant and triumphant that is larger than life, divorced from reality. Yet this *is* the reality. Although, like Paul, we glory only in the cross of Christ, yet the consistent refrain of the Christian witness is that of victory, the victory of the victorious One Himself. He admonishes *us* to "take heart" because *He* has overcome the world (John 16:33). How does this happen? It is through participation in Christ's victory, realizing the power of Christus Victor in the life and work of the church. "For everyone born of God overcomes the world. This is the victory that has overcome the world, even our faith. Who is it that overcomes the world? Only he who believes that Jesus is the Son of God" (1 John 5:4, 5). And John explains the reason for this confident faith, "You, dear children, are from God and have overcome them, because the one who is in you is greater than the one who is in the world" (4:4).

The community of believers, as an organization predicated on the victory of Christ, needs to put such assurance into practice. These are not merely words, a stereotyped, creedal formula. This is the fundamental motivation for the church, the energizing power that led the first evangelists to turn the world upside down. It is the very reason for the church's existence. It lies at the heart of who we are. While this theme is more fully explored in the final chapter of this book, we may profitably remind ourselves here of its fundamental relationship to the victory inherent in Christ.

Why do so many churches spend so much time and energy seeking to implement various programs? Why have we ourselves invested so much of our resources in education, in terms of personnel, time, and funding—a massive investment for the church? Why are we so concerned with people's health and well being, spending so much time operating health-care institutions and helping people through preventative health programs? Why are we so deeply involved in humanitarian aid programs and community services of all kinds? These all represent vast investments of time and energy. And why do we resist the temptation to regard these as ends in themselves?

Why? Because of Christus Victor. We hold that it is His will that we should continue in our communities what He initiated 2,000 years ago, namely to respond to the needs of suffering humanity, to bring comfort and healing, to feed the hungry, to lift high symbols of hope and a better life. We take seriously the belief that the outcome is absolutely sure. We want to raise the quality of life of those around us, at the same time helping them gain sight of the victorious Christ who is already at work, bringing good and destroying the works of the devil.

For all who weep and mourn, who suffer and cry, who despair

and give up hope, ours is to be a message of hope in the present as well as hope in the future. Christ has already gained the victory, and soon the kingdom of righteousness will be ushered in. So, *right now*, we are admonished, "do not be overcome by evil; but overcome evil with good" (Rom. 12:21). The conquest of evil cannot be left until the end. It is also the present responsibility of the church. While final victory is certain, it is the will of the victorious One—and, therefore, the mission of the church—that we enable people whom we meet to experience His "fragrance" here and now, not just by words but through deeds of healing, comfort, and support.

This, then, is the vision of the victorious One Himself. Victory is already a reality, a certainty that emboldens us to engage, to create a profile for the living church, and to declare the victory of Jesus wherever we are. It also sends a signal to the defeated forces of the enemy, the legions of evil, that they are doomed, that their end is sure because they operate in the territory of the One who has already conquered. So in full assurance of faith we can all say with Paul, "I press on toward the goal to win the prize for which God has called me heavenwards in Christ Jesus" (Phil. 3:14).

The last word on the Christus Victor theme must surely belong to the apostle Paul. We have already noted Paul's emphasis on the cosmic dimensions of the conflict between good and evil. In his letter to the early Christian believers in Ephesus he also speaks of Christ's resurrection and ascension in cosmic terms and in the context of the church's mission in the world (Eph. 1:20, 21; 4:8-10). He affirms that Christ ascended "far above all heavens, *that he might fill all things*" (4:10, KJV). The NIV translation of the Greek words, *ta panta*, "all things," captures their awesome immensity—"in order to fill the whole universe."[18] It is almost beyond human comprehension. Yet this, in the divine purpose, is the destiny of the victorious Jesus. The thirty-odd years of Christ's life, which culminated in the cross, was "the key battle" in "the history of the universe."[19] The theme is caught again in the words of one who wrote at length about this age-long conflict and who envisaged its resolution:

> The great controversy is ended. Sin and sinners are no more. The entire universe is clean. One pulse of harmony and gladness beats

through the vast creation. From Him who created all flow life and light and gladness throughout the realms of illimitable space.[20]

It is a prospect glorious to contemplate. Such is the ultimate and eternal outcome of Christ's mighty victory. Praise be to God!

For Further Reading

G. Aulen, *Christus Victor,* trans. A. G. Hebert. New York: Macmillan, 1969.

M. Green, *I Believe In Satan's Downfall.* London: Hodder and Stoughton, 1981.

J. R. W. Stott, *The Cross of Christ.* Downers Grove, IL: InterVarsity Press, 1986.

R. E. Webber, *Ancient-Future Faith.* Grand Rapids, MI: Baker Books, 1999.

Ellen G. White, *The Great Controversy Between Christ and Satan.* Mountain View, CA: Pacific Press Publishing Assn., 1950 edition.

Notes

1. Michael Green, *I Believe In Satan's Downfall* (London: Hodder and Stoughton, 1981), 214. Green also says, "The triumph of Jesus Christ at every juncture over the powers and principalities of evil is a major theme of the New Testament," p. 92.
2. Edward J. Young, *An Introduction to the Old Testament* (London: The Tyndale Press, 1964 ed.), p. 372.
3. David Tiede, *Jesus and the Future* (Cambridge: Cambridge University Press, 1990), p. 39.
4. John 6:35; 8:12, 23, 58; 10:7, 11; 11:25; 14:6, 11; 15:1.
5. R. C. H. Lenski, *The Interpretation of St. John's Gospel* (Minneapolis, MI: Augsburg Publishing House, 1943), p. 978.
6. Gustav Aulen, *Christus Victor,* trans. A. G. Hebert (New York: Macmillan, 1969), p. 4.
7. Ellen G. White, *The Desire of Ages* (Mountain View, CA: Pacific Press Publishing Assn., 1898), p. 756.
8. Lenski, p. 874.
9. Commenting on the view that it is unacceptable to believe in such cosmic forces today, A. M. Hunter says, "There is no metaphysical reason why the cosmos should not contain spirits higher than man, who have made evil their good, who are ill-disposed to the human race, and whose activities are coordinated by a master strategist," *Interpreting Paul's Gospel,* p. 75, cited in Green, p.107.
10. Robert E. Webber, *Ancient-Future Faith* (Grand Rapids, MI: Baker Books, 1999), p. 46.
11. Ellen G. White, *The Spirit of Prophecy* (Washington, D.C.: Review and Herald Publishing Assn., 1969 ed.), vol. 3, p. 101.
12. John R. W. Stott, *The Cross of Christ* (Downers Grove, IL: InterVarsity Press, 1986), p. 228.

13. *Ibid.*, p. 229.
14. William G. Johnsson, *In Absolute Confidence* (Nashville, TN: Southern Publishing Assn., 1979), p. 131.
15. Stott, pp. 251, 239.
16. Webber, p. 127.
17. Ellen G. White, *This Day With God* (Washington D.C.: Review and Herald Publishing Assn., 1979), p. 316.
18. Similarly, the Good News Bible reads "to fill the whole universe with his presence." The New English Bible rendering is "so that he might fill the universe."
19. Green, p. 92.
20. Ellen G. White, *The Great Controversy* (Mountain View, CA: Pacific Press Publishing Assn., 1950 ed.), p. 678.

Jesus and the Great Commission
Bryan W. Ball

In his widely-read book *On Being a Christian*, Hans Kung reminds us that the "most fundamental characteristic of Christianity" is that it regards Jesus as "definitive" and "ultimately decisive." In answering the question "Which Christ?" of the many versions of Jesus currently available, Kung declares that it is the "concrete," "historical" Jesus, whose history can be "located" and "dated,"[1] crucified yet alive, who still calls men and women to faith and discipleship. Thus it will continue until the end of time if those who call themselves His followers today will take seriously Jesus' last words to His disciples—His command to go into all the world with the gospel.

The preceding chapters in this book have brought us face to face again, or even for the first time, with this concrete, historical Jesus, with His words and works, His life, death, and resurrection, with His past and His future, with His promises of wholeness and hope for all who believe. This essential Jesus, the divine-human Saviour, still yearns for men, women, and young people everywhere to come to Him in faith, confess Him as Lord, and accept without reservation His call to discipleship. We have considered the arguments and the evidence, biblical and historical, which compel us to regard Him as credible. We now face an urgent and insistent question: What now? How should we respond? What are we to do with this Jesus who cannot be denied or ignored without compromising our own integrity or rationality?

Jesus Himself has already provided the answer to this most

276 • The Essential Jesus

pressing question. His last recorded words to the disciples who had witnessed firsthand all that He said and did, including His death and resurrection, contain the answer for us as it did for them. Jesus commanded them to go into all the world with the gospel message and make more disciples. The exact words of the Great Commission are unambiguously simple: "Go therefore and make disciples of all nations, baptizing them in the name of the Father, Son and Holy Spirit, teaching them to observe all things that I have commanded you" (Matt. 28:19, 20, NKJV). This, as much as anything else, is essential to our understanding of who Jesus is and what He requires.

The Great Commission raises three fundamental questions, each of them requiring urgent attention if we are serious about Jesus and His will for the church and for the world. What does the Great Commission mean? Who does it include? And how can it be accomplished? In attempting to answer these questions and explore their relevance in the twenty-first century for all professing Christians, we must regard the centrality of mission as foundational to the very nature of the church as well as to Christ's own declared purposes. Jon Dybdhal observes, "If the church ceases to be missionary, it has not simply failed in its task, but has actually ceased from being the church."[2] It would not be difficult to find a dozen similar statements. The church exists for mission.

Before we explore these questions, a word about terminology. Three related words appear in the following pages. Two of them, "mission" and "witness," are used frequently, and often synonymously, although strictly speaking mission is broader than witness. Mission is the task of the church. Witness is what the church and Christians do in order to accomplish mission. Witness can take many forms, one of them being evangelism in both its broad and narrower senses. We shall argue that as witness is essential to mission, so evangelism, both broadly and narrowly understood, is essential to witness. Since all are applicable and necessary in all the world, Max Warren can say that "the word 'missionary' is to be understood as applying to anyone, anywhere,"[3] who is motivated by the Great Commission.

Rediscovering the Great Commission

What does it mean, then, this final word from Jesus to His disciples? How shall we understand it, initially as it was given to the first disciples and then for ourselves, His disciples in the contemporary world? Only as we listen to it carefully, coming direct from Scripture, free from the weight of tradition, bias, or denominational pride, can we grasp again its immense and compelling significance.

The words of Jesus recorded in Matthew 28:19, 20 were delivered at one of several post-resurrection appearances, at most of which Jesus spoke of the task awaiting His disciples. Parallel passages are Mark 16:15-18 and Luke 24:46-49. They reflect similar words spoken by Jesus on other occasions between the resurrection and the ascension, as do also John 20:21, 22 and Acts 1:8. Matthew 24:14 is also particularly relevant. These passages all relate to the Great Commission and Christ's intention for His disciples, and they need to be studied together, although Matthew 28:19, 20 remains the basic text.

While the Authorized Version of Matthew 28:19 begins with the familiar words "Go ye therefore, and teach all nations," most contemporary versions agree that the word here rendered "teach" should be translated, "make disciples of." The Revised Authorized and New International Versions both retain the imperative and read, "Go and make disciples of all nations." Lenski says that "teach" is an "unfortunate and even misleading translation" for those who do not have access to the original.[4] Howard Snyder insists that "disciple-making" means "teaching believers to follow Jesus and live the life of the kingdom that he taught and lived before them," while according to another view discipleship requires "belief in Jesus and transformation of life."[5] So more than instruction is required by the Great Commission. It calls for decision and commitment. It encompasses the entire process of leading men and women to become authentic disciples of Jesus, "obedient followers," to borrow Lenski's pithy phrase.

The other side of this coin, however, is equally significant. Making disciples also includes teaching or the impartation of knowledge. To pass over the debate as to whether this instruction should precede or follow baptism (the answer surely is both), the essential point to grasp here is that true Christian faith is rooted in understanding. A disciple is a person who has been instructed and enlightened in coming to faith. The Greek word in verse 20 (from *didasko*) clearly means to teach, but even the word in verse 19 (from *mateteuo*) carries with it the underlying idea of instruction. Kittel refers to the "unambiguous" sense of teaching or instruction, "the impartation of practical or theoretical knowledge" implicit in this passage and says of verse 20 "the risen Lord made the continuation of this task the life work of his people."[6] It is not possible to be a true disciple of Jesus with an empty mind.

Some contemporary Christian writers are speaking again of apologetics, the defense or explanation of Christian faith. The concept is crucial if the Great Commission is to be accomplished in the Western world. Apologetics proposes the reasons for believing in Christ and for being His disciples and suggests answers to possible objections. Informed Christians become informed through the process of apologetics. Alister McGrath declares that one of the important tasks of apologetics is "explanation," in the context of a secular society that is increasingly ignorant of the basic truths of Christianity and in which "half-truths, misconceptions, and caricatures abound."[7] The world needs to hear, loud and clear, repeatedly and uncompromisingly, what Christian faith is actually about. Apologetics is the teaching function of a church and of Christians who are themselves well-informed.

In Acts 1:8 we find three further elements of the divine mandate for mission. Jesus also said to His disciples, in the context of the promised Holy Spirit, "You shall . . . be witnesses to Me . . . to the end of the earth" (NKJV). We shall return later to two of these crucial factors. For the present, the key word here is "witnesses." It has been frequently pointed out that this word refers to those who testify from personal experience. One of the most trusted New Testament exegetes of the twentieth century says that it "denotes one who declares facts directly known to himself," one who speaks from "his own direct knowledge" about people or events he has observed personally.[8] Kittel further states that Luke uses the word here in a unique sense. The disciples of Jesus were to be witnesses to facts as facts, but also to the meaning of those facts. Their word was to be testimony and evangelistic confession.

The facts in question "are the facts of the history of Jesus. . . which took place in the clear light of history at a specific time and place, facts which can be established and on which one can rely." They must be attested to and their significance must be explained.[9] Those are qualified to be witnesses who could, and who still can, vouch for the objectivity of these facts and explain their continuing redemptive significance. They are witnesses in the legal and biblical senses. On their testimony the lives of others may depend. This is what Acts 1:8 means when it speaks of witness.

Further relevance may be found in John's account. On the evening of the resurrection day Jesus met with a small group of His disciples and began immediately to point them toward the future. "As the Father hath sent me, I also send you," He declared (John 20:21, NKJV). This is probably the genesis of the Great Commission which finds its fullest expression at a later meeting between Jesus and a larger group of disciples and which, as we have noted, is recorded in Matthew 28:19, 20. Lenski relates this text specifically to the Great Commission and renders it "As the Father has commissioned me, I, too, am sending you."[10] While His death and resurrection are still vivid in their minds, on the very day of the resurrection and on the first occasion thereafter when Jesus met with the disciples, He focuses their attention on what their response must be to these momentous events. It demonstrates just how vital mission was both to Him and to them.

There is more here, however, that relates to effective witness. Jesus sends His disciples into the world "as the Father" had sent Him. It is not coincidental that this particular emphasis is found in John's account. It reflects the earlier emphases in this same Gospel where there is repeated reference to the "sending" of the Son by the Father (John 3:16, 17; 6:38, 39; 9:4; 12:49, 50). These texts are all to be seen in the light of John's unique and powerful first chapter where the sent Word becomes flesh and comes down to His own for their enlightenment and redemption. Jesus' own mission has an incarnational character. He was sent from the Father to be one with humankind, to identify and be identified with them. It is a truth of the utmost significance for those who are now sent by Jesus into the twenty-first-century world. To be sent as Christ was sent is to be sent incarnationally into the world. We ignore this truth at great loss, even to ineffectiveness.

Matthew 24:14 presents us with a further factor of great significance in attempting to grasp the intent of the Great Commission for mission in our time. Here, where Jesus refers to the final, end-time gospel proclamation, a particular phrase is used to describe the gospel that is then to be proclaimed "as a witness to all nations." It is not merely "the gospel" without clarification. It is the gospel "of the kingdom." Again, this can be understood adequately—and must be so understood—only in the light of what Matthew has said previously.

Matthew has already written much about the kingdom of heaven or the kingdom of God. There are more than fifty such references in his Gospel, many of them sayings of Jesus Himself. Matthew even uses this same phrase, "the gospel of the kingdom," on other occasions (4:24; 9:35). It was in fact this "gospel of the kingdom" which Jesus Himself proclaimed, the good news about God's kingdom which had already arrived in His person and which figured prominently in His own proclamation. As has been shown repeatedly over the past fifty or sixty years, this was the central thrust of Jesus' own teaching—the kingdom of heaven is at hand (Matt. 4:17; 10:7; Mark 1:15); it has, in Jesus Himself, already "drawn near." The parables of the kingdom (Matt. 13 and 25) are parables of a kingdom that, while yet to come, is also already present. It is *this* kingdom that is at the heart of the gospel. It is the good news concerning *this* kingdom that is to be preached as a witness to all nations in the end-time proclamation.

We must not allow the force of this essential truth to elude us any longer. The kingdom of the future emerges from a kingdom that is already present. They are one and the same kingdom, now in time, then in eternity. To preach only, or even mainly, a future kingdom is to distort the very gospel of Jesus. The church exists as the agent to bring this kingdom continually into being, to demonstrate the presence and the nature of this kingdom and to extend it by mission.

The kingdom, therefore, becomes the focus of true mission, the genesis, the vehicle, and the consummation of the gospel and the Great Commission itself. Beyerhaus sees the church's responsibility to "hasten the visible establishment of Christ's kingdom on earth," noting the relationship of this task to the coming of the Lord. "Only when this work is complete will Christ come to redeem the groaning creation from its present bondage."[11] The gospel *of the kingdom*, proclaimed in all the world, makes this ultimately possible. We must in all honesty ask ourselves if we have been faithful to the gospel which is described in Matthew 24:14. Or have we been content with something less, the message of half a kingdom, the kingdom which is yet to come, perhaps? When Jesus taught the disciples to pray "thy kingdom come" He had more than the distant future in mind.

Finally, the extent of the task calls us again: "Witnesses. . .to the ends of the earth," "to all nations," to the "end of the age." For two millennia the church has, more or less, been driven by this vision. Christian faith can now be found all over the world. It would be easy to think that the task is almost done, and indeed it may be. But we must not forget that the command to preach the gospel and make disciples in all nations applies to peoples and localities where the church already exists, as well as those over the seas. It includes new generations in countries and cultures that have been regarded as Christian for centuries but in reality are not so any longer. In this respect it is imperative to hear again the cry of the lost in the Western world. It is here more than anywhere that the Great Commission needs immediate resurrection. The Christian church here is having little, if any, effect on society. Adventist missiologist, Jon Dybdahl, speaks of the "mission malaise of the First-world church," specifically in Western Europe, North America, Australia, and New Zealand.[12] The secular humanist and the secular materialist are as far removed from the Christ of Scripture as the devout Hindu, the Moslem fundamentalist, and the unenlightened Animist. They, too, must hear. This book then is largely and unapologetically a response to that noxious malaise. It must be countered rapidly if the church, indeed Christianity as a whole, is to remain what it claims to be, the body of Christ with a message for all humankind. While much of what is said here, of course, will also be relevant to the church elsewhere in the world, the "appalling lostness"[13] of the secular millions, to borrow John Stott's evocative phrase, cannot go unheeded.

So from these seminal passages in Matthew 28, Acts 1, John 20, and Matthew 13 and 24, we can recapture what it is that Jesus wanted His disciples to accomplish. There is, of course, much more that can be drawn from these texts and others that are also relevant, and some of it will be said later. But can we not confidently declare that in essence Jesus commanded His disciples to go incarnationally into the world with the gospel of a kingdom already present as well as yet to come; that He bade them witness to all nations and cultures, making other disciples—men, women, and young people who would come to understand who Jesus is and why He came to earth, and who would gladly respond affirmatively to His gospel invitation and in turn become witnesses and disciple-makers? There may indeed be more, but certainly nothing less than this is acceptable, either in understanding the Great Commission or in putting it into effect. It is this momentous task that remains "the central mission," the "great charter" of the church.[14]

Refocusing on Responsibility

We must now turn without flinching to the question of responsibility. It arises inevitably from the very nature of the Great Commission, especially when applied to our own time and to our specific location, wherever that may be. To whom is the Great Commission given? Who are those who are commanded by Jesus to go and make disciples? Are any excluded?

In accepting that the church has a responsibility to witness, it is helpful to remember the relationship between kingdom and church. The church is the created community of the kingdom, and this community is the agent of the kingdom. In bearing witness to the kingdom the church inevitably bears witness to Jesus, for He is the embodiment of the kingdom. Snyder says that the church "exists for the kingdom of God,"[15] a position we can accept more readily when we remember also the eschatological future of that kingdom. Bonhoeffer stated "the Church is the Church only when it exists for others,"[16] i.e. to extend the kingdom on earth by intentional, focused mission and witness by which others accept Jesus and become His disciples.

We have come, once again, to the reason for the church's existence in the world as an identifiable community of believers. Although Jesus spoke much more about the kingdom than He did about the church as such, He nonetheless envisaged the church's existence and its future in declaring that the gates of hell would not prevail against it and that He had entrusted to the church the keys of that kingdom (Matt. 16:18, 19). This is, again, the kingdom about which Jesus spoke so much and which Matthew records so faithfully. *The church now has the keys to this kingdom.* It is an awesome responsibility that many voices throughout the Christian centuries have emphatically sought to underline, including many in our own time. We must not ignore them.

Charles van Engen deplores the current situation in which in the minds of many Christians "church" and "mission" are often seen as distinct and conflicting ideas. He contends emphatically that to understand the church as principally a missionary organization "is not optional," proposing that the church "is being obedient when it can be found out in the main thoroughfares and the streets, inviting everyone to the eschatological wedding feast of the Lamb."[17] Roger Hedlund insists that "we cannot escape the obligation to carry the gospel to the nations," declaring that the Great Commission is "the essential mission of the church."[18] Michael Green says it is "incumbent" upon Christians to spread the good news.[19] Some see a negative attitude to mission in the Western church manifesting itself in a "Little Bo-Peep" mentality that believes that the lost sheep will come home on their own.[20] Clearly, they will not. They must be brought home.

Much of the foregoing reminds us of a statement made many years ago but which now seems remarkably pertinent once again: "The church is God's appointed agency for the salvation of men. It was organized for service, and its mission is to carry the gospel to the world."[21] Few would actually disagree with that. Most, in fact, would wholeheartedly agree in theory. The challenge comes in translating theory into practice, particularly for churches in which it has become comfortable to be nominally Christian and where it is easier for the majority of members to sit in the pews during the worship service and remain silent for the rest of the week.

Perhaps the problem, and its resolution, lies in part at least in the balance between nurture and mission. In recent years there has been an increasing emphasis on nurturing activities designed to keep alive the often-flickering flame of the local congregation. At a time when secularism and materialism increasingly erode the foundations of the faith, it is entirely understandable. The argument that nurture is an essential prerequisite to witness is persuasive. But how far does it go before the balance become untenable? Snyder believes that the church "gets into trouble whenever it thinks it is in church business rather than in kingdom business."[22] The point is clearly valid. It is possible to become more concerned with the life of those in the local congregation than with the death of those in the surrounding community. By "kingdom business" Snyder means activities which are specifically directed at extending the kingdom of God by sharing the good news of Jesus and the kingdom with those who have not yet heard it or not yet responded.

Gavin Reid, an Anglican who became disillusioned with the failure of his congregation to make any significant impact on the community, wrote a book with the provocative title *The Gagging of God.* Proposing that the church, by its ineffectiveness, was actually preventing God's message from reaching the community, Reid suggests three reasons for this situation, the third of which is "the accelerating introversion of practically all forms of Christian activity."[23] If this was true a couple of decades ago, it is more than ever true today. Nurture is the "in" word now. It has climbed the agenda, become more fashionable, more time-consuming and, dare we say it, more ecclesiastically chic, than mission.

It would be easy to conclude that those who spend most of their time and energy, even financial resources, on structure, the nature of ministry, the social life of the congregation, maintenance committees, and the seemingly endless round of camps, conferences, retreats, and workshops have really lost the plot. That might be a harsh judgment since there is nothing intrinsically wrong with any of these concerns or activities. They are in fact all quite legitimate. It is simply that they take up so much time and energy and the best available personnel that there is little left to invest in the real reason for the church's existence. Consequently the church becomes increasingly inward-looking and self-centered, which is the very antithesis of authentic Christian life and the church's reason for being. This unhealthy and unbiblical nexus must be corrected if we are serious about our mission responsibilities. David Watson complains impatiently of the "moribund, introverted ranks" of many churches, observing painfully but truthfully, "we have a private dialogue with ourselves while man plunges suicidally on into absurdity and despair."[24]

It is also necessary to address with purposeful intent the issue of function within the church. The idea that ministry is the sole prerogative of the ordained pastor simply will not do any longer. It is not a biblical view, as has been said frequently in recent years. Some big-city churches may have caught on, but the truth still has a long way to travel before it permeates the whole body of Christ. Ministry is the task of the entire believing community, pastor and people together. Michael Green, in one of his many perceptive and helpful books on the life and work of the church, says in *Evangelism Now and Then* that every-member involvement in the mission of the church is "the biggest difference between the New Testament church and our own." Then he adds, "It is not until church members have the enthusiasm to speak to their friends and acquaintances about Jesus that anybody will really believe that we have got good news to tell."[25]

This seems to have been Christ's original intention. Most commentators agree that the Great Commission was given by Jesus, not only to the remaining eleven disciples, but to the more than 500 believers mentioned by Paul in 1 Corinthians 15:6. This fact, together with Jesus' promise to be with His witnessing, disciple-making followers "to the end of the world," is the basis for believing that the imperative "go ye" in Matthew 28:19 includes "all believers to the end of time." The Great Commission originated in the midst of a large and diverse group of disciples before the church or a set-apart ministry existed. Those who believe, who are themselves disciples, all of them, are to be witnesses and disciple-makers.

Walter Douglas believes, with substantial reason, that we have "a great deal of catching-up to do" with respect to lay involvement in the mission of the church and in ministry to the waiting world. "It is not more or less organization of church structures or the refining or redefining of church polity that we need," he says. *"What is desperately needed is the laicization of the church"* (emphasis supplied). It is a conclusion that many from across the Christian spectrum have reached as they have studied the New Testament teaching on church, mission, and ministry. "Members in the local congregation must be taught that when God calls them into his church, he calls them to serve in the mission of the church."[26] This message has been preached widely now for years, but it is still far from being implemented in many parts of the world.

So where does responsibility lie for ensuring that the Great Commission is fulfilled? It lies, as it always has, with all who are disciples of Jesus. It lies with pastors and with people—and, of course, with leaders of the pastors and the people. None are excluded or exempt. The validity of our claim to discipleship may well be determined by our response.

Regaining the Initiative

Further direction from Jesus can be found in Luke 10, a chapter that invites scrutiny by all who are serious about the Great Commission. In appointing the seventy Jesus said, "The harvest truly is great." There is timeless truth here, relevant to every age in which disciples are called to go out into the highways and byways, as they still are today. To Jesus, the harvest is always great. There are always those who, for whatever reason, are ready to hear the gospel and are willing to receive it. Some may have been opposed or hostile on previous occasions. But now their minds and hearts are open. The Spirit has been doing His silent work. And, of course, witness must be faithfully borne to those who are still ignorant, hostile, or apathetic, regardless of any immediate outcome, since they too might respond later.

How, then, shall we proceed? What can be said that will direct us towards a more successful fulfillment of Christ's commission? It is impossible to answer that question in any detail, and in any case it is not the purpose of this chapter to suggest strategies or methodology. There is something more fundamental, more necessary, than strategy, method, or procedure. Basic attitudes, conviction, and underlying principles must come first and must undergird all strategies and methods. The following five principles are critical to successful mission now, at the beginning of the twenty-first century. Without them any hope of true success is at best minimal.

Witnesses to Jesus

Acts 1:8 contains two further truths essential to the fulfillment of the Great Commission. Firstly, the disciples were to be "witnesses unto Me" (NKJV), although some other versions prefer "witnesses for Me." Lenski is rightly all-inclusive: "Called to witness by me, for me, about me, yea, all about me."[27] Jesus was the supreme object of the apostolic witness. He still is.

How often we have heard that, and how often we have forgotten it in our enthusiasm to witness about our church, our congregation, our distinctive beliefs, our world mission program, our institutions, even our diet. Jesus is the focal point of authentic witness, no matter how valid it is to speak of other things on the appropriate occasion. John Stott adds perceptively that we are not at liberty to communicate a Christ of our own predilection who is not recorded in Scripture, "nor to embroider or manipulate the Christ who is in Scripture, but to bear faithful witness to the one and only Christ there is. . . the authentic Jesus, the Jesus of history who is the Jesus of Scripture."[28] This is the "irreducible minimum of the apostolic gospel."[29]

In his book, *I Believe in the Great Commission,* Max Warren speaks of the "recovery of nerve."[30] He means attempting to fulfill the Great Commission in an age that is outwardly more skeptical and apathetic than any other in history. In this context Warren calls for obedience in discipleship and to Christ's command. "Obedience" is not a popular word today. It contradicts the individualism pervading the popular culture that surrounds us, the culture to which we must bear witness and which so easily infiltrates the church. Yet obedience is nonnegotiable for the true Christian, especially obedience to the commands of Jesus, if witness and mission are again to become a priority. It is, of course, the obedience of love, but obedience nonetheless—specifically obedience to the mission imperatives of Jesus.

In describing the content of authentic witness, David Watson refers to the "objective, historical events" upon which Christian faith is built, pointing out that to concentrate on the "purely subjective side of the Christian faith. . .is but one step away from confusion, deception, agnosticism or even atheism." The strength of the gospel is that it is "firmly rooted in the true, historical events of Golgotha and the empty tomb."[31] Citing John Stott, Watson declares, "If the cross is not central in our thinking, it is safe to say that our faith, whatever it may be, is not the Christian faith."[32] It is what Michael Green means when he says so incisively, "Mission is Jesus-shaped."[33] It is witness to Jesus that is true witness. Anything other, and anything less, must be abandoned immediately and forever.

Yes, it takes nerve to witness to Jesus, deliberately and uncompromisingly, in a post-Christian, post-modern culture, but no more than it did for the first disciples in a pagan Roman or traditional Jewish culture. In spite of all perceived hazards and hostility, Jesus says to His disciples today, as He did in sending out the seventy, "I send you out as lambs among wolves" (Luke 10:3), "to be witnesses *to me*. . .to the end of the earth." The prospect may sometimes be bleak, but it does not release us from our obligations or from His expectations.

A Persuasive Lifestyle

It is almost possible to sense the unease arising in the minds of many as they read the preceding paragraphs. All the old fears and feelings of inadequacy, even guilt, are flowing again. Let me attempt to bring some comfort. We do not need special training, an extrovert personality, facility with words, endless free time, or the latest equipment in order to fulfill Christ's command. Most of us can do it without saying anything. Jesus calls us to *be*, before He calls us to *say* or to *do*. In the Sermon on the Mount He spoke about shining lights and good works leading others to glorify God (Matt. 5:16). Light and good works are both inaudible.

In a culture in which many people have become word-resistant, we can witness simply by what we are. In fact, it is impossible to communicate the gospel effectively with words if those words are not substantiated by a corresponding lifestyle. As the relentless pressure of media exposure creates expectations of a good image, the most effective images are still real people. It is what the atheistic enemy of Christianity, Nietzsche, had in mind when he wrote so scathingly, "His disciples have to look more saved if I am to believe in the Saviour."[34] Michael Green puts it more positively, "If we are not thrilled with Christ and being changed by Him, we can have all the techniques in the world and get nowhere."[35]

Few have understood this challenge better than the late Francis Schaeffer. In *The Church at the End of the Twentieth Century* Schaeffer spoke of the need for integrity in the profession of the Christian faith. He says we "must practice truth" as well as proclaim it. In an age like ours, he argues, we have "removed our credibility before the non-Christian, post-Christian, relativistic, skeptical, lost world" if we compromise our Christian profession by a lifestyle that is less than totally Christian.

> If you think that those who have rejected the plastic culture and are sick of hypocrisy are going to be impressed when you talk about truth and at the same time practice untruth, you are wrong. They will never listen. You have cut the ground from under yourself. We live in a generation that does not believe that such a thing as truth is possible, and if you practice untruth while talking about truth, the real thinkers will just say, "Garbage!"[36]

And, we might add, not only the thinkers. The same conclusion can, and will, be drawn by anyone. Jon Paulien's chief concern here is that the prevailing secular culture is already producing a lifestyle within the first-world church that is barely distinguishable from that within the culture itself.[37]

Snyder even calls for a more radical lifestyle that is plainly and unashamedly counter-cultural against today's secular, hedonistic society. Arguing that affluent Christians are a contradiction in terms and "out of sequence" with the times he claims, "We have forgotten, or rejected the values of simplicity, plainness and frugality held by our forefathers and most of the world's peoples." He then confronts the church with "a difficult choice":

> To follow the way of easy affluence that leads almost inevitably to spiritual poverty or to take seriously the demands of the gospel and become a covenant community that risks taking a counter cultural stand at every point where Christian faithfulness is at stake.[38]

Whether or not we agree, the need for a transparent and consistent lifestyle is beyond question if our witness, corporate or individual, is to be more than "garbage" in the eyes of the watching world. It is a witness that all can bear from now on, even if they never say another word.

Social Responsibility

Jesus also said that believers are to be the salt of the earth and the light of the world. In the context of this passage (Matt. 5:13-16), Stott comments on the two sayings of Jesus known as the Great Commission and the Great Commandment, observing that the Great Commission "neither explains, nor exhausts, nor supersedes the Great Commandment." This commandment to love our neighbor is an "urgent Christian dimension." Stott refers to man as "a psycho-somatic being," pointing out that our neighbor "is neither a bodyless soul that we should love only his soul, nor a soulless body that we should care for its welfare alone," thus reminding us of our responsibility for our neighbor's "total welfare," the physical as well as the spiritual. While such interaction brings credibility to a gospel that otherwise lacks "visibility," that gospel is always defined by "simple, uncomplicated compassion."[39]

For those committed to words and proclamation, the equation of compassion with communication has been a hard lesson to learn. It is much easier to talk than to be involved. Yet it is impossible to study the New Testament objectively without concluding that concern for the needs of others is the hallmark of true Christian faith. A religion which majors only in words, written or spoken, to the exclusion of actual involvement in meeting the needs of the disadvantaged is never authentic Christianity, regardless of how articulate its advocates may be. The incarnate Christ has been described as "the unwearied servant of man's necessity," and the work of His disciples now, as always, is "to feed the hungry, clothe the naked, and comfort the suffering and the afflicted."[40] Social concern and involvement are of equal importance in fulfilling the Great Commission as is verbal proclamation.

This conviction led to the inclusion of a statement regarding

Christian social responsibility in the Lausanne Covenant on world evangelization, a document that still shapes the thinking of many in the evangelical world. Both social action and evangelism "are part of our Christian duty." Both "are necessary expressions of our doctrines of God and man, our love for our neighbor and our obedience to Jesus Christ."[41] Commenting on this clause in the Covenant, John Stott declares, "We must seek not only the spread of the kingdom itself, nor only to exhibit its righteousness ourselves, but also to spread its righteousness in the midst of an unrighteous world. How else can we be the salt of the earth?"[42] The question refuses to go away.

Evangelism and Growth

It hardly needs to be said again that evangelism and growth are crucial to the life and mission of the church. Yet both have attracted unfavorable comment in recent times from some within the church, quite unjustifiably it may be said. In the unambiguous words of one thoughtful and convinced practitioner, "The church is in the growth business, or it will die."[43] This forthright statement calls for serious reflection, particularly as many congregations in some parts of the world are already dying and as the church as a whole in the Western world is more or less stagnant, at best. It is our contention that evangelism, in its broadest sense and as one form of mission and witness, still leads to growth.

It is important to qualify the foregoing by explaining that growth includes spiritual growth and growth in maturity as well as statistical growth. All are essential to the well being and therefore the functionality of the body of Christ. The church *must* grow spiritually *and* in numbers, or it will die. Those who assert that spiritual growth is a necessary prerequisite to membership growth are probably right. But membership growth there must be if congregational death, and ultimately even denominational death, is to be avoided. It is evangelism in the narrow as well as the broad sense that will bring growth, if we understand the word of God aright (Isa. 55:11). It is critical that we rediscover our passion for evangelism, for it is both biblical and necessary.

Evangelism is suspect in some minds primarily because of its

perceived emphasis on numbers. It is a difficult logic to follow given the many New Testament references to quantity (Luke 15; Acts 2:41, 47; 5:14). Be that as it may, we do well to notice van Engen's comment about growth and its measurement by numbers. Using the phrase "yearning for growth," van Engen asserts that "yearning for numerical growth is an essential mark" of the true church. It is a biblical concept, "by which the church has always expressed her nature in 'yearning' to incorporate more and more men and women within the bounds of God's grace." Seen like that, there can be no convincing argument against either growth or evangelism. In fact, where this yearning and subsequent rejoicing over the recovery of the lost are missing, van Engen says "we must ask ourselves whether something is not wrong at the very center of the church's life."[44]

The recovery of the evangelistic imperative begins with Jesus' own ministry, in His delivery of the Great Commission and in His vision of the church to come. The various Greek words used to record these situations all carry the inherent idea of public comment or proclamation of the gospel. This is what Jesus Himself did and what He required of His disciples (Luke 4:43; Mark 16:15; Matt. 4:17). The Greek word from which we derive the word "evangelism" is used in the New Testament of the verbal proclamation of the gospel. For those who regard dialogue as a preferred method for today, it is also worth noting Watson's further comment, "Before any profitable discussion or debate can take place we need to declare the gospel of Jesus Christ."[45]

Lest there be any doubt about the nature of the evangelism here envisaged, it has been clearly defined as "The proclamation of the historical, biblical Christ as Saviour and Lord, with a view to persuading people to come to Him personally and so be reconciled to God." The results of such evangelistic proclamation "include obedience to Christ, incorporation into his church and responsible service in the world."[46] It is intentional, focused, and insistent. Proclamation and persuasion lead to discipleship, obedience, church membership, service, and growth. The outcomes are as assured as the process itself is necessary. We do it or, ultimately, we die.

The Holy Spirit

We have left until last what is arguably the most important single factor necessary to effective witness. It is the *sine qua non* of everything the church undertakes in the name of Jesus—the presence and the power of the Holy Spirit. To do justice to this profound and indispensable theme would require a whole volume in itself. It is possible here only to underline again the essentials of what we have known, at least in theory, for decades.

The necessity of the Holy Spirit in witness begins with Jesus Himself. On the evening of the resurrection day when He first met with His frightened and uncomprehending disciples, He "breathed on them" and said "Receive the Holy Spirit" (John 20:22; to be read with Luke 24:44-48). Lenski makes the important point that this was not, as many have supposed, an "in earnest" bestowal of the gift that would come in its fullness at Pentecost, but a full and real impartation of the Holy Spirit then and there. It had a different purpose from the Pentecostal bestowal. The Spirit was here given to the disciples "for Him to work in them personally," to comprehend and internalize all that had happened in the preceding few days and to grasp what it was that Jesus now wanted them to do.[47] It is a critical distinction. Those who are to receive the power of the Spirit in witnessing must first be open to Him and have their minds changed by His presence. The Spirit does His work in the disciples *before* they can do their work in the world.

The definitive reference by Jesus to the Holy Spirit in relation to the Great Commission is recorded in Acts 1:4-8. The disciples were to receive the Spirit before being witnesses to Jesus in all the world. The inference is clear enough. Without the Spirit they could not be witnesses, at least not effective witnesses, and experience tells us that there is a world of difference between witness and effective witness. The book of Acts is the record of what happened as a result of the fulfillment of this promise at Pentecost. Lenski, again, commenting on this text refers to Christ's witnesses "speaking to the end of time in a great apostolic chorus."[48] It is all made possible, and made possible only, through the presence and the operation of the Spirit.

Stott refers to the "language of human activity" in his book *Christian Mission in the Modern World.* He says pointedly it "is seriously misleading" if such language is taken to mean that "mission is a human work and conversion a human achievement." Speaking of the person yet to receive Christ and enter the kingdom Stott affirms that "only the Holy Spirit can open his eyes, enlighten his darkness, liberate him from bondage, turn him to God and bring him out of death into life."[49] Michael Green observes that the Spirit is "the author, the controller and the energizer of Christian mission."[50] Paulien affirms the Spirit's role as "essential to all effective outreach," calling for sensitivity "to the leading of the Holy Spirit" in all such activities.[51]

The final chapter of Philip Samaan's book, *Christ's Way of Reaching People,* is entitled "By His Spirit." It is a fitting conclusion and an essential emphasis. Samaan speaks of the "pivotal relationship between the Holy Spirit and witnessing" saying, "The New Testament inextricably links the Holy Spirit with the sharing of the gospel." We are compelled to agree. It is impossible, as Samaan together with those cited above and a host of others affirm, to witness effectively without the Spirit's abiding presence, His guidance, and His power. So we ask with Samaan, "How can we ever think that we can bear witness to Christ without the infilling of the Holy Spirit?"[52] It is perhaps the most pressing question of the new millennium.

Despite promises of the Spirit's empowering presence "to the very end of the age," witness to Jesus and His kingdom is a daunting task, particularly in cultures that for the past generation or two have appeared to reject the gospel in favor of more "enlightened" alternatives, or even alternative versions of Christ. But times may be changing, there may be hope, and on this optimistic note we conclude our reconsideration of Jesus' last command to His disciples.

Michael Green and Alister McGrath, two of the most informed and articulate advocates in our time of Christian mission and of the biblical message itself, believe that a new day is dawning, "a day of renewed confidence in the truth of the Christian story." Noting the "barrenness of materialism" and the "hunger for spirituality" evident in our day, Green sees a "massive cultural shift" beginning to take place and believes that "the dogmas of the Enlightenment, which have dominated Western thought for two centuries, are in full retreat." "We are standing," he declares, "at one of the turning points of human thought." It is a "fascinating time to be alive." In this context, McGrath asserts that apologetics and evangelism "are the key to the future of Christianity as it stands poised to enter its third millennium."[53]

While the grip of secularism and materialism remains strong in many quarters, there is evidence that these hopes may be justified. In Jesus' view they are always justified. For Him, the fields are always ripe for harvest, particularly now at the end of time (John 4:35; Matt. 13:39). We may therefore confidently declare our position. Never before has the potential harvest been so plentiful. Never before have the fish been waiting in such abundance to be gathered in. Never before have the sons and daughters of Adam in so many corners of the world been made so aware of the devastating effects of disordered and sinful human nature and the ineradicable hopelessness of the human predicament as in recent times.

Against this background, at the same time full of insecurity and full of hope, Jesus says, "Go *ye* into all the world, and make disciples." What better time, then, than now for unreserved commitment to a revitalized, refocused, Christ-centered, Spirit-inspired proclamation of the Great Commission? We must not hesitate or prevaricate any longer. We *must* go. The survival of the faith, the church, and the destiny of yet unenlightened millions depend on it.

For Further Reading

Michael Green, *Evangelism Now and Then.* London: Daybreak Books, 1992.
Michael Green and Alister McGrath, *How Shall We Reach Them?* Milton Keynes: Word Books, 1995.
Jon Paulien, *Present Truth in the Real World.* Boise, ID: Pacific Press, 1993.
Philip Samaan, *Christ's Way of Reaching People.* Hagerstown, MD: Review and Herald, 1990.
John Stott, *Christian Mission in the Modern World.* London: Falcon, 1975.

Notes

1. Hans Kung, *On Being a Christian* (London: Collins, 1978), pp. 123, 146, 148. Unfortunately Kung cannot always be quoted in support of the biblical Jesus.

2. Jon L. Dybdahl, "Adventist Mission Today," in Jon L. Dybdahl (ed.), *Adventist Mission in the 21st Century* (Hagerstown, MD: Review and

Herald, 1999), p.18.

3. Max Warren, *I Believe In The Great Commission* (London: Hodder and Stoughton, 1976), p.173.
4. R. C. H. Lenski, *The Interpretation of St. Matthew's Gospel* (Minneapolis, MN: Augsburg, 1964), p. 1172.
5. Howard Snyder, *Liberating the Church* (Downers Grove, IL: InterVarsity, 1983), p. 24; Donald Senior and Carroll Stuhlmueller, *The Biblical Foundations for Mission* (Maryknoll, NY: Orbis, 1983), p. 252.
6. G. Kittel (ed.), *Theological Dictionary of the New Testament* (Grand Rapids, MI: Eerdmans, 1964), II, pp. 138, 135, 145.
7. Alister McGrath, "Starting Where People Are," in Michael Green and Alister McGrath, *How Shall We Reach Them?* (Milton Keynes: Word, 1995), p. 20.
8. Kittel (ed.), *Theological Dictionary,* IV (1967), pp. 492, 489.
9. *Ibid.*, p. 492.
10. R. C. H. Lenski, *The Interpretation of St. John's Gospel* (Minneapolis, MN: Augsburg, 1943), pp. 1368, 1369.
11. Peter Beyerhaus, "World Evangelization and the Kingdom of God," in J. D. Douglas (ed.), *Let the Earth Hear His Voice* (Minneapolis, MN: World-Wide Publications, 1974), p. 285.
12. Dybdahl, p. 18.
13. John Stott, *Christian Mission in the Modern World* (London: Falcon Books, 1975), p. 108.
14. Roger Hedlund, *The Mission of the Church in the World* (Grand Rapids, MI: Baker, 1991), 190; *Seventh-day Adventist Bible Commentary* (Hagerstown, MD: Review and Herald), 5 (1956), p. 557.
15. Snyder, p. 24.
16. Dietrich Bonhoeffer, *Letters and Papers from Prison* (New York: Macmillan, 1953), p. 203.
17. Charles van Engen, *God's Missionary People* (Grand Rapids, MI: Baker, 1991), pp. 28, 76, 81.
18. Hedlund, pp. 188, 190.
19. In David Watson, *I Believe In Evangelism* (London: Hodder and Stoughton, 1976), p. 9.
20. Cited in David Haney, *The Idea of the Laity* (Grand Rapids, MI: Zondervan, 1973), pp.141, 142.
21. E. G. White, *The Acts of the Apostles* (Mountain View, CA: Pacific Press, 1911), p. 9.
22. Snyder, p. 11.
23. Gavin Reid, *The Gagging of God* (London: Hodder and Stoughton, 1969), p. 125.
24. Watson, p. 136.
25. Michael Green, *Evangelism Now and Then* (London: Daybreak, 1992), pp. 117, 35.

26. Walter Douglas, "Vocation as Mission," in Dybdahl, *Adventist Mission,* p. 111.

27. R. C. H. Lenski, *The Interpretation of the Acts of the Apostles* (Minneapolis, MN: Augsburg, 1961), p. 32.

28. Stott, p. 48.

29. John Stott, *Explaining the Lausanne Covenant,* Lausanne Occasional Paper, 3 (London: Scripture Union, 1975), p. 13.

30. Warren, ch.7, "The Recovery of Nerve."

31. Watson, pp. 68, 69.

32. *Ibid.*, p. 71.

33. Michael Green, *Matthew for Today* (London: Hodder and Stoughton, 1988), p. 112.

34. Cited in Watson, p. 104.

35. Green, *Evangelism,* p. 22.

36. Francis Schaeffer, "The Church at the End of the Twentieth Century," in *The Complete Works of Francis Schaeffer* (Westchester, IL: Crossway Books, 1982), pp. 4, 33.

37. Jon Paulien, *Present Truth in the Real World* (Boise, ID: Pacific Press, 1993), *passim.*

38. Snyder, pp. 206,194.

39. Stott, *Christian Mission,* pp. 29, 30.

40. E. G. White, *The Ministry of Healing* (Mountain View, CA: Pacific Press, 1942), pp. 17, 106.

41. The Lausanne Covenant, clause 5, in Stott, Lausanne Occasional Paper, pp. 3, 15.

42. *Ibid.*, p. 17.

43. Michael Harper, *Let My People Grow* (London: Hodder and Stoughton, 1977), p. 20.

44. van Engen, pp. 81, 82.

45. Watson, pp. 27, 46.

46. Lausanne Covenant, clause 4, "The Nature of Evangelism."

47. Lenski, *John,* pp. 1373, 1374.

48. Lenski, *Acts*, p. 32.

49. Stott, *Christian Mission*, pp. 123, 124.

50. Michael Green, *I Believe In The Holy Spirit* (London: Hodder and Stoughton, 1975), p. 64. The entire chapter "The Spirit in Mission" is helpful.

51. Paulien, pp. 23, 140.

52. Philip Samaan, *Christ's Way of Reaching People* (Hagerstown, MD: Review and Herald, 1990), pp. 144, 146.

53. Green and McGrath, pp. 7, 12.

The Last Word

"I am trying here to prevent anyone saying the really foolish thing that people often say about Him: 'I'm ready to accept Jesus as a great moral teacher, but I don't accept His claim to be God.' This is the one thing we must not say. A man who was merely a man and said the sort of things Jesus said would not be a great moral teacher. He would either be a lunatic—on a level with the man who says he is a poached egg—or else he would be the Devil of Hell. You must make your choice. Either this man was, and is, the Son of God: or else a madman or something worse. You can shut Him up for a fool, you can spit at Him and kill Him as a demon; or you can fall at His feet and call Him Lord and God. But let us not come with any patronizing nonsense about His being a great human teacher. He has not left that open to us."—C. S. Lewis, *Mere Christianity* (1955), pp. 52, 53.

"Jesus' audacious claims about himself pose what may be the central problem of all history, the dividing point between Christianity and other religions. Although Muslims and, increasingly, Jews respect Jesus as a great teacher and prophet, no Muslim can imagine Mohammed claiming to be Allah any more than a Jew can imagine Moses claiming to be Yahweh. Likewise, Hindus believe in many incarnations but not one Incarnation, while Buddhists have no categories in which to conceive of a sovereign God becoming a human being. . . .

"I must admit that Jesus has revised . . . many of my harsh and unpalatable notions about God. *Why am I a Christian?* I sometimes ask myself, and to be perfectly honest the reasons reduce to two: (1) the lack of good alternatives, and (2) Jesus. Brilliant, untamed, tender, creative, slippery, irreducible, paradoxically humble—Jesus stands up to scrutiny. He is who I want my God to be."—Philip Yancey, *The Jesus I Never Knew* (1995), pp. 260, 263.

"I . . . feel a strong obligation to urge you to make this a front-burner issue in your life. Don't approach it casually or flippantly, because there's a lot riding on your conclusion. As Michael Murphy aptly put it, 'We ourselves—and not merely the truth claims—are at stake in the investigation.' In other words, if my conclusion in the case for Christ is correct, your future and eternity hinge on how you respond to Christ. As Jesus declared, 'If you do not believe that I am the one I claim to be, you will indeed die in your sins' (John 8:24).

"Those are sober words, offered out of authentic and loving concern. I cite them to underline the magnitude of this matter and in the hope that they will spur you to actively and thoroughly examine the case for Christ."—Lee Strobel, *The Case for Christ* (1998), p. 366.